The Growth Advantage

The Growth Advantage

A Business Blueprint for the Ultimate Competitive Edge

Bob Lisser

ROWMAN & LITTLEFIELD
Lanham • Boulder • New York • London

Published by Rowman & Littlefield
An imprint of The Rowman & Littlefield Publishing Group, Inc.
4501 Forbes Boulevard, Suite 200, Lanham, Maryland 20706
www.rowman.com

86-90 Paul Street, London EC2A 4NE, United Kingdom

British Library Cataloguing in Publication Information Available

Library of Congress Cataloging-in-Publication Data

Names: Lisser, Bob, 1959- author.
Title: The growth advantage : a business blueprint for the ultimate competitive edge / Robert Lisser.
Description: Lanham : Rowman & Littlefield, [2022] | Includes bibliographical references and index. | Summary: "The Growth Advantage cracks open the business secrets that teach companies how to achieve that dream of steady, predictable growth through effective planning and solid execution. Readers learn how their company can develop and sustain a blueprint for growth that guides company actions on a daily and weekly basis. Combining elements of culture, strategy, planning, execution, talent acquisition, training, motivation, accountability, and brand differentiation into one book with clear, actionable steps, Bob Lisser brings readers along a journey that starts with a plan and ends with success"—Provided by publisher.
Identifiers: LCCN 2021045533 (print) | LCCN 2021045534 (ebook) | ISBN 9781538161722 (cloth ; alk. paper) | ISBN 9781538161739 (epub)
Subjects: LCSH: Strategic planning. | Small business—Growth. | Business planning. | Success in business
Classification: LCC HD30.28 .L563 2022 (print) | LCC HD30.28 (ebook) | DDC 658.4/012—dc3
LC record available at https://lccn.loc.gov/2021045533
LC ebook record available at https://lccn.loc.gov/2021045534

Contents

Prologue

Strategy Advantage: Be Strategically Brave

ADVANTAGE PRINCIPLE: SUSTAINED GROWTH MAKES PEOPLE STRATEGICALLY BRAVE.

I often get asked, "What is strategy?" Strategy is a fancy way of saying HOW. How are you going to accomplish your top goals and objectives? I call these types of top goals Vital Goals, which means they are vital to your company's success and worthy of your best effort. Whether your Vital Goal is to sustain 15 percent annual revenue growth, qualify for the Boston Marathon, win an Olympic gold medal, lose twenty pounds, or reach the South Pole, how are you going to achieve the goal? The how is your strategy.

The Growth Advantage is a strategic leadership blueprint for sustained and profitable growth. To develop a Strategy Advantage, you need to maximize the following components: **Purpose** (why do you do what you do) + **Opportunity** (what do you sell to whom and where) + **Advantage** (what differentiates you) + **Planning** (what will be done by whom by when) + **Strategy** (how) + **Execution** (now) = **Results**. This seems like a simple equation; it is anything but. It takes a committed effort to improve and maximize your abilities in these areas. Don't panic if you're not hitting on all cylinders. I have never met a company that would get an "A" grade for each component. It is always a work in progress and that's the fun. Plus, the effort is worth it.

Strategy Advantage

Figure 0.1. Strategy Advantage Formula for Results

Why am I writing this book? This is the book I needed thirty-five years ago when I got started in management. I'm writing it for every leader that wants to improve their craft as well as every manager and executive that gets put into a position of leadership without having the leadership skills and training necessary to be successful in their job. Like me, many people get promoted to a higher-level position because they performed in their present position without necessarily having the success skills for their new job. Accordingly, if you promote your top sales representative to a sales management job, make sure you provide the management and leadership training the job requires. If you do not, you might get an underperforming sales manager and lose a top-performing sales representative. This principle is true for all positions.

I'm also writing it for every company leader that is looking for a proven process to sustain profitable growth. If you have a financial question, ask your accountant. If you have a legal question, ask your attorney. If you have a human resource challenge, you can ask a human resource professional. Where do you go if you have a challenge growing your business? My aspiration is that *The Growth Advantage* will be a go-to resource for questions about effectively growing a company.

When I graduated college, landed my first job, and started my career in business, I was so inexperienced I did not even understand what the company I'd just agreed to work for actually did. I paid attention, though; I worked hard, and I learned hard from my bosses, my coworkers, and every resource I could find. I learned what to do, and just as importantly, through many mistakes, I learned what *not* to do. I had a few small successes and built on them with larger successes. The next natural progression for me was to get a management position. In fact, in my first management position, I oversaw thirty-five people and almost all were older and had more experience than me. I had no idea how to manage anything, let alone a whole department of a growing company.

Luckily for me and the company, drive, a little fear, as well as a hunger for knowledge motivated me to learn how to become a successful manager and leader. That drive continued throughout my career; a career that included being a sales representative, a sales manager, a service manager, a general manager, an executive director, and an owner of a company. I have digested hundreds of books and articles, attended scores of training seminars, and paid attention to people I felt were effective leaders. It is an amazing time in that anything you want to learn is readily available in books, articles, web sources, and so forth.

This book is my way of sharing the hard-won wisdom I gained from my experience and education. I have been writing this book for years but actually have been learning what's included in this book for decades. Without a doubt, books changed the course of my life. My hope is that this book can help change the course of yours.

In the next eleven chapters, you are going to learn:

- the importance of becoming Strategically Brave,
- how to create a Growth Culture,
- what a Vital Goal is and how to achieve it,
- the importance of making Vital Goals personal and identifying the Predictive Behaviors that will tell the future,
- how to calculate the math of business,
- how to attain and train talent,
- how to motivate people,
- how to keep yourself and your employees accountable,
- how to identify your company's most profitable place in the market,
- how to maximize your Company Advantage, and
- how to tie everything together and give your employees their best chance at success.

The Growth Advantage is divided into three parts: the Planning Advantage, the Execution Advantage, and the Company Advantage. Each chapter includes details on how you can attain advantages over your competition, thereby building the Ultimate Competitive Edge. These specifics are explained and illustrated with examples, anecdotes, applications, and quotes like this one from Sun Tzu: "All men can see the tactics whereby I conquer, but what none can see is the strategy out of which victory is evolved."

These wise words from the famous Chinese general are referencing military victory, but they are just as applicable to the business world. In my work today as a business consultant and teacher, I moderate Executive Peer Groups where members can discuss plans and strategies as well as share challenges and ideas. Each member becomes a teacher in their areas of strength and a student in their areas of weakness.

Each group has ten to fifteen member companies, and we talk about all elements of success. But in every group, there are people who grow a lot and people who don't grow at all. And in every group, there are people who make a lot of money and people who barely get by. You would think that because they are all getting exposed to the same information they could all capitalize on it and be successful. They could, but they don't—some do not have a success blueprint or the leadership talent on their team to take the ideas, turn them into strategic plans, execute those plans, and make growth happen.

This book covers many of those leadership principles.

ADVANTAGE PRINCIPLE: OUTCOMES ARE NOT A PRODUCT OF OUR CIRCUMSTANCES. THEY ARE A PRODUCT OF OUR DECISIONS AND ACTIONS.

Here's a surprising statistic: "85% of executive leadership teams spend less than one hour per month discussing strategy, and 50% spend no time at all."[1] I've witnessed this problem firsthand. Time and again, I've been directing discussions about strategy when the topic veers into operational matters that are far from vital and should be shuttled to a different level or held for another time. Business teams too often wander to more comfortable issues when confronting high-level obstacles—it is critical that companies keep focus on the most essential decisions and initiatives first.

In today's business climate, executives and managers are being asked to do more and sometimes with less. I empathize with people who say they feel uncomfortable about investing valuable time to read or just sit and think. In my experience, it is a major challenge to get some decision makers to think in strategic rather than operational terms. But reading, thinking, planning, and strategizing is called Leadership Time, and it's a critical part of success.

ADVANTAGE PRINCIPLE: LEADERS ARE MADE, NOT BORN.

There is a fallacy that leaders are born. I disagree! I believe leaders are *made*. From a combination of circumstance and personal drive, leaders are motivated to learn and develop their craft. They learn how to model and inspire optimism, foster a shared purpose, create and execute plans, build unity and commitment, construct and motivate teams, and maximize their advantage. This is true for businesses, families, expeditions, and the military.

I've been amazed at the leadership I've witnessed during the COVID-19 pandemic. My favorite pandemic-era quote, from the leader of a company whose revenue dropped so sharply that they had to close one of their plants, is "Why waste a good disaster?," meaning even though times were tough (he was not belittling the challenges people were facing), we needed to find opportunity and lead our way out of this. That is what worthy leaders do. Strong leadership is always needed, but it becomes especially important during times of crisis when context is changing. Leaders need to stay positive, control the chaos, and stay in the Leaders Quadrant, as we will discuss in chapter 2, "Commit to Your Vital Goals."

Many great companies were founded or thrived during challenging times. Procter & Gamble was founded during the panic of 1837, GE started during the panic of 1873, Disney started during the recession of 1923–1924, Hewlett-Packard was founded at the end of the Great Depression, Bill Gates and Paul Allen founded Microsoft during the recession of 1975, and Uber started in 2009 during the great recession.

A leader that had the drive and also had to step up due to circumstance is Sir Ernest Shackleton. He led twenty-seven men on a journey to be the first to cross Antarctica, and though he failed to reach his destination, he became famous for his leadership abilities. Shackleton and his team departed England in late 1914 with the goal to sail to Antarctica and walk across the continent where another crew would pick them up. Their ship, the *Endurance*, was destroyed by ice floes and sank in November 1915. He and his crew were forced to set up camp on various ice floes, moving their gear and team of dogs along the way.[2] The crew's morale was among Shackleton's greatest concerns, and he encouraged them to play games and participate in celebrations to keep up their spirits.[3] One man wrote in his journal after a celebration that it was "one of the happiest days of my life."[4]

More than one thousand miles away from any other people and with no way to communicate their plight, they survived several months in brutal conditions before boarding the ship's lifeboats and making the perilous trip to Elephant Island. Though they were at least on land, conditions were not much improved, and Shackleton again set off on a single lifeboat with a few of his men to return to the whaling station on South Georgia Island where they started from eight hundred miles to the north. They endured eighty-foot waves and sixty-mile-per-hour winds over the three weeks it took them to reach the whaling station. Once there, only the seasoned whaling captains could truly appreciate the intense journey they had made and honored their achievement. It took Shackleton four more months to get a ship to return to Elephant Island to rescue his remaining crew. It had been almost two years since the beginning of their expedition, and after everything they had been through, not one crew member had died.[5]

Imagine successfully leading a team while stranded on islands and ice sheets in Arctic conditions for almost two years with limited shelter and food supplies. Leading an expedition can be much like leading a business. Shackleton needed to raise capital, manage resources, create flexible plans, find and develop talent, motivate and hold team members accountable, and stay positive in challenging situations. In the end, his team even declared him as being "the greatest leader on Earth." He displayed amazing elements of leadership in areas of hope, shared purpose, planning, adjusting plans, team unity, and brave strategic decision making.

Effective planning and execution are necessary leadership skills required to sustain profitable growth. When a company consistently outgrows industry averages, they are creating a Growth Advantage. This sustained growth makes companies Strategically Brave versus stagnating growth, which makes companies Strategic Cowards. Strategically Brave companies are not afraid of growth, expansion, proactive staffing, saying *yes* to a new idea, saying *no* to a new idea, raising prices, turning away bad business, and so on. Strategically Brave companies that follow solid planning and execution principles typically outpace their industry growth averages many times over on a sustained basis.

Think of strategy as the intelligent allocation of limited resources into an action plan designed to achieve Vital Goals and objectives. Everyone has limited resources, but that should never get in the way of your company's growth. Growth—in my opinion—should always be a Vital Goal because, if done in a strategic way, revenue growth should always increase your resource pool. The principles in this book will help you grow your company strategically, thereby creating a Growth Advantage and becoming Strategically Brave.

A common expression I hear over and over again from my clients is "I should have done this years ago." They're right. Maybe they should have. You may feel the same way when you're finished reading this book. That's fine. But none of us can hide from what happened in the past; we can only focus on executing our plans and strategies now. An old proverb states, "The best time to plant a tree was twenty years ago. The second-best time is now."

Developing and accomplishing a successful growth strategy for your company is not luck—it's a matter of choice and execution. Think about your market, brand advantage, customers, competition, products, facilities, operations, sales, marketing, talent, training, as well as your pricing. What are your top strategic priorities that need to be executed, both short and long term, to achieve your Vital Goals? Prioritize the top one to three in each area. What needs to happen right now and what needs to happen in the future? To build a Growth Advantage, companies need to strategize and prioritize for the present and the future. *The Growth Advantage: A Business Blueprint for the Ultimate Competitive Edge* will show you how.

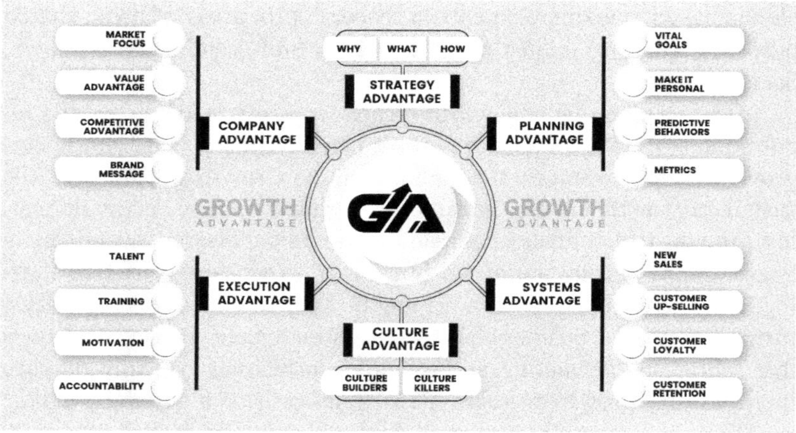

Figure 0.2. Growth Advantage Blueprint

Advantage Challenge: What is your company purpose (why)?
History (past): What elements from your company's past should help shape your future?
Mission (current): What are the reasons for your organization's existence today?
Vision (future): What are the future aspirations of your organization?
Core Values (character): What are the principles that guide your decisions and actions?
Take key words from each of these items that define the company you want to be.
Use the key words to create a Purpose Statement.
Reference the Purpose Advantage Challenge Application (Figure A.1) at the back of the book.

Part I

THE PLANNING ADVANTAGE

ADVANTAGE PRINCIPLE: EFFECTIVE PLANNING & EXECUTION IS THE ULTIMATE COMPETITIVE ADVANTAGE.

The saying goes, "An unaimed arrow never misses." As I travel the country, I find one consistent theme: most executives, managers, and employees are "unaimed," meaning they don't know their company's top goals or how they contribute to those goals. How do I know this? I ask. I've asked hundreds of executives, managers, and frontline employees and have yet to find one company where I get a consistent answer at the top, let alone from the executive team to the front line.

Sure, most employees know their company wants to grow and make money, but they don't know the specific goals, how they contribute to those goals, or the Predictive Behaviors they must perform on a daily, weekly, monthly, quarterly, and annual basis in order to accomplish these outcomes. When employees don't have a specific course of action, they will set their own course, with the best intentions. But when a company has tens, hundreds, or thousands of employees setting their own course, that is *not* a blueprint for success; that is a blueprint for disaster.

Let me tell you a little leadership secret regarding business success. It's not about getting everyone to work harder; my experience and observation show me that everyone is working pretty hard already. It is about getting yourself and your team to spend more time and put more focus on the most important initiatives as well as the behaviors that impact those initiatives. More people doing the most important things more often! This will only happen with effective planning and execution.

Alan Lakein, author of *How to Get Control of Your Time and Your Life*, said, "Planning is bringing the future into the present so that you can do something about it now."[1] So let's consider planning from the perspective of a professional or college football coach. They spend the off-season planning, recruiting, training, coaching, and practicing for the upcoming season, and they spend the week before the game doing the same. Why? So they can bring as much of the upcoming season or the upcoming game (the future) as possible into the present so they can do something about it now. How successful do you think a team's season would be if, instead of spending all this time preparing, the coach just called a meeting right before the game and politely asked each player to play a little harder? The answer is not very. By then it's too late, and the team's results would be in direct relation to the planning effort they'd put in.

Vince Lombardi, one of the most successful coaches in NFL history, said, "It is hard to be aggressive when you're confused."[2] The key to achieving your company's top goals is to make sure you and your employees are never confused about what those goals are or how each individual in the company contributes to accomplishing them. Professional football players spend more than 90 percent of their time planning and practicing for the game and less than 10 percent actually playing it. Coaches like Vince Lombardi knew the power of planning. He knew that planning was the only way to succeed. Do you think he won five championships and two Super Bowls by simply suggesting his players work a little harder?

Yet in business, the ratio of planning to action is reversed. In business and life, we do just the opposite, spending most of our time in the game (95 percent) and spending very little time strategizing, planning, training, coaching, and practicing for the game (5 percent). As the old saying goes, most people spend more time planning their vacations than they do their life.

I am not suggesting that businesses can or should have the same planning ratio as a sports team, but I am guaranteeing that companies would experience a huge increase in effectiveness if they increased their planning ratio over what they are doing now. Planning is a key leadership activity that is too often underutilized. Albert Einstein understood this principle well, saying, "If I were given one hour to save the planet, I would spend 59 minutes defining the problem and one-minute resolving it."[3]

It is only through planning that you can determine and achieve your Vital Goals and know whether you're doing the right things for the right reasons at the right time. In business, companies should *always* work to create or enhance their Market Advantage. I believe that if your company is more effective than your competition at planning and execution, your company will have the "Ultimate Competitive Edge." In fact, if you're not actively maximizing the advantage of planning, you're missing a key opportunity to seize a Competitive Advantage in the marketplace. The Planning Advantage may be the single most important controllable aspect to both your personal and your business life.

Although we typically plan in time frames of one year, five years, or even longer, we need to make sure we're breaking the activities (behaviors and results) and everything that contributes to that plan into the shortest time frames possible (weeks, days, and even hours). If contributing employees on your team clearly understand what behavior needs to be accomplished every day and week, then as long as they're held accountable to those behavior goals, the quarterly, annual, and five-year goals will be achieved—like magic.

The goal of the Planning Advantage chapters is to make sure everyone knows your Vital Goals, how they contribute to those goals, what Predictive Behaviors they need to do on a daily and weekly basis, and how you're going to keep score. We'll talk about accountability in chapter 10, "Accountability Advantage," but for now consider this: you can only hold people accountable if they know what they are being accountable to. From my experience, companies that follow this process will profitably grow their businesses well above their industry averages. This in turn leads to a financial advantage the competition simply cannot compete with.

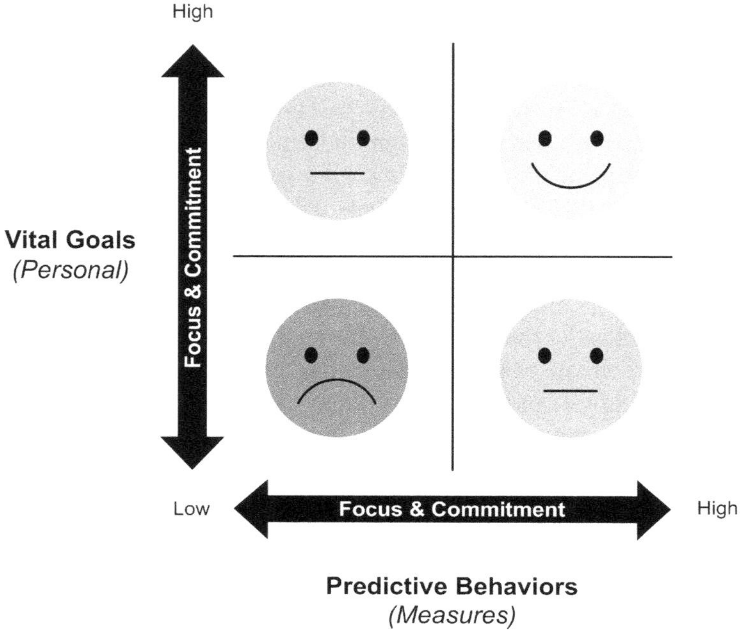

Figure I.1. Planning Advantage Grid

The figure I.1 is a visual representation of what we will be covering in Part I: The Planning Advantage.

- **Bottom Left**: Focus on and commitment to the Vital Goals and Predictive Behaviors is low. In this quadrant, goals are not being achieved because no one knows what the goals are or the behaviors required to accomplish the goals. I see too many companies living in this quadrant, and this is where you should hope your competitors operate.
- **Top Left**: There is focus on and commitment to the Vital Goals but no focus on and commitment to the Predictive Behaviors. This is typical in companies where result goals are established but not behavior goals. This is a formula for mediocrity. We can't manage results; we can only manage behaviors.
- **Bottom Right**: There is focus on and commitment to the Predictive Behaviors but low focus on and commitment to the Vital Goals. This is unlikely because it is rare for companies to focus on behaviors but not the goals. It is also almost impossible to determine required behaviors without knowing the bull's-eye.

- **Top Right**: Focus on and commitment to the Vital Goals and the Predictive Behaviors is high. Companies and people that have focus on and commitment to their Vital Goals as well as focus on and commitment to the Predictive Behaviors that will propel them to accomplish those goals have a smile on their face. Why? Because they will have the "Ultimate Competitive Advantage" in life and in business. If you had that, why wouldn't you be smiling?

Chapter One

Create a Growth Culture

ADVANTAGE PRINCIPLE: INTENTIONAL CULTURES WITH CLEAR BEHAVIOR EXPECTATIONS PRODUCE RESULTS.

Tony Hsieh's company culture at Zappos, the online shoe and apparel retailer he founded, is hard to miss. When you walk in the door, you see a spaceship where employees can take naps and a Ping-Pong table people can use during their breaks. Employees dress as they please, and every department has a nickname. Executives are known as "Monkeys."[1]

None of this zaniness happened by accident. Zappos's company culture was intentionally created to attract culture fit talent. The company understands that younger generations are attracted to more than compensation; they are attracted to an enjoyable work environment where employees are valued and the company has a purpose. Zappos created an intentional customer-obsessed company culture, based on a specific set of core values, that attracts the talent they need to support their desired objectives.

According to their website, they "aim to inspire the world by showing it's possible to simultaneously deliver happiness to customers, as well as employees, vendors, shareholders and the community, in a long-term, sustainable way."[2] Zappos's vision is to deliver happiness through the four Cs: Commerce, Customer Service, Company Culture, Community. CEO Hsieh celebrated it. He said, "They can copy the look and feel of our website and even the brands we have signed up. They can't copy our culture. That's our Competitive Advantage."[3] Zappos's culture was so successful Amazon paid $850 million dollar to acquire it.

Whatever you are trying to accomplish in business and in life, to achieve it you must create a culture that supports the outcome(s) you desire. This is true whether you are trying to build a growth culture in business, a winning sports team, or a healthy culture in your personal life. The choice is yours. You can either intentionally create the culture you want, or you can just let it evolve on its own, outside of your control. Either way, a culture *will* be formed. If you don't actively promote a healthy culture, the culture that evolves on its own will often have unhealthy consequences. In business, to sustain a successful culture, it is crucial that the culture be positive, winning, rewarding, and fun and produce desired results so that your most successful employees—Culture Fit Employees—will just naturally want to be part of it.

Now, not every company's culture has to have spaceships and Ping-Pong tables. The key to building an effective culture for your company is to base it on your company's purpose, core values, vision, and desired objectives. Culture underpins every action in a company. That's precisely why a positive culture—so often neglected—is vital to a company's success and why it's the focus of the first chapter in this book. Every element of this book will help you turn your company's culture into a Business Advantage.

Advantage Challenge: With this in mind, picture yourself walking in the door on a Monday morning ready for the week ahead and greeting your coworkers. What is *your* company's culture? Be brutally honest in your assessment. Does your company's culture contribute to sustained, profitable growth? Is it positive and winning? Or is it fraught with drama and negativity? The bottom line: if you don't like your company's culture, change it, intentionally!

Creating a deliberate culture that produces the results you're striving to achieve is a key element of creating the Ultimate Competitive Edge. Just as with the other advantages detailed in this book (Planning, Execution, and Company), companies that decide who they want to be, have a clear vision, know their purpose or "why," know how to develop and execute strategic plans, and live by defined core values will always have an advantage over competitors who don't purposely develop and evolve their culture. Despite this importance, company culture is too frequently neglected.

Often, company leaders have already wondered out loud, "What happened? We used to have a strong corporate culture that produced great results. Now we don't. Where did it go wrong?" Business context is always changing, and accordingly, cultures need to evolve along with those changes. These are what I call "Culture Shifts," where, in essence, a company needs to get better at executing the key elements of being a growing, results-driven company. A Culture Shift might be needed because of growth (changes in company size or market share), changing goals, a more competitive landscape, economic fluctuations, or poor results.

As conditions change and companies grow, leadership, talent, and ability need to grow at the same pace. If you want to have a culture that supports sustained growth, you are going to need to be responsive to the triggers that require culture evolution. A Culture Shift is not a onetime thing. Below are several triggers that may require a Culture Shift.

Culture Shift Triggers

Changing Company Size—As a company gets larger, its culture needs to evolve if leaders expect to profitably grow and achieve objectives at the same pace they have in the past. This is true whether your annual sales are in the millions or the billions. I've worked with many leaders of companies with annual revenues in the $6 to $10 million range who are stumped when growth stalls.

The number one reason is that talent and leadership skills have not kept up with growth. They do not have a company culture that develops leadership outside of the owner or family. The managers of these companies are *doers*, not leaders (see chapter 2, "Commit to Your Vital Goals," for more on this). Their company culture needs to evolve. As they continue to grow, the leaders can't personally touch and be involved in everything like they used to when the company was smaller. They need to groom an executive team they can trust to produce coveted results. In fact, the number one priority of every CEO, executive, and manager should be to develop an exceptional group of direct reports they can trust to live the culture and get the job done. As companies grow, their revenue, culture, and talent requirements continuously advance. Additionally, the larger a company gets, the less busy leaders need to be with demand activity—activity that chooses them. They need time to be leaders and focus on planned activity—leadership activity they choose.

Changing Market Share—I've worked with companies that have varying levels of market share, ranging from single digits to 90 percent, and although the initial growth planning process is similar for all companies, there is one difference. Companies with large market shares—over 50 percent—may be destined for growth stagnation if they don't grow their market opportunity pool. Business happens where opportunity and advantage intersect (see chapter 11, "Company Advantage," for more on this topic). In order to sustain growth, it is essential that there is adequate market opportunity. If there are no fish in the lake, it is going to be a bad day of fishing.

A Changing Economy—I started my company, Growth Advantage, in May 2009. The stock market was bottoming out, and the United States had entered the Great Recession. Was I a little nervous about starting a new business in these circumstances? You'd better believe it. But I quickly learned that many companies that had been consistently growing until 2009 then hit a stall or even started going backward. These once-successful companies could be successful again; they just needed to make a major culture shift—quickly. Eventually, my nervousness disappeared. What a great time to start a consulting business focused on profitable growth!

Today, we are operating in the wake of the COVID-19 pandemic, which forced many companies to make Culture Shifts to survive. I wish it were not the case, but it seems we go through at least one of these extreme Culture Shift challenges every decade. This means however successful your company is, you can never "set it and forget it." You must always be evolving your culture.

One culture challenge that may be a greater part of some companies' future is employees working remotely. It is extremely difficult to instill core values and engage people in the company culture when they are not regularly in the office and their primary contact is with their immediate manager. Jamie Dimon, the JPMorgan Chase & Co. chief executive officer, said, "It's time to get people back to the office. The firm has noted productivity slipping from employees working at home and that remote work is no substitute for in-person interaction."[4] I've seen similar outcomes firsthand. When employees work remotely, the planning and execution principles we discuss in this book become even more important but also more challenging to implement. Make sure remote workers are constantly communicated with, are engaged, have specific goals, are held accountable to those goals, are included and involved, and are provided the proper training and tools. Some companies are evolving to a "best of both worlds" approach where employees split their time between working from the office and working remotely.

A More Competitive Landscape—The changing competitive landscape can have a major and sometimes even catastrophic impact on a business. Ask BlackBerry, Blockbuster Video, Borders Books, Circuit City, or the owner of any family drugstore after a Walgreens opens across the street. BlackBerry had to reinvent itself; Blockbuster, Circuit City, and Borders are no more; and many family drugstores across the country have closed. And yet more cell phones are being purchased today than ever before, more movies are being watched, more electronics are being purchased, more books are being written and read, and our aging population is consuming more prescription drugs than ever before. The competitive landscape in which these companies once existed changed, and they and their culture did not evolve fast enough. Company cultures should perpetually drive innovation and advantage investment.

Changing Company Goals—Sometimes the status quo is just not good enough, and this can be tough for business leaders to face. This is common in sports, where team owners or university presidents want to goose the win-loss record, so they bring in a new coach. The new coach demands a culture change, and hopefully positive results soon follow. Nick Saban and Alabama's Crimson Tide are good examples. Saban has developed a culture of success, where winning the national championship is not just something to strive for but rather the expectation. Your company can also develop a winning culture and build on it for success by working on your Planning Advantage, Execution Advantage, and Company Advantage.

One of my clients summed this concept up well. After growing at an improved pace for a couple years, he stated, "This is the new normal," meaning they are committed and will do whatever it takes to sustain these improved results. They never want to go back to the old standards.

Poor Results—All the triggers noted above can and will contribute to declining results if not addressed. When growth stalls or declines, a lot of bad things start happening. The more capital intensive your business, the worse it gets. I've found there is nothing quite like declining orders and declining profitability to inspire a company to want to make a Culture Shift. Always shift with the tide, and this is less likely to happen.

Advantage Challenge: How does your company's culture contribute to successfully facing business context changes? Which triggers are affecting your company, and what is your plan of action?

All cultures have some positives. A great way to start making a Culture Shift is to look at what's working and build from there. Observe the behaviors prevalent in your organization now; then imagine how people would act if your company were at its best. What are the behaviors and values already displayed by the Culture Fit Employees that you would like all employees to emulate? Culture is behavior driven, and it's critical to focus on a few behaviors that will have the desired impact for your company. These behaviors are Culture Builders; must align with your company's purpose, brand, strategy, and objectives; and are defined by an explicit set of core values. Culture Builders will become the norm with a continual focus on a company's Vital Goals and implementing an execution strategy to achieve those goals. Engaging in behavior management and tracking, regular training, and making people accountable for progress are critical.

Conversely, all cultures have negatives that hinder progress. These are behaviors that are killing your company's culture and sabotaging its results. These I call "Culture Killers." Culture Killers, often hiding in plain sight, include frequent complaining, unproductive busyness, excuse making, dysfunctional meetings, complacency with the status quo, accepting Below Baseline performance, and lack of accountability. Grand change, change that brings sustained growth, always comes from *dissatisfaction* with the status quo.

Here, in the Culture Builders/Culture Killers chart, are some examples of Culture Builders and Culture Killers. As you read through this list, assess your own company's culture. Which Builders need work? Which Killers need to be addressed?

Culture Builders	Culture Killers
Having a Clear "Why" (Company Purpose)	No "Why"
Living Core Values	No Core Values
Defined Team Rules	No Team Rules
Team Trust	Lack of Trust
Strategic Thinking & Planning	No Strategic Thinking & Planning
Specific Goals (Alignment)	Non-Specific or No Goals
Behavior Tracking & Management	No Behavior Tracking or Management
Action & Progress	Lack of Progress
Focused Measurement (KPIs)	Too Little or Too Much Measurement
Accountability	Accountability Deficit
Productive Meetings	Dysfunctional or No Meetings
Training & Reinforcement	Too Little Training
Employee Engagement	Low Engagement
Positive & Winning Attitude	Bad Attitudes & Complaining (Too Busy)
Staying Hungry	Becoming Satisfied
Focus (Less is More)	Un-focused (More is Less)

Figure 1.1. Culture Builders and Culture Killers

ADVANTAGE PRINCIPLE: GRAND CHANGE COMES FROM DISSATISFACTION WITH THE STATUS QUO.

Be honest with yourself. Do Culture Builders dominate your company, or is your company outweighed and bogged down by Culture Killers? I have yet to work with a single company that was not comprised of both. The companies that stall are companies satisfied with the status quo. The companies that show sustained growth pay attention to their workplace culture, plan for it, monitor it, address the Culture Killers, nurture the Culture Builders, and consistently evolve their culture, as necessary.

It's human nature for most of us to be resistant to change. So when you begin to make a shift in your company's culture, you will encounter resistance. That does not mean, however, that your people can't or won't change. It just means you must be intentional and consistent as you work toward a winning and results-driven culture.

To sustain growth, your company needs to attract the best and brightest, and like the employees at Zappos, these people are only going to want to be part of a culture that's winning, rewarding, producing results, and celebrating success. I have a name for a company's best and brightest employees: Brass Ringers. These are the Culture-Building employees who do whatever it takes to produce Brass Ring results. These are the employees you want in your company! They aren't going to want to be in a negative culture where everyone is afraid to make a mistake. You want Brass Ringers? Create a winning culture that will attract and keep them.

The University of Wisconsin's Badger football team is a great example of culture building. Before 1990, the team did not have a consistent history of winning. Then they hired Barry Alvarez. As coach and then athletic director, he built a consistently winning football program by building a team unmatched in the running game. The Badgers can now claim the college running back with the most career yards (Ron Dane, a Heisman trophy winner), the running back with the most career touchdowns (Monte Ball), the running back with the second most yards in one game (Melvin Gordon), as well as a few Rose Bowl appearances. These players are Brass Ringers, and the bowl appearances and victories are a Brass Ring result.

When the Badgers are recruiting elite running backs, they have a pretty convincing pitch because they built a culture and a system that supports success at running the ball and winning football games. In his autobiography, *Don't Flinch*, Alvarez said, "You have to have a feel for your players. I think that's one of my strengths as a coach, and always has been. You have to know what buttons to push; when to push them and when to back off."[5]

This is a perfect example of a culture reinforcing positive outcomes and positive outcomes building culture. UW's football team has qualified for a bowl game and its men's basketball team has earned an invitation to the National Collegiate Athletic Association (NCAA) tournament for more than fifteen years straight. That is the longest streak in NCAA history.

Now you're ready to embrace a positive, winning growth culture in your company, right? Super! But it is not enough to *say* you want it; you must do the work. You have to *create* the culture you want by establishing core values (rules to play), executing plans (producing results), and, most importantly, determining what behaviors are going to drive that culture and holding employees accountable to those behaviors.

Workplace cultures are behavior driven, and the behaviors of everyone, from executives to frontline employees, must support the culture you are working to build. Executives might think it is the frontline employees bringing down a company's culture, but that is not typically the case. Often, executives themselves can unwittingly destroy the very success they are trying to grow. It's absolutely critical that leaders model the behaviors they want to see in their employees. It is even more important that they hold team members accountable to the behavior goals and core values they establish.

Too often, managers set behavior expectations for their teams but fail to model the behavior or hold the team accountable. Here's an example: A sales manager spends a day in the field with a sales representative who has a goal of fifteen prospecting attempts each day. Then, because it's a busy day with many appointments, the manager ends up dropping the fifteen-attempt requirement. The message the sales rep gets is that you only have to make your prospecting calls when it is convenient.

Conversely, consider a family business—a company I've worked with extensively—that prides itself on honesty and lists integrity as one of its core values. Many companies say they pride themselves on honesty, but when put to the test, they fall short. They talk the talk, but don't walk the walk. One day, the owner of this family business and I were meeting when one of the managers asked if the owner could sign off on some large customer credits, which the owner promptly did. An hour later, in passing, the manager told the owner not to worry about the credits because the customer had already paid the bills in full. The owner was visibly appalled. "I don't care if they already paid," he told his manager. "If the customer deserves the credits, make sure they get them."

That is a perfect example of a leader modeling the core values he wants his company to live by, through his own behavior. In that moment, he sent his manager a clear message that the company's values were more important than dollars and that he would not compromise those values for a short-term gain.

A key part of building a Culture Advantage is to establish Predictive Behaviors (covered in chapter 5) that you want to ingrain in the culture and you want teams to complete every day/week. These behaviors should be as specific as possible. A manager should design their week around key leadership activities such as planning, key initiatives, accountability, motivation, talent acquisitions and development, relationship building (employee and customer), metric review, and contributing to growth. I would specify days and times for each activity. It may look something like this:

- **Mondays (accountability):** conduct weekly meetings (team and one-on-ones), track and review identified key metrics, hold team members accountable.
- **Tuesdays (talent):** talent acquisition and retention, coach and train (scheduled), motivation activities.
- **Wednesdays (relationships):** engage with employees, talk to customer decision makers (specific number each week), contribute to growth.
- **Thursdays (business):** work on plans, strategy, culture; review finances; focus on "Big Projects."
- **Fridays (yourself):** plan your days/week (specific time), focus on personal development, schedule time to think.
- **Every day (energy):** model core values, convey a positive and winning attitude, enhance positive interactions, regulate team energy, tie everything together.

I work with many companies whose executives say they want to build a profitable growth culture, a culture that includes a consistently producing sales culture, but saying it or wishing it is not going to make it happen. In order to build a strong sales culture in a company shifting to a strong growth culture, you need to define and measure the Predictive Behaviors that will consistently produce the results you want. Although these behaviors may vary by company and industry, below are some *measurable* elements that will build a winning, productive sales culture:

Every day/week I will:

- make **designated number of** prospecting attempts (phone);
- make **designated number of** prospecting attempts (in person);
- make **designated number of** attempts (other);
- ask for **designated number of** referrals;
- network for **designated number of** leads;
- generate **designated number of** web and social media leads;
- schedule **designated number of** discovery calls (first appointments with prospects);

- conduct **designated number of** presentations to prospective customers;
- sell **designated number of** new customers;
- spend **designated number of** hours in training sessions, reading, practicing, role-playing;
- sell with honesty and integrity; and
- have a positive attitude.

If a management team, sales team, or any team follows a ritualized process like this, and if each member of the team is held accountable to it, the team will produce consistent results and help build a winning culture. Most sales reps fail not because they can't sell, but because they don't follow a detailed plan with behavior requirements.

In addition to engaging with defined, measurable behaviors, having a winning attitude is also a key part of success and should be infused in your company's culture. But fostering a winning attitude can be tricky. Because it is not quantifiable, attitude is one of the hardest elements to change and manage. Sales reps often have to make a hundred or even hundreds of prospecting attempts in order to generate one new customer. Being continually rejected can be frustrating and demotivating. In order to be successful sales reps, they need to keep a positive attitude, much like Jim Carrey displays in the movie *Dumb and Dumber*.

Jim Carrey's character, Lloyd, a chauffeur, is in love with Mary, a businesswoman he's been hired to drive to the airport. Initially, Mary is not at all interested in Lloyd, but Lloyd is persistent, nonetheless. "What are my chances?" he asks Mary. "Not good," she briskly replies. Lloyd considers this for a moment and then asks, "Not good, like one out of a hundred?" To which Mary says, "I'd say more like one out of a million." Instead of being crushed, Lloyd seems energized. "So you're telling me there's a chance? Yeah!"

Although an extreme example, that is the kind of winning attitude a company with a positive, successful culture should instill in its people. This type of culture will attract and keep Culture Fit Employees. Positivity is not reserved for the boss. Regardless of your position, you contribute to winning culture. It is essential to have a winning culture to sustain results.

Once you establish core values, behavior requirements, and result objectives, it is critical that the desired behaviors are modeled and employees are held accountable immediately. Years ago, I was working on changing a company's growth culture, and an important part of that change was going to come from the service department. Growth had stalled, and our objective was plain: increase growth. One of the key elements of achieving that objective was improving the company's customer enhancement or upselling existing customers. We wanted to build a culture that prioritized upselling existing customers as an integral aspect of growth. This company did business in an industry that serviced its customers weekly. The owner and I ran some numbers and determined that by getting each service person to make *one* upselling attempt per day, the company would add 5 percent or more in additional growth in an industry that averages 3 percent to 4 percent growth. No other change would have a bigger effort-to-impact ratio. This task would only take five to ten minutes per service employee per day and, if done, would actually *double* their growth.

Before the initiative, the customer upselling culture of this company might be summed up as "we take what we can get." We wanted to evolve into a customer enhancement culture as a "condition of the job," meaning everyone on the service team would do their upselling behavior every day and be accountable or else experience negative consequences.

The one upselling attempt was what I call a Key Predictive Behavior, meaning if done consistently and well, this behavior would produce predictive results. I asked the service team to execute this behavior every day. Most followed through, and the new element of this culture—the Key Predictive Behavior—started to build momentum.

But remember, it's human nature to resist change. A senior service employee came into my office one day and informed me that he wasn't going to participate. Upselling existing customers simply wasn't for him. He hadn't done it in the past, and he wasn't going to start now. When the steps to change the culture at the company were first rolled out, I had already explained to all the employees why upselling was important to the company and, therefore, to their individual success. The employee refusing to participate understood the plan, he understood the behavior, but he was still refusing to change.

"Gary," I said to him, with obvious disappointment in my voice, "I really hate to see you go." There are going to be times when the person in charge of building the culture of a company cannot negotiate. If you allow team members to tell you what they *won't* do, you will have no success in telling them what they *must* do. My response to Gary might seem harsh, but it wasn't meant just for Gary. My response also sent a strong message to the rest of the team. Gary was testing the new culture, and his test failed. When his bluff was called, Gary performed the Key Predictive Behavior without another conversation or meeting and remained with the company.

Don't get me wrong—I always work toward full employee buy-in to a Culture Shift, but once a decision is made on that shift, it is a leader's job to follow through and expect 100 percent participation. The only way to know if any process works is to do it perfectly and expect nothing less. UCLA coaching legend John Wooden agrees; he said, "Give me 100 percent. You can't make up for a poor effort today by giving 110 percent tomorrow. You don't have 110 percent. You only have 100 percent, and that's what I want from you right now."[6]

Or as Bill Murray said, "Whatever you do, always give 100 percent. Unless you're donating blood."[7]

The daily Key Predictive Behavior required of Gary (and the other service personnel) took only five to ten minutes a day, was within his ability, would improve the company's culture, and would improve his own success. It was not optional. Would legendary UCLA basketball coach John Wooden have won ten national championships in twelve years if he had let the players decide which plays to keep in the playbook and which to eliminate? Definitely not. If you're a leader who wants to win, and by win, I mean have a growth culture with 100 percent buy-in at your company, you will need to make your point.

Evolving your company's culture will not happen overnight. It will not happen in a week or even in a month. Establishing your company's Culture Advantage is an ongoing process. Companies able to overcome a bad economy, a competitive landscape, loss of market share, and poor results are going to be those companies that continuously work on evolving with the change. They are companies that intentionally develop a culture of engagement with momentum and clear expectations and that use their culture as a true business advantage.

But remember, a Growth Culture doesn't just happen. The remaining chapters of this book include the leadership principles needed to build a Culture Advantage.

Advantage Challenge: Committed to making a workplace culture adjustment? Great! In order to do that, you need to identify and rank your company's Culture Builders and Culture Killers. Which Culture Builders needs the most work/improvement? Which Culture Killers are the biggest obstacle? Then go to work addressing them one at a time.
Reference the Culture Advantage Challenge Application (Figure A.2) at the back of the book.

Chapter Summary

- Advantage Principle: Intentional Cultures with Clear Behavior Expectations Produce Results.
- Whatever you are trying to accomplish in business (and in life), in order to achieve it, you must create a culture that supports the outcome you desire.
- Business context is always changing, and cultures need to evolve along with those changes.
- As a company gets larger, its culture needs to evolve if executives expect to profitably grow at the same pace they have in the past.
- When the competitive landscape changes, change with it.
- A great way to start making a Culture Shift is to look at what's happening inside your company that fits the culture you want and build on it.
- Owners, executives, and managers must model the behaviors they want to see in their employees.
- Pay attention to and address Culture Builders and Culture Killers.
- Advantage Principle: Grand Change Comes from Dissatisfaction with the Status Quo.
- Evolving your company's culture will not happen overnight. It will not happen in a week or even in a month. Establishing your company's Culture Advantage is a never-ending process.

Chapter Two

Commit to Your Vital Goals

ADVANTAGE PRINCIPLE: PLANNING TRUMPS WISHING.

First Lady Eleanor Roosevelt said, "It takes as much energy to wish as it does to plan."[1]

Whenever we blow out the candles on a birthday cake, we're supposed to make a wish. As kids, we often had grandiose wishes like a new bike or a trip to Disney World. Wishing seldom worked, of course, but for that split second, we were able to suspend disbelief and think for a moment that some higher power would honor our wish and make that dream come true.

Sadly, too many people and companies treat their desire for success like a wish, spending valuable time and energy wishing for success, hoping to realize their Vital Goals through some cosmic power that honors good intentions. If they would only spend that same amount of time and energy identifying their Vital Goals and developing the strategic plans to achieve them, they would inevitably be much more successful. Then their wishes might actually come true.

First, a definition. Let's break down the term "Vital Goals" into its two component parts:

Vital—an element or condition *necessary* to the existence, continuance, and well-being of something that is indispensable or essential to survival.

Goal—the *result* of achievement toward which effort is directed.

Therefore, **Vital Goals** are results necessary to the existence, continuance, and well-being of something indispensable—like your company's profitable growth and survival—and worthy of your best efforts.

Is profitable growth vital and worthy of your best effort? I hope the answer is *yes*. The phrase "worthy of our best efforts" is a critical element of this definition. Imagine for a moment that every employee at your company was focused on and spending more time doing the behaviors worthy of their best efforts. Imagine that you were focused on the priorities that would have the biggest impact on your business and personal life. It is an exciting image, isn't it? From my experience, the results can be amazing when there is this type of focused, companywide commitment.

Face it, there is nothing so useless as doing proficiently that which should not be done at all. The challenge for leaders and employees alike is to distinguish busyness from productivity. Too often I see busy employees who are unproductive. The tasks they're engaged in might be urgent, or at least they might seem urgent, but they are not vital. This all too common disconnect is caused by a lack of focus on the behaviors worthy of our best efforts. Sales representatives are a good example of this. I frequently see sales reps who aren't hitting their quotas and should be out doing the Predictive Behaviors that will bring results. Instead, they are sidetracked by time-wasting activities that make them look busy but are not productive.

A running joke in the training world: Why do theaters show so many movies on weekday afternoons? They're for salespeople!

ADVANTAGE PRINCIPLE: SUCCESS SHOULD NOT BE MEASURED BY BUSYNESS; IT SHOULD BE MEASURED BY ACCOMPLISHMENT.

Any critical activity—from building a business, to raising a family, to winning football games, to losing weight—will not be achieved without proper planning that includes prioritizing the vital (actions that require our best efforts) over the urgent (actions that are pressing but unproductive).

Take heart. If you're just realizing that you, your managers, and your frontline people are not focused, it isn't too late to change. The best time for your company to identify your Vital Goals and the Predictive Behaviors was perhaps years, months, or maybe only weeks ago. The second-best time is now. *Now* is the time for you and your company to engage in meaningful planning. *Now* is the time for you and your company to start prioritizing the Vital Goals and do the right things for the right reasons at the right time and in the right way.

Vital versus Urgent—Do You Know the Difference? Most leaders instinctively know that more time and energy must be spent on Vital Goals and less on whatever unforeseen tangent seems urgent at the moment. Take a close look at the chart below, adapted from Dwight D. Eisenhower's Urgent/Important Principle.[2]

By categorizing how you and your employees utilize time, you can begin to understand some of the key differences between productive and busy. Controlling where and how we spend our time is one of our greatest gifts if we capitalize on it.

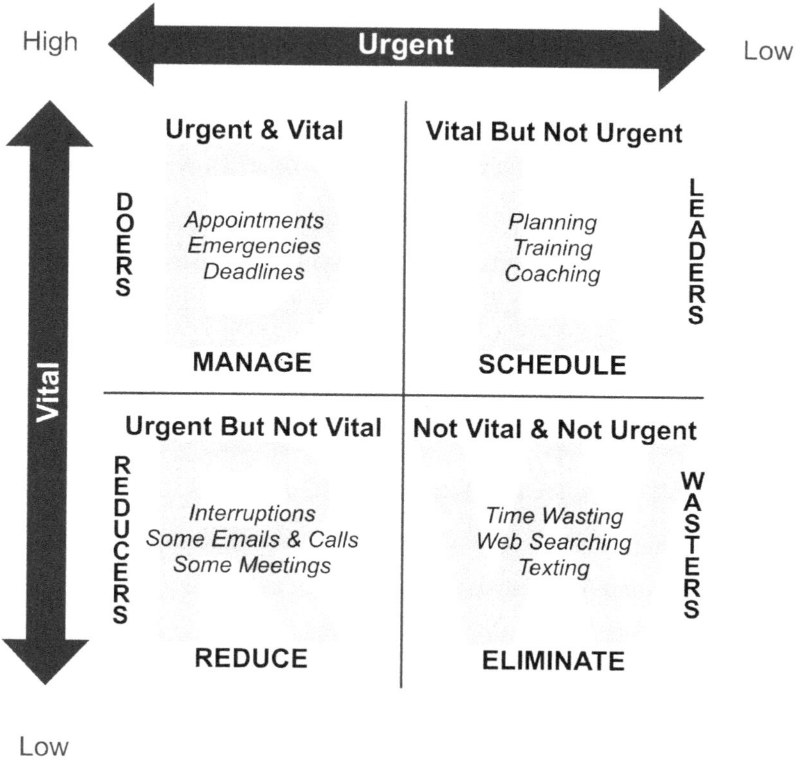

Figure 2.1. Vital-Urgent Grid

The tasks that make up our daily and weekly activities that seem urgent at the moment too often take precedence over those that are vital for results and long-term success. Why? Because of the common belief that if we're really busy, we have to be effective, right? Wrong! I wish that were true, but it's not.

During one consultation, I met with one of my client's key employees. This employee had kept a detailed log of everything she'd done throughout her days and she wanted to show it to me. Why? So that she could show me how busy she was. I looked at her log and agreed she was indeed very busy. And yet she wasn't productive. Once the client put a new plan in place that spelled out the Vital Goals and Predictive Behaviors the team needed to get busy doing, guess what? She refused to follow the plan. As a result, she did not stay with the company very long. Urgent does not equal Vital, and busy does not equal results.

One of the most overlooked advantages of planning, of identifying Vital Goals with specific Predictive Behaviors, is that talented employees will thrive and employees that don't fit your company's culture will weed themselves out. When this happens, human resource management becomes much easier and real leadership becomes self-evident.

How are your employees spending their time? How are you spending your time? Spend time reviewing the Vital-Urgent Chart. This will help you better understand not only the difference between Vital and Urgent in your own life but also how to use your time to better manage your outcomes. Think about the differences between the four quadrants for a moment and consider how they apply to your life and your business. Read on for a detailed examination of each quadrant and look for Talent Overkill tasks to delegate, time wasters to eliminate, and leadership activities to schedule.

Quadrant D—Urgent and Vital (Doers Quadrant)

Examples of activities both urgent and vital are:

- achieving your Vital Goals;
- a water pipe leaking in your second-floor restroom;
- your annual meeting is next week, and you need to write your speech;
- it's April 14 and you don't have your taxes complete;
- an important client is on the verge of leaving you for your competition;
- a growing theft problem in your business;

- an appointment with a valuable prospect who plans to make a decision this week;
- a sudden downturn in your plant's productivity; and
- three hundred deliveries scheduled to be made today.

Planning strategy: This is the **Doers Quadrant**. I call it that because these are tasks that must get done in a timely manner. They are both Vital and Urgent. The challenge is to manage the activities in this quadrant, so this quadrant does not manage you or your team. It is okay for the *appropriate* team members to be busy with **Quadrant D** activities. It is not okay for them to be impossibly busy, spending *all* their time here and still not getting the job done. Manage your **Quadrant D** situations and steer the outcomes so they align with your company's Vital Goals.

If you and your team are spending all of your time in **Quadrant D** and you still can't keep up, you are either not being honest with yourself as to where you are spending your time or you're not properly staffed. No one has the energy to give their best effort 100 percent of the time and still accomplish tasks with excellence. **Quadrant D** activities should be acted on in a timely manner by the *correct employees*, allowing leaders to spend more time and be more focused in **Quadrant L.** Leaders need to spend their time in **Quadrant L**, not **Quadrant D.**

Quadrant L—Vital but Not Urgent (Leaders Quadrant)

Examples of activities that are vital but not urgent are:

- strategic planning,
- educating yourself or your team,
- budgeting for the upcoming year,
- spending time with your children,
- completing a company growth plan,
- developing a marketing strategy,
- database management,
- sales prospecting,
- conducting training and follow-up training reinforcement,
- customer loyalty surveys,
- coaching and accountability sessions, and
- writing a book.

These are all vital activities but *not* urgent in the sense that we must do them today or even this week. Customers don't call and complain that we haven't gotten to our **Quadrant L** activities, yet **Quadrant L** activities can have a huge impact on customer loyalty. **Quadrant L** activities are vital activities that we too often put off. If you put them off for too long, they may never get done at all, which will truly limit your success. In fact, some people don't see **Quadrant L** activities as work at all! Have you ever been at a training seminar or a planning session and felt like you were just sluffing off? You must change that mindset. If you are going to develop into a true leader, **Quadrant L** activities are the most critical work you do.

Planning strategy: I call **Quadrant L** the **Leaders Quadrant**, or the **Difference Maker Quadrant**, because this quadrant is where the Difference Makers in life and in business live; the leaders who understand their Vital Goals and know they should be spending more of their time in this quadrant. They understand their role is not in "doing" but rather in "leading." By spending adequate time on things like thinking, reading, learning, planning, training, coaching, and accountability, they will make their company stronger and give their company an advantage in the market.

A great metaphor that applies to this quadrant is that these executives know not to scuff up the playing floor with their dress shoes. In other words, effective leaders can't also be the doers, in the same way that effective coaches can't also be the players. They are two different skill sets, and each requires focus for a company to realize success. When strategizing about how to reach **Vital Goals**, many of the activities necessary will fall into **Quadrant L**. But too many leaders never get to **Quadrant L** because these activities are not necessarily urgent. **Quadrant L** is for planned activities, and it is critical that you schedule them. The best leaders schedule items in **Quadrant L**, thereby making them urgent.

I often get asked how much time people should be spending in each quadrant, and it varies by position, industry, and company. Typically, the higher you are on the organizational chart and the larger your company, the more time you should be spending in the **Leaders Quadrant**. Leaders like Jeff Bezos, Mark Zuckerberg, or Tim Cook spend 90 percent of their time in the **Leaders Quadrant**. An upper-level manager may strive for 75 percent, while a middle-level manager may aspire for 50 percent of their time spent on leadership activities. Whatever the percentage, more is better, provided **Quadrant D** activities are also completed efficiently and effectively 100 percent of the time by the appropriate people.

ADVANTAGE PRINCIPLE: TIME SPENT ON LEADERSHIP ACTIVITIES COMPOUNDS LIKE INTEREST.

Quadrant R—Urgent but Not Vital (Reducers Quadrant)

Examples of urgent but not vital activities are:

- a team member poking their head into your office to talk about their day;
- unstructured meetings, unimportant e-mails, meaningless reports, and unproductive telephone calls;
- completing a task that is not your responsibility or performing tasks that should be delegated (Talent Overkill).

These are tasks that are staring you in the face all day long. They're urgent (or a coworker is trying to make them seem urgent) but not one bit critical to achieving your Vital Goals. A common source of such activities is other people trying to pass the "monkey on their back" to you. Sometimes it's appropriate to politely say *no* to people or to encourage them to solve the problem themselves.

This is the **Reducers** or **Delegators Quadrant** because these tasks need to be delegated or reduced in quantity. Often, they are activities being completed by the wrong person or by employees who are too expensive for busywork. I call this Talent Overkill, and every company commits this common sin. When an executive is doing tasks that could be completed by an administrative employee and doesn't have time for the Quadrant L leadership activities of training, coaching, and planning, that's Talent Overkill. It is also a Culture Killer.

Planning strategy: Activities in this quadrant need to be reduced, and, when possible, delegate those that cannot be reduced. One of the most effective and efficient executives I know spends very little of his time on a computer. He has someone else check and prioritize his e-mails. He dictates all his directives to his staff. These strategies may seem trivial, but they're not. They are Difference Maker activities because they allow the leader to spend time where he can have the greatest impact on the company's success. In fact, this is one of the most efficient and effective people I have ever worked with, which in return made me want to hire him for more projects. It is no surprise to me that he is a huge success.

We're all human, and none of us will ever eliminate all of our **Quadrant R** activities, but you owe it to yourself and to your company to keep your time in this quadrant to a minimum. Steve Jobs may have been one of the best at applying this principle. To keep focus, he would ask his employees, "How many times did you say *no* today?" In Jobs's opinion, the more nos the better. To have extreme, laser-like focus, Jobs was always willing to reject a lot of opportunities, even if they sounded great. Saying no is a deeply uncomfortable but really effective thing to do. It's more than a practice—it's more than a habit—it's a really wonderful ability.

Quadrant W—Not Vital and Not Urgent (Wasters Quadrant)

Examples of not vital and not urgent activities include:

- surfing the Internet;
- checking news headlines and stock quotes during business time;
- talking to team members about weekend plans during productive time; and
- texting, gaming, and social media communications not business related.

London Reuters reported that "employees who fritter time away on Facebook, Twitter, and other social media websites are costing British businesses billions. British employment website myjobgroup.co.uk said it polled 1,000 British workers and found that nearly six percent, or 2 million, of Britain's 34 million-strong workforce, spent more than an hour a day on social media while at work, amounting to more than an eighth of their entire working day."[3]

If I can get people to spend one hour on **Quadrant L** activities instead of social media, their lives change dramatically for the better. The people wasting this hour every day think they are getting away with something, and they are—they are limiting their own success and the success of their companies.

Planning strategy: Eliminate! Eliminate! Eliminate! Leaders, eliminate these activities from the productive time of your business day. Shift the time to **Quadrant L**. This is the time-wasting quadrant, and with computers, Internet, texting, Facebook, Twitter, and so on, there are more activities than ever poised to steal our time. It is imperative that you, as a company leader, eliminate these time wasters from your enterprise. I am not suggesting that people become robots, but there is a time and place for these activities and that is not during productive business hours. As an example, Zappos is a company that has a specific time allotment for when people need to be productive and when they can play.

New technologies are also making remote work, or working from home, a growing trend in the workplace. Due to more temptations, if not managed effectively, this can make controlling time-wasting activities a challenge. To avoid these pitfalls, make sure remote workers have structure, clear expectations, regular communication, and weekly accountability meetings and, by all means, use tools and technology to keep everyone focused.

Now that you've familiarized yourself with **Quadrants D**, **L**, **R**, and **W**, you can use this concept to evaluate where you are spending your time and improve your results.

Are you busy or productive? Are you a leader or a time waster? Be honest in your assessment. Do it now. Timing is a critical variable in the planning equation.

Advantage Challenge: To be successful in reaching your Vital Goals, you must take deliberate action. What Quadrant L activities do you need to improve on? Do more of? Add to your arsenal? Where will the time come from?
Reference the Time Management Advantage Challenge Application (Figure A.3) at the back of the book.

Effective planning and execution is the Ultimate Competitive Advantage. It is only through planning that you can know your Vital Goals and whether you and your team are doing the right things for the right reasons at the right time. Do you think your competition is engaged in effective planning? Do you think your competitor's employees know their employer's Vital Goals? In business, you should always work to enhance your Market Advantage. I believe that if your company outplans and outexecutes the competition, you'll have a huge Competitive Edge. In fact, if you're not actively maximizing the advantage of planning, you're missing a key opportunity to seize this advantage over your competition in the marketplace. The above quadrant exercises can help with that.

It is not an overstatement to say that the Planning Advantage may be the single most important controllable component of your career. If properly applied, planning can be an important aspect to success in the rest of your life, too.

So why don't employees focus on the most important things? We assume they know what's most important, but often they don't. Research has determined somewhere between 5 percent and 15 percent of the workforce know and understand their company's top goals—from my experience that figure is generous. Keep in mind: employees can't achieve a Vital Goal if they don't know what it is! Managers can't hold people accountable to phantom goals.

Too many employees are simply unfocused. They've got too many activities, and they don't have adequate time and resources to do the job. Employees are also asked to do too many different kinds of activities. When they're asked to do too many things, they don't do anything well. Lack of focus or too much change is another obstacle to success. Companies are flip-flopping and not consistent with their goals. Although innovation is critical in business, there is so much emphasis on new ideas and change in the business world that owners think it is their job to constantly introduce new ideas, when they are not executing the last five new ideas they already introduced. If you're not executing well on your core business activities, chances are that more new ideas—unless they are related to execution—are probably not the solution.

There is a simple secret to getting your team to focus. The more you focus (fewer initiatives), the more you and others can accomplish with excellence. Now, I get that there's always a multitude of things going on in a business day, but, once again, if we can narrow the focus to be more on our Vital Goals, people will achieve more with excellence and have more control and greater outcomes.

How many Vital Goals should a company have? Although there's no clear answer, I generally believe the fewer the better. Keep them to a minimum. Companies that try to wrangle too big a footprint or master too many enterprises likely won't accomplish any with excellence, which puts them at a competitive disadvantage. Effective CEOs, like Steve Jobs, limit the top initiatives their leadership teams focus on each year. Walk into an Apple store and it is amazing how few products they sell (outside of accessories and content), yet the volume of their sales revenue is huge and growing.

In my experience, a company can't be focused on more than one to four Vital Goals at any given time. Four may even be too many; three is a more manageable number. Consider how that number multiplies when you start breaking it down into each department's contribution and then each individual's contribution. It expands exponentially. If you try to pursue more than three goals, you run the risk of diluting your resources and scattering your focus. I also like to keep the department and individual goals in that ratio when possible. This can be a challenge when a select department has two or three elements that contribute to one of the company's Vital Goals. Always try to narrow the focus when possible. I believe in having at least one or two training goals to support the Vital Goals. Also, determine what tools your team needs to complete the goals efficiently.

Lastly, once you establish your Vital Goals, you must keep that focus and not switch gears every week, every month, or every quarter. You must be consistent with your goals and with your message, or people will stop taking you seriously. Without laser focus, a team's energy is zapped and goals are seldom achieved; with it, anything can be accomplished.

ADVANTAGE PRINCIPLE: COMMIT 100 PERCENT TO VITAL GOALS. IT IS THE EASIEST COMMITMENT TO KEEP.

Peter Drucker said, "Unless commitment is made, there are only promises and hopes . . . but no plans."[1] If you want to make sure your Vital Goals are achieved, you and all contributors on your team need to commit to them 100 percent and point all efforts and actions toward achievement. If you make less than a 100 percent commitment, you leave room for debate, interpretation, and doubt. When you're interested, you do something only when it's convenient. When you commit, you accept no excuses, only results; and 100 percent commitment is the easiest commitment to keep.

With my clients, I ask for a recommitment to the goal(s) during every visit. This is an important step toward improving outcomes. Once you commit to a Vital Goal, you are not just committing to the goal itself; you are also committing to the actions and Predictive Behaviors required to accomplish that goal. Consider these truisms:

- While most people are interested in successes, top performers are committed.
- While most of us are interested in exercise, people who run marathons and complete triathlons are committed.
- While all executives and managers are interested in being leaders, effective leaders commit to their craft. Remember, leaders are made, not born.

Now that you've determined your Vital Goals, you've got to make sure that you have the discipline to include *all* the steps that are going to help achieve those goals. You need to make sure Vital Goals are specific, detailed, and based on Predictive Behaviors with buy-in from your employees. You've got to make sure you're focused, you can measure results, and you're prepared to adjust to get to the final outcomes you want to achieve.

Advantage Challenge: Brainstorm your company's potential Vital Goals. Prioritize the top one, two, and/or three goals worthy of your best effort. Eliminate all the rest. As you work though the book, establish Baselines and Brass Rings for each goal, as well as a plan for achieving each of these goals. Examples of Vital Goals I've seen include: Growth, Profit, Net Promoter Score (NPS), Return on Invested Capital, Customer Retention, and so on.
Reference the Vital Goals Advantage Challenge Application (Figure A.4) at the back of the book.

Chapter Summary

- Advantage Principle: Planning Trumps Wishing.
- Too many people and companies treat their desire for success like a wish, hoping to realize their Vital Goals through good intentions.
- Vital Goals: Results necessary to the existence, continuance, and well-being of something indispensable (like your company's profitable growth and survival) and worthy of your best efforts.
- Advantage Principle: Success Should Not Be Measured by Busyness; It Should Be Measured by Accomplishment.
- A challenge for leaders and employees alike is to separate busyness from productivity.
- How are your employees spending their time? How are you spending your time? Knowing the difference between what's truly vital to results and what may be merely momentarily urgent can be the cornerstone to success.
- Advantage Principle: Time Spent on Leadership Activities Compounds Like Interest.
- It is only through planning that you can know your Vital Goals and whether you and your team are doing the right things for the right reasons at the right time.

- Keep in mind: employees can't achieve a Vital Goal if they don't know what it is! Managers can't hold people accountable to phantom goals.
- Advantage Principle: Commit 100 Percent to Vital Goals. It Is the Easiest Commitment to Keep.
- Once you establish your Vital Goals, you must keep that focus and not switch gears every week, every month, or every quarter.
- You must be consistent with your goals and with your message, or people will stop taking you seriously.

Chapter Three

Be Specific

ADVANTAGE PRINCIPLE: THE MORE CLEARLY YOU AND YOUR TEAM SEE THE GOAL, THE MORE LIKELY YOU ARE TO ACHIEVE IT.

Let's get specific. Having specific goals with deadlines attached are critical elements toward achieving goals and maximizing growth, but too often I see companies (and individuals) failing in this area. Frequently, when I ask people what their company's top goals are, I get vague answers like "enhance growth," "improve profits," "sell more business than we lose," "increase sales," "reduce costs," and "hire more talent." These all sound like reasonable goals, but in truth they actually say very little and, therefore, have a negligible chance of being achieved. The comedian Jane Wagner said it well: "All my life, I always wanted to be somebody. Now I see that I should have been more specific."[1]

Vagueness is the enemy of achievement. General goals don't get taken seriously, while specific goals clarify what bull's-eyes people should be aiming at and hitting. This is because goals that lack clarity open the door to interpretation and don't provide the necessary benchmarks against which success can be measured. Unproductive employees can hide behind a company's unspecific goals, no matter how well intentioned the goals might be. As a leader, you should be doing all you can to eliminate hiding places. When a company has dozens, hundreds, or even thousands of confused employees with good intentions but no bull's-eyes, success and profitable growth will *not* be sustained. Bull's-eyes will *not* be hit.

ADVANTAGE PRINCIPLE: AN UNAIMED ARROW NEVER MISSES, BUT IT DOESN'T HIT MANY BULL'S-EYES.

This chapter will show you how to make your Vital Goals specific. To see concrete examples of why unambiguous goals are important, contrast the general goals in the list below with their more specific counterparts. Which goals do you think are more likely to be achieved?

- Improve service versus improve Net Promoter Score (a gauge of customer loyalty) from 45 percent to 65 percent by (deadline date)—see NPS description in sidebar.
- Increase sales versus increase new sales 20 percent by (deadline date).
- Expand the sales force versus have (specific number) of sales reps producing (specific $) per time period.
- Enhance our SEM (search engine marketing) versus generate ten new customers through website and social medial leads weekly.
- Reduce lost business versus retain 95 percent of existing customers annually by revenue.
- Exercise more versus exercise one hour per day six days per week.
- Lose weight versus lose twelve pounds in the next twelve months (one pound per month).
- Enhance growth versus grow revenue 15 percent annually (double the size of the company in five years).
- Enhance cash flow versus increase operating profit to 20 percent annually.
- Make steady improvement in the space program versus land a man on the moon by the end of the decade.

ADVANTAGE PRINCIPLE: A SPECIFIC VITAL GOAL IS A DREAM WITH A DEADLINE.

W. Edwards Deming, economist, engineer, and Automotive Hall of Fame inductee, said, "It's not enough to do your best; you must first know what to do and then do your best."[2] Four problems I see with goal setting are: (1) no goals, (2) goals are too general, (3) goals are set

"Net Promoter Score" is a customer loyalty metric developed by Fred Reichheld, of Reichheld, Bain & Co., and by Satmetrix. It was introduced by Reichheld in his 2003 *Harvard Business Review* article, "One Number You Need to Grow,"[3] and is detailed thoroughly in his books *The Ultimate Question*[4] and *The Ultimate Question 2.0*.[5]

The Net Promoter Score, or NPS, breaks your customers into three basic categories: Promoters, Passives, and Detractors. By asking your customers this simple question, "How likely is it that you would recommend [your company] to a friend or colleague?" and rating their answers on a scale of 0 to 10, you can categorize the answers as follows:

- **Promoters** (score 9–10) are loyal customers who will keep buying and refer others, fueling profitable growth.
- **Passives** (score 7–8) are satisfied but unenthusiastic customers who are vulnerable to competitive offerings.
- **Detractors** (score 0–6) are unhappy customers who can damage your brand and impede your company's growth through negative word-of-mouth.

To calculate your company's NPS, take the percentage of your customers who are Promoters and subtract the percentage who are Detractors. NPS is a great predictor of customer loyalty, which in turn is a great predictor of profitable growth.

too low (safe), and (4) goals are set too high (unachievable). All four of these problems limit growth and success. That is why I use precise performance classifications when setting specific goals. These classifications give employees an achievable goal and a stretch goal and most importantly communicate what is unacceptable.

ADVANTAGE PRINCIPLE: IF YOU WANT TO INCREASE YOUR GROWTH TRAJECTORY, INCREASE YOUR STANDARDS.

When setting goals for both results and behavior, I classify performance using the following categories:

Brass Ring Goals and Performance—A stretch goal for companies and individuals. Brass Ring goals are achievable but require a superior level of performance. My management philosophy for Brass Ring producers is: **"I work for you."** My goal is to sustain this performance and keep this talent. In the elements of growth classifications, which we will discuss in detail in the next chapter, it is my goal to have 25 percent or more of a team be Brass Ring. Sure, we wish 100 percent of the team was Brass Ring, but I have yet to see it achieved, and if your company does, it is likely your Brass Ring goals are set too low.

Baseline Goals and Performance—The minimum acceptable standard for the company, for a department, or for a contributing individual. Baseline Goals should be reasonably achievable for everyone on the team. My management philosophy for Baseline performers is: **"You work for me."** Although we should always strive to get everyone to Brass Ring results, in most positions, Baseline results are acceptable. In fact, many of my clients would love to have a full team of Baseline producers! One exception to this is at the executive level. All executive-level employees must be Brass Ring leaders or have the potential to become Brass Ring. In the elements of growth classifications that I will discuss in the next chapter, it is my goal to have 50 percent or more of the team Above Baseline—75 percent including Brass Ring.

Below Baseline Performance—An unacceptable standard of performance. Coming in Below Baseline is unacceptable and should have consequences. My management philosophy for Below Baseline performers is: **"I'm moving in."** As their manager, you should have contact with these employees as frequently as possible until they get their productivity Above Baseline. Too often I see companies set goals that are not being achieved and no one is held accountable. This means the goals are not taken seriously and become useless. In the elements of growth classifications discussed in the next chapter, it is my goal to have 25 percent or less of the team Below Baseline. This may sound easy, but I assure you, it is not.

ADVANTAGE PRINCIPLE: YOU SET THE STANDARD BY WHAT YOU TOLERATE.

Establishing specific Vital Growth goals is only the first part of the growth planning process, but it is a critical part of achieving the sustained growth that exceeds industry standards. As you can see in the

Compounded Growth

Growth	5%	10%	15%	20%	25%
Starting Annual Revenue	**$10,000,000**	**$10,000,000**	**$10,000,000**	**$10,000,000**	**$10,000,000**
Year 1	$10,500,000	$11,000,000	$11,500,000	$12,000,000	$12,500,000
Year 2	$11,025,000	$12,100,000	$13,225,000	$14,400,000	$15,625,000
Year 3	$11,576,250	$13,310,000	$15,208,750	$17,280,000	$19,531,250
Year 4	$12,155,063	$14,641,000	$17,490,063	$20,736,000	$24,414,063
Year 5	**$12,762,816**	**$16,105,100**	**$20,113,572**	**$24,883,200**	**$30,517,578**
Year 6	$13,400,956	$17,715,610	$23,130,608	$29,859,840	$38,146,973
Year 7	$14,071,004	$19,487,171	$26,600,199	$35,831,808	$47,683,716
Year 8	$14,774,554	$21,435,888	$30,590,229	$42,998,170	$59,604,645
Year 9	$15,513,282	$23,579,477	$35,178,763	$51,597,804	$74,505,806
Year 10	**$16,288,946**	**$25,937,425**	**$40,455,577**	**$61,917,364**	**$93,132,257**

Figure 3.1. Compounded Growth

following Compounded Growth chart, revenue growth acts much like compound interest. In the chart, you can see how growing 5 percent to 25 percent annually can compound over five years and ten years.

This example company has a starting annual revenue of $10,000,000. Grow 10 percent annually and revenue doubles every seven years. Grow 15 percent annually and revenue doubles every five years. Grow revenue 25 percent and revenue doubles every three years. Whatever your industry's growth standards are, if you follow a proven growth strategy, you should be able to exceed those industry averages. Now, I know it probably sounds scary to grow and double your revenue, but I can assure you that growing in the right way almost always enhances profit. I've worked with a number of companies that were concerned that the cost of growing at a faster pace would reduce profitability, yet, in virtually every case, profit rose as well. These outcomes helped to make these companies Strategically Brave.

Advantage Challenge: Ask yourself? When would you like to see your company revenue double in size? Do you have a strategic growth plan? Are you prepared?

Once you establish your Specific Vital Goals, don't keep them to yourself! It is imperative that you shout your goals from the rooftops and make sure they are understandable, achievable, and measurable. Write the goals down, pass them around, post them, publish them, and communicate them to everyone from, the executive team to the front line. If everyone needs to sing from the same song sheet for your company to be successful, then you'd better make sure everyone knows the melody by heart. Jack Welch, in the book *Jack: Straight from the Gut*, said, "Like every goal and initiative we've ever launched, I repeated the message over and over again until I nearly gagged on the words. The organization had to see every management action aligned with the vision."[6] Your company needs to see every decision and action aligned with the Vital Goals. If you don't feel like you have repeated the message too much, you have not repeated it enough.

One of humankind's most spectacular scientific achievements, landing a man on the moon, is also a great example of how specific goals can make a difference. John F. Kennedy made sure the world knew the goal, which then put a substantial amount of pressure on NASA toward achieving it.

Just five months after he was elected, President John F. Kennedy put a deadline on a nation's dream: "I believe that this nation should commit itself to achieving the goal, before this decade is out, of landing a man on the moon and returning him safely to the Earth."[7] That was 1961. America's space program was still in its infancy and far from being on track to achieve anything, much less a moon landing.

President Kennedy, in his speech, said the following:

> It is time . . . for this nation to take a clearly leading role in space achievement, which in many ways may hold the key to our future on earth. I believe we possess all the resources and talents necessary. But the facts of the matter are that we have never made the national decisions or marshaled the national resources required for such leadership. We have never specified long-range goals on an urgent time schedule, or managed our resources and our time so as to insure their fulfillment. . . . I believe that this nation should commit itself to achieving the goal, before this decade is out, of landing a man on the moon and returning him safely to the Earth. No single space project in this period will be more impressive to mankind or more important for the long-range exploration of space; and none will be so difficult or expensive to accomplish.[8]

In 1950, NASA's goal was "Make steady improvement in the space program." When Kennedy was elected, he made this the goal: "Land a man on the moon by the end of the decade." In his historic speech to Congress, he clearly articulated (1) the lack of a Vital Goal for the space program, (2) the lack of a critical timeline to achieve this goal,

(3) the lack of commitment to a goal, and (4) the lack of commitment of adequate resources to achieve this goal. In his decree, the president identified the Vital Goal, set out a distinct timeline for achieving that goal, and asked Congress for the resources to do it. In a word, he made it specific.

What happened? Those of us who are old enough to remember it were sitting in front of a television set on July 21, 1969, and will never forget the moment astronaut Neil Armstrong said, "One small step for man; one giant leap for mankind," and planted his foot on the lunar surface. We had accomplished what many believed was impossible, and we had done so within eight years of President Kennedy's identification of the US space program's Vital Goal. Armstrong and his Apollo 11 team then safely returned back home. Like most goals, the moon landing never would have happened without specific goals and a clear deadline.

The computing power in today's average smartphone far exceeds what was available to Mission Control back in 1969.[9] You live in an era when you have virtually unlimited access to previously unimagined twenty-first-century technology. So ask yourself: How much can I accomplish today by identifying my Vital Goals specifically and completely and then setting out a plan to achieve them?

Questions to consider when gauging whether a Vital Goal is specific:

- **Are goals specific (dream/deadline)?**—Is there a clearly defined outcome with a deadline that everyone on the team who contributes to the goal knows and understands?
- **Are you absolutely committed?**—Are you and your team members committed to expending the energy and resources required to accomplish this goal? Failure is not an option.
- **What is the upside (pleasure)?**—Are the benefits of achieving this goal worth the energy and resources required? Does the upside outweigh the downside in everyone's mind?
- **What is the downside (pain)?**—Are the energy, effort, and resources worth it or do they outweigh the benefits of achieving the goal? Any time an employee (even subconsciously) believes the downside outweighs the upside, they will not exert the energy required to achieve the goal.
- **Is it achievable?**—Is the goal achievable and do the contributing team members believe their contribution is achievable? For someone

to be motivated to do anything, they must believe what they are being asked to do is doable. Great leaders excel in this area.
- **Is it measurable?**—Is there a quantitative way of gauging progress and knowing when the goal is achieved?

I've seen companies make amazing strides by prioritizing Specific Vital Goals, but it is critical that you don't just pull these numbers out of the air. It is imperative to have a detailed plan not just for achieving the goals but also for establishing them in the first place. Saying you are going to grow your business by 10 percent Baseline and 20 percent Brass Ring sounds good, but it will only be meaningful and achievable if you have a detailed plan and everyone involved knows what their contribution must be.

The next chapter will show you how to establish your goals thoughtfully versus plucking a number from the past, or worse, out of the air randomly.

Advantage Challenge: Are your Vital Goals specific? Ask the following questions: Are they specific (dream/deadline)? Are you absolutely committed? What is the upside (pleasure)? What is the downside (pain)? Is it achievable? Is it measurable? *Reference the Be Specific Advantage Challenge Application (Figure A.5) at the back of the book.*

Chapter Summary

- Advantage Principle: The More Clearly You and Your Team See the Goal, the More Likely You Are to Achieve It.
- Advantage Principle: An Unaimed Arrow Never Misses, but It Doesn't Hit Many Bull's-eyes.
- Advantage Principle: A Specific Vital Goal Is a Dream with a Deadline.
- To calculate your company's NPS (Net Promoter Score), take the percentage of your customers who are Promoters and subtract the percentage who are Detractors. NPS is a great predictor of customer loyalty, which in turn is a great predictor of profitable growth.
- Advantage Principle: If You Want to Increase Your Growth Trajectory, Increase Your Standards.

- Brass Ring goals are achievable but require a superior level of performance. My management philosophy for Brass Ring producers is "I work for you."
- Baseline goals and performance are the minimum acceptable standard for the company, for a department, or for a contributing individual. My management philosophy for Baseline performers is "You work for me."
- Below Baseline performance is an unacceptable standard of performance. My management philosophy for Below Baseline performers is "I'm moving in."
- Advantage Principle: You Set the Standard by What You Tolerate.
- Once you establish your Specific Vital Goals, don't keep them to yourself! It is important that you shout your goals from the rooftops and make sure they are understandable, achievable, and measurable.
- It is imperative to have a detailed plan not just for achieving the goals but also for establishing them in the first place.

Chapter Four

Make It Personal

ADVANTAGE PRINCIPLE: SHORTEN TIME FRAMES, REMOVE HIDING SPOTS, AND MAKE GOALS PERSONAL.

Pick up a business magazine on any newsstand or visit a business news website and you'll find all sorts of articles celebrating the accomplishments of successful companies. Company achievements can be impressive, but it is important to understand that companies by themselves don't accomplish anything—they are artificial entities; it is the *people* working for those companies who have the power to achieve Vital Goals. That is why business goals must be made personal, in the shortest time frame possible, from the executive level to the front line.

ADVANTAGE PRINCIPLE: ACHIEVE BUSINESS SUCCESS BY HAVING MORE PEOPLE DOING THE MOST IMPORTANT THINGS MORE OFTEN.

And yet it has been my experience that too many employees don't work up to their best potential. Not because they are bad people with bad intentions, but, as already noted, they don't know their company's Vital Goals and expectations. If they don't know their company's Vital Goals, how can they know their personal goals and contributions? How can anyone possibly do their best if they don't even know what their best is supposed to be? What they don't know and understand they can't achieve.

Advantage Challenge: In a prior chapter, we challenged you to prioritize your Vital Goals. Now, ask everyone on your team if they know the company's Vital Goals, their personal goals, and how their personal goals contribute to the accomplishment of the company's Vital Goals. Work on it until the answers from everyone on your team are specific and consistent.

In this chapter, I will discuss how to translate a company's Vital Goals into individual employee goals by identifying the contributing elements, making goals personal for each contributor, and shortening the time frames for goals and accountability—which, in return, removes hiding spots. Typically, after completing this exercise, company leaders realize that they can grow and accomplish more than they thought possible. By identifying their elements of growth and establishing personal goals, many companies that had meager growth expectations of 2 percent to 5 percent realized they could exceed their industry standards and grow annually by 8 percent to 15 percent or more on a sustained basis.

Never pick goals at random or base them on what you've accomplished in the past. The key is to work the process backward. Once you decide that growth is a Vital Goal and establish preliminary growth expectations, you need to determine the elements that contribute to growth and make the goals personal by establishing the Baseline and Brass Ring goals for each contributor in each element. By making the goals personal, Vital Goals become specific versus picking a number out of the air or adding a percent or two to last year's results. In most cases, by planning this way you will find that the goals increase dramatically, thereby exceeding the Vital Goal expectations. Or you might realize the opposite: because you don't have enough contributing elements or contributors in each element, you won't achieve your goals even if everyone on the team exceeds their standard. I've had this happen at training sessions where people come up to me afterward and say that when making these calculations—making it personal—they realized they don't have enough contributors to hit their established goals.

In order to accomplish any Vital Goal, careful attention must be given to detail. Consider the man who many believe coined that famous line "God is in the details." In 1938, German architect Ludwig Mies van der Rohe was named director of the Armour Institute in Chicago, a place of higher learning that was becoming known as an emerging center for a new breed of progressive architects. Mies's first task upon arrival at his new job? Change the curriculum. Mies required architecture students return to a back-to-basics education in order to get their degree.[1] How could they design masterpieces if they did not know how to draw? How could they have command over the construction of skyscrapers if they did not know how to build a simple house? How could any building be built properly if every contractor did not have a copy of the blueprints and know their role?

The meaning to Mies's famous quote is important, just as working out the details for achieving Vital Goals is important. Whatever one does, it should be done thoroughly with everyone knowing their role and taking a personal interest in the details. Imagine building a house or facility without each contractor and their workers knowing the blueprint for the desired outcome of what the building should look like and knowing their role and time frame for completion. Envision the outcome if you asked the framers, the carpenters, the plumbers, and the electricians to describe what they were building, their contribution, and the expected completion date and they all gave different answers! The outcome of this project might be interesting, but it would not meet expectations. This is a truism for architecture and building, of course, but it has a direct application to business outcomes. This is why I call the Growth Advantage planning and execution model a "Blueprint."

Now comes the hard part. Getting started! American author and humorist Mark Twain knew the secret to that stumbling block. He said, "The secret of success is simply getting started, and the secret of getting started is to break complex, overwhelming tasks into small manageable tasks, and then starting on the first one."[2] How do you make goals personal, so your company achieves its Vital Goals?

Follow these steps:

1. Start by forming a Vital Goal Team. If growth is the Vital Goal, create a Growth Team. A Vital Goal Team should be made up of a small group (six to twelve) of the executives, managers, and other impactors of the Vital Goal. Have a team for each Vital Goal.

2. Determine preliminary Baseline and Brass Ring goals. I like to establish preliminary goals and have a benchmark to determine if those numbers are met or exceeded in the planning session. What accomplishment for the year would make the team happy? If the preliminary growth goals are determined to be 10 percent Baseline and 20 percent Brass Ring, but after completing the steps below, during the planning session, the Baseline goal is 4 percent and the Brass Ring 6 percent, we still have some work to do. We may need to increase the personal goals, the number of elements, or the number of contributors. I'm typically pleased when the goals established after the planning session are higher than the preliminary established goals. Keep in mind, most companies achieve results that are somewhere between their Baseline and Brass Ring.

3. Identify the elements of growth (or the elements that contribute to the achievement of any Vital Goal). Besides determining the elements that will contribute to your company's growth, also determine how many contributors you need in each element. Determining the number of contributors is as critical as establishing the goals for each element. For example, in financial services, real estate, and insurance, it is not just important to grow new sales; it is important to grow the number of contributors producing those results. If you don't grow the number of producers, eventually growth will stagnate. You can do this by adding contributors in existing markets or you can expand markets. I was working with a company that doubled in size, and one of their key elements of growth was new sales from their sales department. They wanted to continue to grow, and yet they refused to expand their sales team at the pace of their growth. Well, you can guess what happened to their growth. It eventually stalled until we expanded the number of producers.

I also feel it is beneficial to expand the number of elements that contribute to your growth or contribute to the achievement of any Vital Goal. The more people and elements contributing to any outcome, the more consistent and sustainable the results will be. I've seen many companies add elements of growth that they previously were not focusing on, and those elements became key contributors to sustainable growth.

Three ways you can increase revenue are (1) increase your number of customers (new customers and customer retention); (2) increase the frequency with which customers purchase (repeat sales); (3) increase the average dollar amount of each purchase (price increases, add additional charges, exchange existing product or service for a more expensive product or service, combine the original product with one or more related products—package, or offer new or additional products or services).

Elements of growth might include:

- **New Customers (addition of new customers):** Regardless of what your company sells—software, advertising, subscriptions, insurance, financial services, real estate, cars, copiers, or services—the addition of new customers is a crucial element of healthy growth. Whether you are adding new customers with sales representatives (outside, inside, retail, etc.), with new stores or locations, through your website or social media, through Amazon or Shopify, or in any other way, it is important to grow the number of contributors to this element at the same pace as your growth. As an example, if you're consistently growing at 12 percent to 15 percent annually (and if that is in line with your future growth plans), depending on the percent of your growth coming from this element, you will need to grow your number of contributors and/or contributions from this element at this pace as well. In order to generate new customers, you need to create shifts in the market, become visible to a market that is oblivious, become relevant to a disinterested market, become credible for potential customers to be open to your product or service, build trust for them to be receptive, provide value for them to show interest, and convey an advantage for them to take action.
- **Customer Enhancement (upselling existing customers):** This is an undercapitalized element of growth. The customers themselves should be looked at as a market, and accordingly, we should sell our existing customers everything we offer. I have seen many companies who were not focusing on customer upselling, and when they added this as an element of growth, it became a key contributor. I asked an incredibly successful company that was very effective at upselling customers if they ever run out of upselling opportunity, and they said *no*. They believed they could double the size of their company without adding one new customer. Just imagine if you could do this in your company! Well, maybe you can. Companies not utilizing this element are leaving a substantial amount of profitable growth on the table.
- **Price Increases:** Getting fair price increases can be a significant element of maintaining a healthy business, and if you are providing value to your customers and investing in your market advantage, you should be getting these increases. Netflix is spending a substantial amount on quality content for their customers (billions), so they increased prices. They were butchered in the press, but guess what? As their value to cost is amazing, their metrics and stock price continued

to improve. If you're afraid to increase prices fairly, your company may have other issues you need to address.

- **Added Charges:** Car rental companies, airlines, mobile phone companies, and many other industries use this element as a mechanism for growth and short-term profit. Be careful. Companies get addicted to these types of charges, and if abused, they can impact customer loyalty negatively, which in the long run may have a negative impact on profitable growth. When all the other airlines were adding baggage charges, Southwest Airlines did not and turned not charging for bags into a Competitive Advantage. This element of growth can be effective when done fairly, but it can also be effective if you're the contrarian in your industry.
- **Customer Retention and Repeat Sales:** Customer retention is a "keystone" element of profitable growth. It is obviously much easier to sustain growth when you build customer loyalty, retain customers, and generate repeat sales. I've worked with companies that were losing more than 10 percent of their customers annually, which meant they needed to add 10 percent through other elements before they even started growing. Once retention was improved, they not only found that growth improved but also became more sustainable and profitable. Some companies, like satellite or cable TV and Internet service providers, mobile phone service, and linen service companies, utilize contacts that have repeat sales built into their business model. Others, because of their offering and advantage, like Amazon with one-click purchasing of almost anything with free shipping, have customer retention and repeat sales built into their model. Either way you need to always work on customer loyalty with your offering, service, and innovation. Purchasing from Amazon is easy, and being easy to do business with is a great customer loyalty builder. The best way to generate repeat sales is to earn it.
- **Economic Impact (growth or shrinkage):** Although this is an element of growth you can't always make personal or control, it should be factored into your growth goal calculation and be included in progress calculations and reports. The better your company is at sustaining the other elements of growth in your plan, the less you have to be fearful of this element. Companies that consistently outpace historic and industry averages typically do the same during economic downturns.
- **Other:** This list can be unlimited depending on the industry your company is in.

4. Make Vital Goals Personal. Every contributor in your company needs to know how *they* contribute with personal goals. In order to achieve any Vital Goal, their personal contribution for achieving it needs to be understood. Sounds simple, right? And yet too many managers and too many companies don't do it! I am often in training sessions where participants come up to me after the session and tell me they were not aware that what they do has such a big impact on their company's growth.

Let me share a story I think illustrates the importance of making things personal. When I moved back to Wisconsin, I moved to a small town, and while I was there, the Green Bay Packers won the Super Bowl, the Wisconsin Badgers won the Rose Bowl, and the local high school football team won the state championship. As you can probably imagine, children were outside playing football in every yard you drove by.

Well, I happened to be at the high school one day, and I sat and watched the coaching staff work with the team. I found it fascinating and enlightening. The head coach worked with one player for the majority of the time, making sure this player knew what his role was for every formation and for every play called. The coach was not only making sure this student knew his role on every play, but he was making sure the rest of the team knew that position's role on each formation and play, too. The coach was Making It Personal because in football if one player takes the play off or makes a mistake the results can be game changing. Now imagine if every coach did this at every practice! That is what they did, and that is why they won state championships. They created a winning culture on the practice field by clarifying roles and expectations. Do this in business—build team accountability though awareness—and the results can be just as exciting as winning a state championship.

5. Shorten Time Frames. By that I mean set, manage, and hold team members accountable to their goals in the shortest time frames reasonable—days and weeks versus quarters or years, plays versus games. Effective leaders know the longer you let underperformance go unmanaged without an accountability nudge, the more likely underperformance will become a habit. If I could manage by the hour, I would! Underproducers and new employees especially need to have their work expectations broken down into the shortest time frames feasible. This way, you never get too far off course without making needed adjustments, and nonperforming employees can't hide. I am not suggesting you should not have five-year strategic plans, annual growth and profit goals, or quarterly project goals. I'm also not suggesting that you should not empower your employees. You should! The key is to break those goals into personal, bite-sized chunks for each contributing employee. Because effective leaders are helping to make people and, accordingly, the companies they work for more successful, they make these types of employment requirements a positive and not a negative.

Accountability is a good thing, and the closer the feedback comes in relation to the outcome, the more effective it is. If you are a parent, you'll know exactly what I mean by this. When your toddler learns a new word and pronounces it right for the first time, you praise them immediately, not a week or a month later! By then your approval will have lost all meaning. If a teenager does not follow the rules and they don't experience immediate consequences, it is likely this behavior will be repeated. The same goes for business behavior.

6. Remove Hiding Spots. The bigger a company gets, and the more remote the workers are, the more hiding spots there will be. That's just the way it works. People don't always set out to find hiding spots, but if they do not know their goals, do not know how they contribute, and are not held accountable, they will disappear into a hiding spot. They will exist instead of produce. In a three-person company, everybody knows what everybody else is doing, and conversely, if something is not getting done, it is obvious who is responsible for the oversight. Conversely, when there are tens, hundreds, or thousands of employees, nonproducers can slip between the cracks. In companies focused on growth, leaders need to know what everyone is doing and producing every day, every week, every month, especially as the company grows. The larger a company gets, the less efficient it can become if it doesn't follow proven leadership principles. Additional staff does not always produce additional output at the same pace. But once hiding spots are gone, Brass Ring and Above Baseline employees will stand out in a good way. Below Baseline employees will stand out in a bad way and either step up, move on, or be let go. Chip Heath and Dan Heath in the book *Switch* said it well: "Big-picture, hands-off leadership isn't likely to work in a change situation, because the hardest part of change—the paralyzing part—is precisely in the details."[3]

All six of the above steps will help you work toward demystifying your company's growth into something understandable, measured, and personal. Your job is to make sure everyone knows his or her specific role, and that is key. Alfred North Whitehead, philosopher, said, "We think in generalities, but we live in detail." As a leader, you've got to live in the details, especially when talent is increasingly hard to come by.

When I first meet with the owners or leaders of companies, I always ask them by what percentage they would like to grow. Interestingly, their answer is typically very conservative. But when they form a Growth Team (a group of executives and contributors from the various departments that contribute to growth) and determine how much people can contribute (based on individual Baseline and Brass Ring goals) in the various elements of growth, the goals are typically *two to five times as high* as what they originally thought. The best part is they typically achieve those results and outpace their historic and industry average.

One of my early client's growth had stalled, which is a death knell for a capital-intensive business. When I asked the executive team how much they wanted to grow, they said they would be very happy with 4 to 5 percent growth. At the first planning session with the Growth Team, we made objectives personal, and they set their Baseline growth goal at 12 percent and the Brass Ring growth goal at 30 percent. Keep in mind this was in an industry that was averaging low-single-digit growth at best.

I won't lie to you: I walked out of that meeting a little scared, thinking that we had set the bar too high and that their goal was going to be difficult for them to achieve. Then I reminded myself that we had not plucked a number out of the air. These goals were established in a detailed planning session where we Made Goals Personal based on reasonable standards for all contributors.

The end of the story? This company *doubled* their revenue in a little more than six years by exceeding their Baseline goal each year, and more than 60 percent of that growth came from new elements. Extraordinary? Yes, and all it meant was taking the extra planning time.

When people know what is expected of them and there is nowhere in the company to hide, goals are achieved at a greater magnitude and with greater consistency. Making it personal and removing hiding places typically make more would-be contributors actually contribute. And although everyone loves a Brass Ring producer and most people think that is where the magic comes from, the reality is that for consistent growth, the majority of the team must just stay Above Baseline (75 percent plus) if you are staffed properly.

Clients I work with submit behavior and result numbers to Growth Advantage monthly (internally they capture them daily or weekly).

There have been companies I've worked with where an astonishing 90 percent of the contributors to the Vital Goals were Below Baseline when we started! Obviously, that is a formula for failure. As already noted, it is my goal to get 75 percent or more of the team Above Baseline with 25 percent being Brass Ring. However, if 90 percent are Below Baseline, one of three things is happening: (1) the Baseline goals are set too high, (2) there is no blueprint to achieve the goals, or (3) there are no metrics or accountability. If 100 percent of the team is Above Baseline, you are either a very blessed company or the goals are set too low.

As a rule of thumb, the better defined your details are, the more effective you can be at communicating the Vital Goals of the organization. God may indeed be in the details, but so is your success. Details help you know exactly what needs to be accomplished in order to achieve your Vital Goals, and that precision is exactly what you need to succeed.

Advantage Challenge: Determine your growth goal (or any Vital Goal) by:

1. Start by forming a Vital Goal Team.
2. Determine preliminary Baseline and Brass Ring goals.
3. Establish all the elements that will contribute to the goal.
4. Decide how many contributors you will have for each element.
5. Establish weekly Baseline and Brass Ring goals for each contributor.
6. Calculate annual outcomes by multiplying the number of contributors in each element times the goal and then times fifty-two weeks.
7. Sum all the element totals.

Chapter Summary

- Advantage Principle: Shorten Time Frames, Remove Hiding Spots, and Make Goals Personal.
- Advantage Principle: Achieve Business Success by Having More People Doing the Most Important Things More Often.
- Establish Specific Vital Goals by making goals personal.

- Translate a company's Vital Goals into individual employee goals by identifying the elements of growth, making goals personal for each contributor, and shortening the time frames for goals and accountability—which, in return, removes hiding spots.
- First, identify the elements of growth (or the elements that contribute to the achievement of any Vital Goals). Also, determine how many contributors you need in each element.
- Second, make the Vital Goals personal. Every contributor in your company needs to know how they contribute with personal Baseline and Brass Ring goals.
- Third, shorten time frames. By that I mean set, manage, and hold team members accountable to their goals in the shortest time frames possible—days and weeks versus quarters or years.
- Fourth, remove hiding spots by applying the first three principles.
- When people know what is expected of them and there is nowhere in the company to hide, goals are achieved at a greater magnitude and with greater consistency.

Chapter Five

Use Predictive Behaviors to Tell the Future

ADVANTAGE PRINCIPLE: TODAY'S BEHAVIORS PREDICT TOMORROW'S RESULTS.

If you've been part of a typical planning session, now is usually the time people assume they're done. They've established their Vital Goals and Made the Goals Personal. At this stage in the planning session, company leaders typically charge out of the planning meeting primed to get started, work harder, and hope to achieve their new goals. Did you see the word "hope"? A company's Vital Goals remain a hope unless you take the next step: planning Predictive Behaviors.

Most planning sessions stopped long ago, but we're just getting started.

When folks rush out of their planning session too early, they're *missing the most critical element of planning.* That element is identifying the routine, repeated behaviors you and your employees must perform to achieve your Vital Goals. What actions must be made on a daily or weekly basis? What will these consistent behaviors lead to? Results. Results you never dreamed could be possible. Results that are within your grasp if you take the time to tackle Predictive Behaviors.

PREDICTIVE BEHAVIOR

Anatole France, a poet, journalist, and novelist, said, "It is by acts and not by ideas that people live."[1] Leaders get results by guiding employees into consistent, deliberate actions in the shortest time frames feasible. Focusing on consistent, deliberate actions that are proven to get the desired results is the most important element toward building your Ultimate Competitive Edge. We call those actions "Predictive Behaviors."

A Predictive Behavior is an action that if completed habitually will tell the future. For example, if a salesperson makes an average of one hundred prospecting calls a week, she may talk to thirty contacts and gain six first meetings with potential new clients. Three of those will be worth presenting to, and one will turn into a new customer. The Predictive Behavior of contacting prospects leads to the Predictive Result of gaining more new clients and eventually more new sales for the company. To build customer loyalty, Predictive Behaviors might include ease of ordering (one click), return policies, time to reach a human on the phone, issue resolution (effort and time), frequency of personal touches, rewards and incentives, or, in the world of Chick-fil-A, saying, "It's my pleasure" instead of "You're welcome" or "No problem."[2] It is a differentiator and, oddly, one that very few other retailers have been able to replicate. Chick-fil-A makes it more than a statement that associates are required to say; it is a culture they are immersed in from the time they start.[3]

Notice that contacting prospects is extra important because it is the first step that sets a chain of results in motion. That's called an "Initiating Predictive Behavior." No matter how good her selling skills are, if this salesperson doesn't do enough of the Initiating Predictive Behavior, she will not maximize her results. The all-important Initiating Predictive Behavior may not be prospecting calls. It may be a combination of actions. For some companies, it's referrals, networking groups, Google Ads, or customer contacts through marketing, Internet, website, or social media leads. No matter what the first step is, predicting tomorrow's results by focusing on today's behavior is one of the most powerful Growth Advantage principles.

ADVANTAGE PRINCIPLE: PREDICTIVE BEHAVIOR IS A BEHAVIOR THAT IF COMPLETED HABITUALLY WILL TELL THE FUTURE.

Automobile industry mogul Henry Ford, inventor of assembly line manufacturing, understood this principle well. He understood that he could build cars faster and more cheaply if he focused on individual actions (tightening one bolt on a wheel so many times per hour/day) versus the end result (a completed car). In 1913, Henry Ford established the first assembly line for the mass production of an automobile. Ford's innovation reduced the time it took to build a car by over 80 percent and allowed his company to produce more than all other auto manufacturers combined. Further, his profit margin increased while lowering the cost to consumers. The cost of the Model T dropped to $250 in 1924, the equivalent of approximately $4,000 today.[4]

Nick Saban, the current head football coach of the University of Alabama, also focuses on behavior, not outcomes. His philosophy changed ten years before he was featured on a 2008 cover of *Forbes* magazine as "The Most Powerful Coach in Sports."[5] At that time, he coached the Michigan State Spartans, and they were a twenty-seven-point underdog against the undefeated Ohio State Buckeyes. He decided not to focus on the outcome of the game but to focus on the process of playing the best football. To accomplish this, he told his players to focus on each play as if it had a history and a life of its own. "Don't look at the scoreboard," he said. "Don't look at external factors you can't control." He called this "The Process."

Saban's "Process" has attracted widespread interest and was featured in the documentary *Nick Saban: Gamechanger*. The results speak for themselves: Michigan State won the game against top-ranked Ohio State. Saban has since led the Louisiana State University Tigers to the Bowl Championship Series (BCS) national championship in 2003 and the Alabama Crimson Tide to both the BCS and AP national championships in the 2009, 2011, and 2012 seasons and the College Football Championship in 2015, 2017, and 2021. He has won seven National Championships (2003, 2009, 2011, 2012, 2015, 2017, 2021) and is the first coach in college football history to win a national championship with two different schools. His Vital Goal every year is to win the national championship, but he still coaches his players to focus on "The Process"—his Predictive Behavior.[6]

Simple Predictive Behaviors can have a huge impact on complicated issues and change the world. The Carter Center (www.cartercenter.org), founded by President Jimmy Carter, has been instrumental in working to eradicate Guinea worm disease (dracunculiasis). This parasitic roundworm infection is contracted when people consume water contaminated with Guinea worm larvae. Larvae then mate inside a human's abdomen, female worms mature and grow, and after about a year, the now one-meter-long female Guinea worm creates a lesion on the skin and emerges from the body. The excruciating process often takes weeks and leads many people to immerse themselves in water to relieve the burning pain. Contact with water stimulates the emerging worm to release its larvae into the water and the cycle of infection continues. People affected are incapacitated for extended periods of time, unable to care for themselves or provide for their families.[7]

The Carter Center works closely with many international organizations and local communities on the Guinea Worm Eradication Program with the Vital Goal to wipe out this disease through community-based education and behavior change. In 1986, an estimated 3.5 million people a year in twenty-one countries throughout Africa and Asia were affected by the disease. In 2019, cases were reduced more than 99.99 percent, with only fifty-four reported infections. Education, commitment, and Predictive Behaviors as simple as filtering drinking water and keeping anyone with an emerging worm from entering water sources have prevented at least eighty million cases and eliminated the disease in seventeen countries. Guinea worm disease could become the second human disease, after smallpox, and the first parasitic disease to be eradicated. It would also be the first disease eradicated through the power of behavior change alone, without the use of a vaccine or medicine.

Just like Henry Ford, Nick Saban, and the Carter Center, we can anticipate tomorrow's results by zeroing in on *today's* behavior. This ability to predict the future gives great comfort to leaders. Suddenly the future comes into focus. We know what growth the company can achieve simply by looking at the impact of Predictive Behaviors.

ADVANTAGE PRINCIPLE: WE ALL HAVE THE POWER TO CONTROL THE FUTURE.

To make Predictive Behaviors work, companies must (1) identify key Predictive Behaviors, (2) commit to these key behaviors, (3) perform the behaviors with boring consistency, and (4) turn the Predictive Behaviors into habits. The results will be anything but boring.

Again and again, I'm shocked by how quick companies can change for the better and start achieving unparalleled results. The basis for such transformative change comes from good planning. At the heart of that good planning is a commitment to Predictive Behavior.

Identifying Your Predictive Behaviors

I like to share this story of two established Realtors. They were an extremely professional mother and daughter combo who were part of the "country club crowd." Both women had been in the real estate business many years and enjoyed huge success. They undoubtedly received many leads and referrals from friends and past clients, so the last thing you would expect is for them to spend time telephone prospecting. And yet that's what they did. Every week, this dynamic pair was "dialing the phone," in other words, reaching out to potential clients to keep filling their pipeline. This deliberate, consistent behavior was a key reason they maintained success. Half a day or more every week, no matter what, these women practiced excellent Predictive Behavior skills that led to real-world results.

Let's look at Predictive Behavior for losing weight. There is an abundance of resources for identifying Predictive Behaviors in this area. As an example, the National Weight Control Registry notes Predictive Behaviors such as weighing yourself once a week, modified food intake, watching less than ten hours of TV per week, and exercising an average of one hour per day.[8] These Predictive Behaviors help people stay on track with maintaining a low-calorie diet and staying physically active. Other examples of weight loss Predictive Behavior might be calories consumed, carbohydrates consumed, steps taken per day, or a time range when food is consumed (intermittent fasting).

Another weight loss group, www.loseit.com, guides you regarding how many calories you can eat to hit a specific weight loss goal. Their website includes a tool for recording the calories you eat and even reports your progress.[9] I input metrics for a 252-pound male with a desired weight of 200 pounds and the goal of losing one pound per week. The site tells how many calories should be consumed each day, which in this case is 2,408 or less. Like most Initiating Predictive Behaviors, from that point on, the choice to do them or not is in the hands of the person trying to accomplish the goal. Will they only follow the plan when it is convenient? Or are they committed to losing the weight, meaning they will accept no excuses, only results? Weight loss, like most Vital Goals, demands a strong commitment. The good news is that with most Predictive Behaviors in business, you don't have your body fighting back. Competition is easier to deal with than a body telling us it is hungry. Pizza is the toughest competitor I've ever faced!

What are *your* Predictive Behaviors? They will vary based on your Vital Goals. There can be many Predictive Behaviors for a given goal, but we want to focus on a limited number of Initiating Predictive Behaviors that have the greatest impact. Some will be obvious. Some may take research. Here's a sampling of research ideas to pinpoint your Predictive Behaviors:

Research tips to find YOUR Predictive Behaviors:

Personal Experience—Jumping in and doing is one way to identify Predictive Behaviors. You can't become a scratch golfer in a training seminar. You need to combine lessons with a lot of experience on the course.

Peer or Expert Experience—Unless you're attempting to be the first person to reach the South Pole, there are typically others who have achieved what you are trying to achieve. Seek out the best and learn their Predictive Behaviors.

Research (online, periodicals, books, training seminars, etc.)—Books have changed my life, and they can change yours. Whatever it is you want to be the best at, read applicable books and articles thirty to sixty minutes each day. You should also participate in correlating training sessions.

Industry Peer Networking Groups—I facilitate Industry Peer Networking Groups, and these networking groups are a great way to get empirical evidence on effective Predictive Behaviors. If you don't have any in your industry, start one.

Consultants (my favorite)—Find a consultant in the specific area of expertise where you are looking for help. Their payback should always exceed their costs.

Trial and Error—Keep trying until you find the right combination and quantity of Predictive Behaviors that will lead you to the Brass Ring results you are after.

Don't worry too much about picking the perfect Predictive Behaviors at first. What's important is to identify some with potential and get started. You'll discover the correct ones over time after you commit, perform them with boring consistency, and measure your results. Also beware of the worst mistakes people make regarding Predictive Behaviors:

1. setting Predictive Behavior goals too high, making them unachievable;
2. setting Predictive Behavior goals and then not doing them faithfully; or
3. not correlating the Predictive Behavior with the desired result.

Committing to Your Predictive Behaviors

Every time I visit a client, I ask their commitment level to their Vital Goals and Predictive Behaviors. You must ask yourself this question often. Commitment is essential to make Predictive Behaviors work their magic.

When it comes to planning, you don't need a perfect plan. You need to *act* perfectly. In other words, come up with a good plan, then commit to executing it perfectly. Commit to the Vital Goal and carry it out by doing the Predictive Behaviors. Commit to measuring the results. If you act with commitment to your plan, then you can always adjust as you move forward and make your good plan a better one. But you won't get anywhere if you don't make a firm commitment. As the saying goes about a breakfast meal of scrambled eggs and bacon, the chickens were involved. The pig was committed. Be like the pig. Go whole hog.

This sounds easy but it is not. Committing to performing Predictive Behaviors every day versus doing them when it's convenient makes all the difference. It's also the key to building your Ultimate Competitive Edge. I attended a writers' conference and was amazed by the commitment many of the attendees had to their love of writing. Most had families, jobs, and full lives besides writing books. They would get up early in the morning before anyone else was up and before they had to leave for their jobs and spend one or two hours writing each day. Now that is commitment to a dream. They opened my eyes to the commitment it would take to complete a book.

PERFORMING WITH BORING CONSISTENCY

Once you've identified the Predictive Behaviors you need for success and committed to them, you must perform these behaviors with boring consistency. You can't just be interested; you must *commit*. Stick to the numbers you choose.

Did you commit to a Facebook and LinkedIn post each week to drive traffic to your website and generate new sales? Then insist on one post on each site every week. Did you commit to reading thirty minutes each day? Then be accountable to reading thirty minutes each day. Did you commit to making one hundred prospecting calls a week? Then insist on one hundred. Did you commit to ten thousand steps each day? Then take ten thousand steps. Did you commit to visit your best customers once each quarter? Then visit them once each quarter. It is the only way you will know if the behavior leads to the desired result. I personally do better when I make daily commitments versus saying I am going to do something three times each week. It takes excuses off the table.

Commitments may involve staffing positions, too. Did your plan call for ten people in a position doing the behavior? If you only have eight on staff, then you need to hire two more. The idea is to consistently achieve or exceed your minimum goal (Baseline). This accomplishes two things: (1) it makes people live up to the goal you committed to, and (2) it lets you evaluate results based on the activity. That's the only way you will learn if they work. Performing with consistency allows you to examine the numbers and determine if you've set the right number. If numbers jump all over the place from week to week, it's hard to compare, and you'll never know if you've set the right number of Predictive Behaviors to achieve the desired result.

ADVANTAGE PRINCIPLE: PERFORM PREDICTIVE BEHAVIORS WITH BORING CONSISTENCY AND THE RESULTS WILL BE ANYTHING BUT BORING.

Turning Behavior into Habit

Aristotle, a Greek philosopher, said, "Excellence is an art won by training and habituation. We are what we repeatedly do. Excellence, then, is not an act but a habit."[10]

Now it's time to turn Predictive Behaviors into habits. Habits help ingrain behaviors, so people naturally perform them on an unwavering basis. With a habit, there's no thinking involved (e.g., *Should I do this?*). It's just like brushing your teeth. After you get up, you always shower and brush your teeth. It's a habit. When a behavior is important enough—and all your employees' Predictive Behaviors should be important since you've just linked them to your company's Vital Goals—make it a habit. Habits can be altered with astonishing results. As Charles C. Noble, an American major general and engineer who worked on the Manhattan Project and led construction in Nuremberg after World War II, said, "First we make our habits, then our habits make us."[11] Expect your employees to act in ways that best align with your Vital Goals by helping them turn Predictive Behaviors into ingrained habits.

Our brains do not distinguish between good and bad habits. Our brains form habits from the actions we do frequently. If we frequently reach for a handful of chips when we come home from work, that act becomes a habit. If we take the dog for a walk as soon as we come home from work, then our arm will automatically reach for the leash instead of the chips. The challenge is to turn actions that are better for us in the long run (healthy eating, exercise, reading a book) into habits and not succumb to short-term pleasure (eating chips, flopping on the sofa, watching "KUWTK"). Successful people make these tough choices. They choose long-term benefit. But the secret is it's no longer a tough choice every day (chips or exercise?). Once an action is performed frequently enough, the brain takes over and the action shifts to the unconscious brain. You're taking the decision out of the equation. The act becomes a habit.

As a manager, one of your most important jobs is to identify Predictive Behaviors for your employees (and for yourself) and make them into habits. How? By creating triggers that stimulate specific actions.

Triggers could be a cue, a nudge, a craving, or a stimulus. Once the action occurs, there needs to be a reward. The reward will help to make the action more automatic, thereby creating the habit. Here is how the Habit Cycle works:

Triggers:

Cue—A signal or a prompt that reminds someone to do something. Daily cues such as a database notice, call reports, or whiteboards remind people (either consciously or unconsciously) to perform

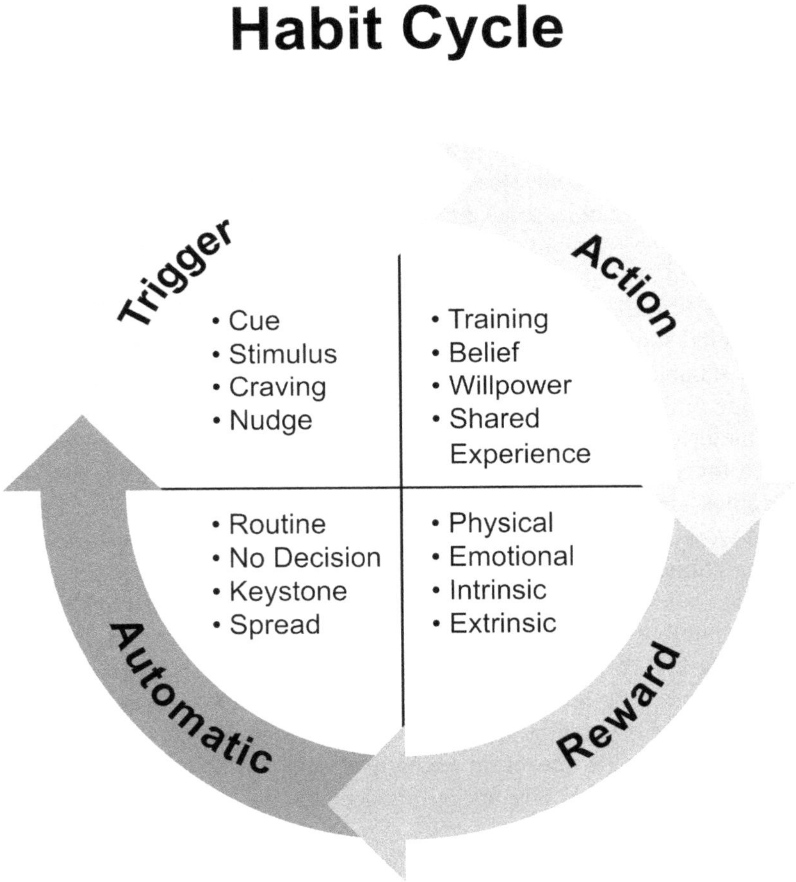

Figure 5.1. Habit Cycle

Predictive Behaviors habitually. This small signal is a huge advantage builder. There are mobile device apps that provide cues for almost every behavior imaginable including exercise, diet, and healthy living. Real-life example: one sales representative put a specific number of business cards in her pocket every day, and she did not finish prospecting until the cards were gone.

Nudge—Managers are really "nudgers." A manager should check in and make sure each employee is performing Predictive Behaviors. The key is to make it more uncomfortable not to do the Predictive Behavior than to just do the Predictive Behavior. Real-life example: weekly accountability meetings are a great nudge when they focus on Predictive Behaviors and the associated results. If an employee falls Below Baseline, those nudge meetings should shift to daily. During these meetings, make the employee report to you their behavior and results for the week. Athletes have trainers to nudge them to do the proper training every day so they can achieve the strived-for results. Humans are naturally motivated to avoid being uncomfortable.

Stimulus—A stimulus is an incentive that stimulates or acts as an enticement for someone to perform an act. For someone to be motivated to perform Predictive Behaviors on a consistent basis, they must believe it is worth it. This concept will be covered in more detail in chapter 9, "Motivation Advantage." Real-life example: paid time off can be a great stimulus. I once incorporated a plant incentive where production employees could leave early on Friday and still be paid for forty hours provided the entire plant achieved some specific deadlines and metrics. This was a perfect example of a win-win for everyone involved; it was the best my plant ever ran.

Craving—A craving is a physical response the brain gets when it's addicted to something (smoking, coffee, drugs, exercise). Unfortunately, most addictions involve bad habits, although some people claim to be addicted to the high of exercise. Cravings are powerful triggers in habit formation but do not play a key role in management in a business setting. I wish I could get people to crave doing their business Predictive Behaviors.

You should ask yourself what the triggers and accountability nudges are in relation to every Predictive Behavior. Luckily, management is made simpler since habits help make these actions automatic, but the manager still needs to be on top of these critical employee actions.

After a trigger spurs the action, you need a reward that helps to make the behavior automatic, and this completes the "Habit Cycle."

There are intrinsic rewards such as purpose, recognition, respect, appreciation, and achievement, as well as extrinsic rewards such as commission, time off, bonuses, pay increases, and prizes. The key is to find out what is meaningful for each employee.

John Wooden, UCLA basketball coach, knew the power of turning Predictive Behaviors into habits. A coach for twenty-seven years, he drilled his teams on excellent habits, starting with the absolute basics: how to put on their shoes and socks. Why focus on such a small behavior as that? Because Coach Wooden knew that shoes and socks put on in the right way could prevent his players from getting blisters. Without blisters, his team was free to play their best and focus on the game. "That's your first lesson," he said. "With blisters, you'll miss practice. If you miss practice, you don't play. And if you don't play, we cannot win."

Coach Wooden knew that thirty minutes invested in teaching adults to tie their shoes and smooth the wrinkles from their socks was time well invested. He trained his team on good behavior and expected them to adopt his shoe-tying method for every future game and practice. "If you want to win championships," Wooden said, "you must take care of the smallest details."

Coach Wooden seldom talked about results (winning games). Instead, he focused on executing the right behaviors. When Wooden's coauthor, Steven Jamison, was asked what his secret was, he said, "Wooden taught good habits." Coach Wooden has unprecedented results. He won ten national championships (a record), seven in a row (a record), eighty-eight consecutive victories (a record), thirty-eight consecutive playoff wins (a record), four perfect seasons (a record), and had only one losing season in forty-one years (his first one).[12]

Establishing Vital Goals, making goals personal, and enforcing Predictive Behaviors may sound like micromanagement, but in reality it empowers freedom—provided employees understand what they are supposed to be doing and do it. Predictive Behaviors, like Coach Wooden's shoe-tying behavior, need to be identified and, yes, managed on a daily, weekly, and monthly basis in order to achieve Vital Goals.

ADVANTAGE PRINCIPLE: PASSIVITY IS THE ANTITHESIS OF LEADERSHIP. LEADERS CREATE DELIBERATE ACTION.

Motivation

Motivation is an important element when turning Predictive Behaviors into habits. If you want employees to be motivated to execute their Predictive Behaviors as habits, make sure they can solidly answer the following four questions: What is expected of them? Can they do it? Is it worth doing? Why? We'll discuss these four magic motivation questions in detail in chapter 9, "Motivation Advantage." For now, remember employees need to know what it is we want them to do, believe they can do it, believe it's worth doing, and understand why they are doing it.

Another key element of motivation is progress. As Teresa Amabile and Steven Kramer described in the *Harvard Business Review*, the top motivator for people is progress. Workers feel good when they see they're making progress toward a goal. With progress, "emotions are most positive and their drive to succeed is at its peak,"[13] they write. Predictive Behaviors make management easier because they give workers clear daily and weekly goals. Employees stay motivated because they can see their progress. It's clear and constant.

South Pole explorers Roald Amundsen and Robert Falcon Scott approached the idea of steady progress and predictive behaviors vastly differently. Amundsen, a seasoned Norwegian adventurer with a well-trained team of men and sled dogs, set a steady pace averaging fifteen and a half miles a day in his bid to reach the South Pole first in 1911.[14] Scott, also a seasoned adventurer, took a less predictable course. He strayed from his Vital Goals: reach the South Pole first and stay alive. Instead, he collected heavy geologic specimens en route even though the primary objective was reaching 90° south. Although this negatively impacted the focus on his main goals, his discoveries did ultimately contribute to science and his legacy.[15]

Scott used dogs and ponies on his team, although the ponies were ill suited to Antarctic conditions of −20°F to −50°F, and Scott and his men were not well trained in handling sled dogs. Scott pushed forward hard on good weather days, driving his team of men and animals to the point of exhaustion, then holed up in his tent on bad days. The dogs and ponies were dead even before Scott's final push for the South Pole, so Scott and his men had to haul the sleds themselves.[16]

Amundsen, on the other hand, refrained from pushing his team harder on good weather days. He emphasized steady habits and rest. He ventured out on stormy days, too, noting in his journal, "It has been an unpleasant day—storm, drift and frostbite, but we have advanced 13 miles closer to our goal."[17] I would love to hear a sales rep return to the office on a winter's day and say: "Storm, drift, and frostbite but I made thirteen prospecting attempts today." I would know that sales rep was a keeper.

You might already know the end of the story. Scott reached the South Pole on January 17, 1912, only to find Amundsen's team had beaten him by more than a month. Scott's party turned back, exhausted and suffering from frostbite and starvation. All five of them died on the return journey. Scott's last words in his diary read, "We took risks, we knew we took them; things have come against us, and therefore we have no cause for complaint, but bow to the will of Providence, determined still to do our best to the last."[18]

Amundsen won by planning. He kept strictly to his Vital Goal, used a well-trained team, and advanced toward the South Pole using Predictive Behavior. Each day his team moved forward approximately fifteen and a half miles, and he reached the South Pole on the day planned.

Examples of Predictive Behaviors:

- New sales: Twenty prospecting attempts per day and ask for two referrals (in person, phone, social media, etc.).
- Reach the South Pole: Travel fifteen and a half miles per day regardless of conditions.
- Lose weight: Eat 2,408 net calories or less each day (depending on weight and goals).
- Upsell existing customers: One attempt by each service employee each day.
- Improve fitness: Exercise thirty to sixty minutes each day.
- Improve accountability: Weekly team and one-on-one accountability meetings.
- Google search engine optimization: Produce high-quality content, improve your metadata, include inbound and outbound hyperlinks, use keywords.
- Improve customer loyalty: Make a loyalty contact with every customer once each quarter.
- Achieve anything: Focus on it one to two hours per day.

- Expert on a topic: Read thirty to sixty minutes every day.
- Live longer: Eat seven to nine servings of fruits and vegetables each day and have a glass of wine.

Predictive Behaviors Will Vary by Goal, Company, Individual, and Market

The Growth Advantage is a business strategy, but its basic concept is simple. To accomplish sustained results, you need to clearly know where you want the company to go and fully understand the Predictive Behaviors and resources needed to get there. That's what this chapter is all about—focusing on the behaviors your company can follow to lead to the results you want. Many of my clients report back to me after a couple years. They've had a chance to turn Predictive Behaviors into habits and watch the results. "We finally get it!" they say. "All we needed to do was to focus on the behavior, and the results will follow."

Sustained growth *is* a challenge. Most companies don't do it. Only the successful outliers do. You can become an outlier by focusing on behavior. Predictive Behavior(s), carefully chosen and ingrained in habit, will make the challenge of sustained growth achievable and will change your destiny. Samuel Smiles, a Scottish author, summed it up well: "Sow a thought, and you reap an act—sow an act, and you reap a habit—sow a habit, and you reap a character—sow a character, and you reap a destiny."[19]

Advantage Challenge: Identify Predictive Behaviors for each element of your growth. Select one element of growth by department and by position. Note the Baseline and Brass Ring result goals. Establish initiating Predictive Behavior goals and all follow-up behavior goals.

Reference the Predictive Behaviors Advantage Challenge Application (Figure A.6) at the back of the book.

Chapter Summary

- Advantage Principle: Today's Behaviors Predict Tomorrow's Results.
- A company's Vital Goals remain a hope unless you take the next step: planning Predictive Behaviors.

- Advantage Principle: Predictive Behavior Is a Behavior That if Completed Habitually Will Tell the Future.
- Advantage Principle: We All Have the Power to Control the Future.
- Predictive Behaviors are the key to achieving any result.
- First, identify and commit to your Predictive Behaviors.
- Advantage Principle: Perform Predictive Behaviors with boring consistency and the results will be anything but boring.
- Measure and correlate the behaviors with the desired results.
- Finally, turn them into habits by creating triggers that stimulate specific actions. Triggers could be a cue, a nudge, a craving, or a stimulus.
- Once the action occurs, there needs to be a reward.
- Rewards will help to make the action more automatic, thereby creating the habit.
- Our brains do not distinguish between good and bad habits. Our brains form habits from the actions we do frequently.
- Advantage Principle: Passivity Is the Antithesis of Leadership. Leaders Create Deliberate Action.

Chapter Six

Do the Math

ADVANTAGE PRINCIPLE: UNDERSTANDING THE MATH OF BUSINESS GIVES YOU AN EDGE.

The book *Influencer: The Power to Change Anything* summarized the importance of keeping score: "Keeping score produces clear, frequent feedback and can transfer tasks into accomplishments that can generate intense satisfaction."[1] The United States' National Science Foundation maintains a permanent scientific research station at the South Pole called the Amundsen-Scott. It was built in 1956, and its name honors two Antarctic explorers, Roald Amundsen and Robert Falcon Scott. As introduced in the prior chapter, in 1911 Amundsen and Scott led separate expeditions in a race to be the first to the South Pole. Amundsen emphasized the importance of stable, productive companions, and he and his crew figured out that if they traveled a conservative but steady number of miles per day (fifteen and a half miles a day), they would arrive at their goal as scheduled. Scott was in a hurry, and his progress was much more erratic, traveling many miles one day but then none the next. Amundsen, with his steady, measured miles, won out, and his expedition was the first to arrive at the South Pole on December 14, 1911. Amundsen beat Scott by five weeks, and all his men survived the experience. Scott and his team also made it to the South Pole—an impressive achievement—but they sadly perished on their return journey home.[2] While Antarctic adventures may seem alluring, it was actually the time spent on Predictive Calculations, and not just personal bravery, that got Amundsen to his Vital Goal. Amundsen won, in part, with math and Predictive Calculations.

What does this have to do with business? Well, an old axiom states: "That which gets measured gets done." In a Growth Advantage world, the axiom changes to: "That which gets measured frequently, in the shortest time frames feasible, and with the right standards (Brass Ring and Baseline) gets done consistently." Think about it. A football game without a score is no game at all. A diet without tracking calories and carbohydrates, time spent exercising, or weighing in will never be successful for weight loss. And a perilous expedition would go awry if the distance traveled toward the ultimate goal isn't measured. It follows that a business without the capability to track the behavior and results of its people is destined for underperformance. Some feel measurement is overrated; I couldn't disagree more.

It is critical to measure key metrics as they relate to your Vital Goals, Personal Goals, and the Predictive Behaviors that support those goals. Like the Three Little Bears in the Goldilocks parable, there are three kinds of companies:

Company One has too many measures, and their challenge is dealing with an overabundance of metrics and reports. They have so many measures the outcomes aren't visible or accessible, and their employees don't pay attention to them. For example, one company I worked with handed me two very thick three-ring binders of key metric reports on day one. The reports had good data, but there were so many reports that I am pretty sure I am the only one that took the time to review all the reports in those binders. Reports unviewed at regular intervals are useless.

Company Two has too few measures, so there's no way to hold people accountable. Employees and managers have no way to gauge performance. In the Peer Groups I moderate, we collect financial performance data annually. For some companies, this exercise is simple and the data they provide is perfect. For other companies, this exercise is a challenge, and the data are questionable. This is critical data that every leader should have at their fingertips, and running a company and not having this data readily available and accessible is incomprehensible. You can probably guess which companies are achieving greater success.

Company Three: "Ahhh, their metrics are just right." Company three has the proper quantity of measures (result and behavior) that are available, easily accessible, as well as visible and produce clear, frequent feedback that transfers activity into accomplishments. As with Vital Goals, less is more with key metrics.

A word of caution: most companies and leaders (including me) want all their metrics to be collected and calculated automatically, which unfortunately can also make them invisible. Technology is a wonderful thing, and I love all that it can do, but data can get swallowed into a black hole. That is why critical data needs to be accessible, visible, and meaningful. In other words, make sure it is touched, posted, and reviewed regularly! There is nothing wrong with using a marker and a whiteboard to post metrics the "old-fashioned way." I was working with a client, and after about a year, the lightbulb lit up. He said, "I finally get it. If I focus my energy on the Predictive Behaviors and Measures, the results will follow." Exactly! Accordingly, he started having his employees post their Predictive Behavior on the whiteboard outside his office on a daily basis and their results improved dramatically. Measurements like these promote employee accountability, focus, and motivation, which allows smart companies to adjust and evolve over time.

This chapter introduces two new concepts: "Predictive Measures," which are the measures of Predictive Behaviors we discussed in prior chapters, and "Result Measures," which are the measure of the results. Both concepts—Predictive Measures and Result Measures—are needed for tracking and achieving sustained results. Companies are too often Result Measure heavy, which is looking backward, versus Predictive Measure focused, which is forward looking and, as with Predictive Behaviors, will tell the future.

Weight Loss—To illustrate this point further, let's take the common goal of losing weight. Say it is January 1, and your New Year's resolution is to lose twenty pounds by December 31. In a calorie control plan, the Predictive Measures are the daily calories consumed minus the calories burned (frequency and duration of exercise), which will give your net calories. The Result Measure is the actual weight loss or gain. A Predictive Behavior relating to weight loss is to weigh yourself and track these metrics daily. Let's not forget there can be more than one way to achieve a goal. For people who follow a low-carb weight loss plan, their Predictive Measure is carbs consumed daily and their Result Measure is weight lost. The key is to define the Predictive Measures necessary to succeed on the diet and keep track of them daily and weekly. If you do, congratulations because your Result Measure will be that you lost the twenty pounds!

New Sales—Now, let's say you are a new sales representative, and you are hungry for success. For new sales, your Predictive Measures might be prospecting attempts, prospecting contacts, referral leads, network leads, website leads, social media leads, first appointments with a new prospect, presentations, new account closing rate, and/or average sale. The Result Measures are a lot more cut and dried; they are your actual sales. Too many sales representatives fight the behavior measures, not understanding they are a critical element of their success. They actually are the keys that open the door to their personal accomplishment as well as the company's success.

Upselling Existing Customers—If you have ever gone to a restaurant or a fast-food burger place, you have heard the refrain, "You want fries, dessert, or a drink with that?" That is because fast-food company managers know that if their frontline employees ask that question one hundred times to one hundred customers they will make a few additional sales. That might not seem like much, but those are sales they wouldn't otherwise have, and it cost the employee nothing to say the familiar phrase. Multiply the additional sales by every fast-food restaurant in every town every day, and the results are significant. The Predictive Measure is simply the attempts, and the Result Measure is the increased sales. Whether you're a fast-food restaurant, a software provider, a manufacturer, or in a service industry, track and correlate the attempts with the results and you can determine if there is value in the activity. Perform the behavior and measure it. If it does not produce the desired results, go back to the drawing board. Without measurement, you will never know.

Customer Loyalty—A perfect example of a Predictive Measure is Net Promoter Score (NPS). Remember Fred Reichheld's metric from chapter 3? It is the measuring method that breaks your customers down into three basic categories: Promoters, Passives, and Detractors. By asking your customers, "How likely is it that you would recommend my company to a friend or colleague?" and rating their answers, companies can find their NPS. Companies that have higher NPSs typically have better customer loyalty/retention, grow more, and are more profitable than companies that have lower NPSs.[3] It's that simple. NPS is the Predictive Measure, and customer retention, growth, and/or profit are Result Measures. Building loyalty is also one of the best ways to enhance sales with existing customers.

Something to keep in mind when you establish Predictive Behaviors and Predictive Measures is that the most important ones are the

Initiating Predictive Behavior and correlating *Initiating* Predictive Measure. These are the activities that get the ball rolling and initiate the result outcome. For sales, that might be a prospecting attempt. For Amundsen, it was putting in the appropriate miles every day. For a dieter, it might be calories consumed.

Measurement is *the* activity that brings facts into focus. Where a leader's skill comes into play is in how those measurements are communicated and used. It is imperative that leaders communicate why they are measuring performance, which is to help guide success. Measurement is a powerful tool of achievement. If people are resistant to measurement, it is likely that they don't want to do the work it takes to be successful but want to be able to hide instead. Remember, hiding spots are exactly what we want to remove. Metrics are critical leadership success indicators.

So far, in this blueprint to business growth, I have detailed the advantages of planning, having clear goals, making goals personal, shortening time frames and removing hiding spots, and focusing on Predictive Behaviors. The math of business functions in all these areas and is *the* element that reveals how everything we are doing is actually working.

Are you getting where you want to go? Math will give you the answer. That is one reason why clients submit numbers to us at Growth Advantage monthly. (1) It makes clients follow through and actually capture and report on the key metrics they agree on during the planning sessions. (2) It removes hiding spots as I then submit a monthly write-up reporting how each individual, department, and the company as a whole is doing in relation to their behavior and result goals. (3) It provides an accountability nudge as I review these numbers with the respective teams during each follow-up visit. (4) These numbers not only tell the client how they are doing, but they also tell them if the Growth Advantage Blueprint is working for their company.

I could not be as effective a consultant without these metrics, just as a leader cannot be effective without proper metrics.

Aldous Huxley said, "Facts do not cease to exist because they are ignored."[4] Effective leaders want the truth, even when that truth hurts. That's because knowing the truth is the only way you will know how your company and your people are really doing. Amundsen chose crewmates he knew would tell him the truth when he asked them for updates on critical expedition elements and who would hold each other accountable. He could only make the necessary adjustments if he knew the facts. Back in Antarctica in the winter of 1911, incomplete information would have gotten him and his men killed. Not knowing the truth in business isn't quite so dire, but it can still be a death knell for companies. Not knowing the truth of who is doing what behaviors, how often, and how well could cause a business to languish and its employees to not reach their full potential. Math tells the truth. Some companies do customer satisfaction surveys and ask customers to give them a good score on the survey—they don't want the truth—those surveys are useless. Other companies like Enterprise Car Rental do customer surveys and want the truth.

ADVANTAGE PRINCIPLE: METRICS THAT DON'T SEEK THE TRUTH ARE USELESS.

Enterprise Car Rental uses Enterprise Service Quality Index, or ESQi, as a Predictive Measure. ESQi identifies the underlying attributes that will have the greatest effect on customer satisfaction (courtesy, professionalism, timeliness of service, ethical standards, and core values). Every month, they measure ESQi for each local branch through telephone surveys of hundreds of thousands of customers. Branches earn a ranking based on customers who say they were completely satisfied with their last Enterprise experience. ESQi results are published companywide, which makes the surveys a focal point for all customer service activities, and they use the results to improve performance at their locations worldwide.[5] This transparency allows everyone to see how they performed and where they rank in comparison to everyone else. Dedicated to promoting from within, the ESQi score functions as an important gauge for Enterprise career advancement.[6] You will never hear an employee at Enterprise ask you to give them a good score on the survey. Why? Because they've built a culture where they want the truth. Don't be a leader that discounts negative data, amplifies positive data, or puts a positive spin on ambiguous data. Blaming external factors for setbacks rather than accepting responsibility is a Culture Killer.

Why measure?

- Measurement allows us to **make better decisions**, grounded in reality (not conjecture), with an emphasis on predicting and tracking results. It is important to remember that facts exist whether we track them or not. With better tracking, we are helping to make people and companies more successful.

- Metrics **enable better planning** because they give us practical parameters by which we can establish achievable goals. Measurement allows us to adjust and evolve over time. It is my experience that when planning with proper metrics, goals expand and become sustainable.
- Metrics **foster greater accountability** for the commitments we make and the contributions made toward the Vital Goals of the organization. In fact, it is impossible to hold people accountable without directed key metrics. Measurement provides an accurate context and greater accountability for all that we do.
- Measurement enables us to **learn and adjust** our strategy more quickly and effectively to respond to the professional—as well as the personal—challenges we face. As Confucius said, "When it is obvious that the goals cannot be reached, don't adjust the goals; adjust the action steps."[7] If I need to travel fifteen and a half miles per day to get to the South Pole on time and return safely and I am only averaging thirteen miles, I better start doing eighteen miles per day until I'd get back on schedule.
- Most of all, measurement enables us to **improve our performance** by providing a standard against which we can accurately gauge that performance.

If you have ever taken college classes, you can probably relate to this image: The semester is nearing an end, and the professor is about to post student grades. Today, they may be posted online, but not so long ago she would have posted them in public on the classroom door. Picture students standing around, anxious to see how they did. Is the whole class there waiting when they are posted? *No.* The top performers that believe they did well are waiting for the grades to be posted. Generally, people don't want to be ranked near the bottom of anything. If they do, they are not the kind of people you want on your bus, your team, or working for your company. You want the people who are waiting to see their grades. The people who know they flunked are probably in their dorm rooms partying or packing. This is an example of a simple but effective way to post results.

The vital signs you choose to measure may differ from industry to industry and firm to firm, but the criteria for an effective math scoreboard is the same for all of us:

- **Use few measures** in charting the score. The more variants you have, the easier it is to obfuscate, and the scorecard is something that everyone in your company must easily understand.
- **Clearly illustrate** the key points in your scoreboard. We want to make sure it is inviting to read and easy to understand for everyone on the team.
- In the same vein, the scorecard must be **instantly understandable**, making its critical points apparent to everyone at a glance, not after hours or even minutes of scrutiny, just like when a teacher posts test scores on the classroom door.
- The scorecard must be **highly visible**. Think about putting it in the lunchroom, employee lounge, or major public gathering area. If your employees all have buy-in to the results of your company, they all have a stake in what's shown on the scorecard.
- It must be **easily updatable** so that progress can be quickly and cleanly shown. There is great technology available that can transmit updated metrics to screens throughout your company, or you can use an old-fashioned but effective whiteboard.
- Finally, it must be designed to **motivate players to win**. The numbers in scoreboards must be seen as a positive challenge, not as a negative detriment. When done properly, metrics should inspire performance and should be used as a tool to help people succeed—and managers should introduce it that way. Treat it as a critical part of your growth strategy and people soon will see the value of the math scorecard, as well as come to appreciate how clearly it quantifies your goals and objectives. If we have the ability to see it, we can believe it and that much sooner start to achieve it.

A Sales Funnel that shows the progress of sales performance can be seen as a type of math scorecard. The display of potential customers and their potential contribution to the company can become almost like a board game as your sales staff works to close the gaps and increase the real-time numbers. There may be aspects of a jigsaw puzzle to this metric as challenging or nonresponsive customers are analyzed based on their revenue potential and as strategies are designed to overcome their resistance.

Laying it all out in a very public way helps spur motivation and promotes understanding and acceptance of company goals and objectives. A Sales Funnel is the ultimate Predictive Measure as you should be able to look at it as a gauge of future success. The scoreboard should give you a good idea of not just how you've done but how you are doing going forward.

One key when doing scoreboards is to use real metrics as much as possible. If a sales representative has $1,000,000 of active prospects they are working on in their funnel, and their historic closing rate from the funnel is 25 percent, their predictive funnel is $250,000—not $1,000,000. Ask a sales representative what they expect to close, and they will say 90 percent or higher. Yet few actually have a closing rate that high.

The Art of War, the ancient military text attributed to Sun Tzu (500 BC), states, "The general who wins a battle makes many calculations in his temple ere the battle is fought. The general who loses a battle makes but few calculations beforehand. Thus do many calculations lead to victory, and few calculations to defeat."[8]

The math of business isn't sexy, and sometimes it is hard work to capture and post the data. But if you understand its application, you will always have the edge over competitors, thereby leading to victory. Decide if you want to win in the marketplace or just play. If you want to win, you need a way to keep score.

Advantage Challenge: Are you ready to start measuring performance in your company? Good! Now, imagine for a second that you are a patient in a hospital. You have a chart at the foot of your bed, and you are attached to a set of high-tech machinery that monitors your vital signs. Think of a math scoreboard as a very public way to measure your company's vital signs. What are the vital signs you need to track (result and behavior) to achieve your Vital Goals?

Pick one Vital Goal. What are the associated departmental goals, position goals, and Predictive Behaviors? What are the results and Predictive Measures for these goals?

Chapter Summary

- Advantage Principle: Understanding the Math of Business Gives You an Edge.
- That which gets measured frequently (shortest time frames) and with the right standards (Brass Ring and Baseline) gets done consistently.

- It can be as bad to have too many measures as it is to have too few.
- It is critical to measure key metrics as they relate to your Vital Goals (behavior and results).
- Predictive Measures track Predictive Behaviors; Result Measures track results.
- Measuring allows us to plan better and make better decisions, fosters accountability, and produces better results.
- Effective leaders want the truth and use measures to get it.
- Measurement enables us to improve our performance by providing a standard against which we can accurately gauge that performance.
- Advantage Principle: Metrics That Don't Seek the Truth Are Useless.
- The numbers in scoreboards must be seen as a positive challenge, not as a negative detriment.
- Laying it all out in a very public way helps spur motivation and promotes understanding and acceptance of company goals and objectives.
- The math of business isn't sexy, and sometimes it is hard work to capture and post the data. But if you understand its application, you will always have the edge over competitors, thereby leading to victory.

Part II

THE EXECUTION ADVANTAGE

ADVANTAGE PRINCIPLE: AN EXECUTION ADVANTAGE IS ONE OF THE ULTIMATE ADVANTAGES.

In *The Mind of the CEO*, Jeffrey Garten paraphrases former America Online CEO Stephen Case, saying, "A vision without execution is a hallucination."[1] Although strategy, culture, planning, and everything else we discuss in this book is critical, without execution, it all becomes a disappointing effort. We can shoot for any bull's-eye in a planning session, but the "rubber meets the road" when it comes to executing the plan. An Execution Advantage is one of the Ultimate Advantages a company can hold over its competition.

The president of one of my clients started out in a frontline position. He worked hard, educated himself, and climbed the corporate ladder one rung at a time. He is well versed at strategy, planning, and so on, but his real strength is execution. If he and his team plan for something to get done, it gets done. This strength sets his company apart from their competition. His performance and metrics outperform his market competitors by a wide margin. He is a very high-paid executive that has never cost the owners of his company a penny; he has made them millions based on their Execution Advantage. Even though they are demanding, these types of executives are usually loved by their direct reports because they deliver results.

There are four elements of the Execution Advantage we will explore in the next four chapters:

- **Talent Advantage**—Do you have enough quality talent to accomplish your objectives and are you staffed for planned growth?
- **Training Advantage**—Does your team have the proper training and reinforcement to provide them with the needed knowledge and abilities?
- **Motivation Advantage**—Is your team motivated to complete their Predictive Behaviors and model Core Values on a consistent basis?
- **Accountability Advantage**—Does your company have an accountability culture that delivers results?

Chapter Seven

Talent Advantage

Obsess about Talent

**ADVANTAGE PRINCIPLE:
SPEND A LITTLE MORE TIME RECRUITING AND DEVELOPING TALENT, AND YOU WILL SAVE A LOT OF TIME MANAGING TALENT.**

Jim Collins, in his wonderful book *Good to Great*, said, "Great companies practice a principle of getting the right people on the bus, the wrong people off, and then pointing the bus in the right direction."[1] Attaining the right talent is a critical element of accomplishing anything you want, whether in business, sports, or life. This chapter explores the top hiring mistakes companies make and offers Predictive Behaviors for building a Talent Advantage; a process to identify, attract, select, and retain talent. Learn to avoid common mistakes such as relying on the interview as the only screening tool, hiring reactively, and not defining the attributes and qualities you seek. This chapter unpacks each Predictive Behavior for finding and keeping the best people. We will explore how not to wait until the last minute to hire, and thus be forced to take whomever you can get, and instead come up with an effective strategy for attracting the best talent, at the best time, for your business.

The Beatles got it right: "Help, I need somebody. Help, not just anybody." Talent is everybody's "job one"! Even if your company has a human resources department, finding talent is still the responsibility of everyone on the team: the CEO, the company president, executives, and the direct manager. In fact, if you are an executive or manager, building a quality talent pool of direct reports should be your highest priority. Having the proper talent is a key leadership principle that allows companies to win in the marketplace. The ability to make good decisions regarding talent represents a reliable way to enhance your Competitive Advantage since few organizations are good at it.

Company leaders may be envious that behemoths, such as Apple, Google, Amazon, and Facebook, are able to spend exorbitant sums on hiring and gobble up a disproportional amount of the top talent. True, most companies cannot spend what these global corporations do on recruiting, but I've found that with a magnetic culture and good hiring strategy, any size company can build a Talent Advantage. You just have to develop a strategy for acquiring talent, the same way you've developed a strategy for being effective in every other aspect of your business.

You can only catch the fish that are in your lake, with the bait that you have. So let's upgrade the bait and catch the best fish available.

Some Startling Statistics Regarding Hiring

25 Percent or Fewer of New Hires Are Brass Ring Performers

By now, you know what the term "Brass Ring" means when it comes to business growth and goal accomplishment. A Brass Ring goal is a stretch goal. A Brass Ring employee is a consistently top performer. Now, of course you want all your people to be Brass Ring, right? It is blasphemy for me to say otherwise. Well, I am here to tell you the truth: that is just not realistic for most if not all companies. It is extremely rare to get 100 percent of your hires to be Brass Ring, and actually, that's okay. I've worked with many top-performing companies and have yet to see a company with 100 percent of their contributors to any Vital Goal all be Brass Ring. Not every manager, production employee, customer service representative, salesperson, programmer, or route driver you hire will be Brass Ring.

This may vary based on how good you are at recruiting and developing talent, but normally, if you can get a quarter of your talent to be Brass Ringers, 50 percent Above Baseline, and 25 percent striving to get there, your company will be growing and accomplishing other goals at a rate well above your industry standards—provided you are properly staffed. If I could have 75 percent Above Baseline growth contributors at all of my clients, many would have more growth than they could handle. That only applies when companies stay fully staffed in key contributing positions.

There is one exception to this truism and that is your executive team. They must *all* be, or have the potential to become, Brass Ring leaders. If you can't give all of your top executives an "A" rating (or rate them as having the potential to become an "A"), it will show in your results. If you can do this, you will have a huge advantage in the marketplace. One of the priorities I focus on when working with owners or executives of companies is getting them to build a Brass Ring team of executive direct reports. Without such a team, it is difficult for either of us to achieve success. With a Brass Ring team, nothing can stop us!

The Job-Hopping Generations

According to a Gallup report, 21 percent of millennials say they've changed jobs within the past year, which is more than three times the number of nonmillennials who report the same, and 60 percent of millennials are open to a new job. Gallup estimates that millennial turnover costs the US economy tens of billions annually.[2] This is a scary statistic if you consider that millennials make up more than 35 percent of the workforce and this percentage is climbing. However, the idea that millennials and Gen Z created this trend is a common misconception. Every generation job hops in their youth in the search for the right career fit, higher pay, or career advancement. In good economic times when there are more jobs, more types of jobs, and more ways to access available jobs, retaining millennials is the same problem we are going to have with attracting and retaining all talent. That is why, as we discussed in chapter 1, "Create a Growth Culture," it is important to develop a magnetic culture that attracts and retains talent. Younger generations look for purpose, learning, flexibility, growth opportunities, as well as a positive and rewarding culture.

Hiring Is Less Accurate Than Flipping a Coin

Barry Deutsch, coauthor of *You're Not the Person I Hired!*, has reported on what he called the 56 percent Hiring Failure Rate Problem.[3] "When companies hire a six-figure executive, they expect them to 'hit the ground running' and produce results quickly. But according to their research and surveys of more than 20,000 hiring executives over the past 15 years, and a review of the published literature on the subject of executive failure, roughly 56 percent of newly hired executives fail within two years of starting new jobs."[4] This failure is an expensive proposition.

40 Percent of Sales Hires Fail

According to *Topgrading for Sales*, a practical guide and the industry standard, 40 percent of newly hired salespeople fail to make their quotas.[5] Too many new sales hires never hit their target or leave their jobs within the first couple years. I asked a billion-dollar company in a sales-driven industry what percentage of newly hired salespeople hit their quota for a period of time, and their answer correlated with my experience yet was still surprising. It was 25 percent. This is a company that has good hiring practices, sales training, marketing, and database management. Imagine what the percentage would be if they didn't. This is why you must always be filling your talent pipeline.

I find this figure particularly troubling. All the more so when you learn that, according to CSO Insights, 25 percent of companies take more than a year to ramp up their new sales hires. That means companies are paying new employees for months, and sometimes for a full year, who will never succeed! It's easy to see how hiring wrong quickly becomes a very costly venture. *Topgrading for Sales* estimates a wrong sales hire can cost a company as much as $500,000 or more a year if you factor in lost opportunity (five times base compensation).[6] Even if you use a conservative estimate like $50,000, underperformance and

Employee Turnover Costs			
Employees	100	100	100
Annual Turnover for Established Employees	50%	30%	10%
Positions to Fill	50	30	10
Success Rate of New Hires	50%	70%	90%
Total New Hires	100	43	11
Cost of Mis-Hires	$50,000	$50,000	$50,000
Total Employee Turnover Cost	$5,000,000	$2,142,857	$555,556

Figure 7.1. Employee Turnover Costs

turnover is very expensive. Whatever the actual figure is for your company, multiply it by the number of people who have quit or whom you have fired. It can cost millions.

We all are going to make hiring mistakes, which becomes very costly. See the Employee Turnover Costs table in figure 7.1. I believe it is valuable to look at turnover two ways: (1) turnover of established employees and (2) turnover of new hires. Combining hiring costs, training costs, turnover costs, and lost opportunity costs, I am using a very conservative number: $50,000. Accordingly, investing resources to become a better recruiter, selector, and retainer of talent has a great payback.

Another side of this coin to consider is that zero or low turnover may not be a good thing either. I've visited companies that were not growing or making much money but were proud of their low turnover. There may have been a number of leadership issues causing their poor results, but having the wrong people in the wrong seats was probably a driving factor. These companies may need a little turnover.

Top Hiring Mistakes and How to Fix Them

Hiring Mistake 1: Not Committing Enough Time and Not Making the Acquisition of Talent an Obsession

Whatever amount of time you are currently spending on finding and recruiting talent, increase it. Don't completely pass this responsibility off to the human resources department or other managers. The more time you spend doing this, the more the long-term payback is going to be for you and for the company. Acquire quality people and the experience of managing and leading them becomes much more positive and rewarding. Stick with subpar talent and you will pay for it with your time and results. Commit enough time and resources to talent acquisition and you will build on your Talent Advantage.

"Everyone you meet is another interview," quipped Jack Welch, past CEO of General Electric.[7] For example, if you're out on a Saturday afternoon shopping at a hardware or retail store and the retail clerk helping you is presentable, energetic, and a "go-getter," give her a business card, tell her about your company, and ask if she'd be interested in coming in for an interview. Go out and find the people you need instead of waiting for them to come to you. Some companies have special business cards designed to pass out in these situations.

I was leaving a parking garage with a client once, and he was telling me about the attendant: how enterprising he was, working multiple jobs and putting himself through college. Yet this CEO had multiple human resource needs and never considered this individual. I quickly encouraged him to call this individual in for an interview. Always be on the hunt for talent! As an example, if you manage the sales department, you should meet with every sales representative that cold-calls your company.

Hiring Mistake 2: Not Defining Attributes and Qualities Required for the Position

Know the attributes and qualities you want in your ideal candidate before you begin recruiting. Warren Buffett of Berkshire Hathaway says, "I look for three things when hiring people: first personal integrity, second intelligence, third high energy level. But if you don't have the first, the other two will kill you."[8] Herb Kelleher from Southwest Airlines said, "What we are looking for first and foremost is a sense of humor."[9] If you've ever flown Southwest, you'll know that it is apparent having a sense of humor is a big part of their culture.

Once you have identified the attributes and qualities that fit your culture and predict success in the designated position, make sure you have elements built into your selection process that verify the candidate has these skills and characteristics.

Hiring Mistake 3: Hiring Reactively

Don't act like talent needs are a surprise; you will always have them. If you've ever watched *Glengarry Glen Ross*, you've heard Alec Baldwin describe the "Salesperson's ABC": Always Be Closing.[10] Well for leaders, this should be "ABH," Always Be Hiring. You need a talent pipeline that is constantly in motion and delivering talent to your company to replace turnover—the talent that is leaving or being let go. Plan for it.

Let's say a company needs one hundred people in a specific position at all times. Now, let's say that company has 40 percent turnover with established employees in this position and a 50 percent success rate for new hires. That means the company needs to have, at all times, at least forty interns being trained and at least twenty prequalified candidates. Most companies know their talent requirements and their turnover and success rate, yet still do not recruit proactively. Ask prequalified candidates to stay in touch and to keep pursuing the job. This principle applies to every position.

If you wait until you have an opening to hire, and it takes thirty to ninety days to get someone hired, another ninety days to get them trained, and months before they start producing, in a high-turnover position, you'll never catch up. Instead, if you have turnover in a position, you should take a proactive approach, create a talent pipeline and Always Be Hiring. That's what top-performing companies do to maintain their Talent Advantage, and if they are going to compete for the best people, that's what all companies need to do too.

Hiring Mistake 4: Not Terminating Below Baseline Performers

You might think terminating Below Baseline performers has no relation to hiring, but it actually does. People who don't hire well are always behind, so they become reluctant to terminate Below Baseline performers—who have no potential to become Baseline or Brass Ring. They have the attitude of "Hey, at least there is someone in the position, even if they aren't doing a very good job." Employees pick up on that mentality, and it sets a low standard for everyone. So not terminating low performers can easily spill over and become a hiring mistake as well as a Culture Killer. Brass Ringers won't want to be a part of this culture. If you hire proactively, you will become more comfortable removing employees who are not performing, which will set a higher standard for your company.

Hiring Mistake 5: Relying on the Interview as the Only Screening Tool

I cringe whenever I hear a business leader say, "Oh, I have a good gut," as it pertains to interviewing and hiring. I have worked with thousands of employees, and I could not have predicted from the interview or initial meeting who would be a top performer and who would fail. Relying on instinct may sound good, but it is simply not going to get the job done. I've found the reverse is actually true. As a young manager, I was at a sales awards banquet, and when they called the top producers on stage, I remember thinking, "Wow, most of these people don't fit the image I have of a top-producing sales representative." This experience changed my paradigm instantly. So, yes, do thorough interviews. Just don't make decisions to hire based on the interview process alone, and don't fall in love with the candidate before you do additional screening.

Hiring Mistake 6: Asking Interview Questions Without Having a Desired Answer

In law school, professors train trial attorneys to never, ever ask a witness a question if they don't know the answer. The same is true of hiring. If you're going to ask the applicant a question, don't just ask for the sake of asking. Ask questions for a reason. Ask questions to confirm the candidate has the attributes and qualities you want in your ideal candidate. Know what answer you are looking for (and not looking for) before you even ask the question. Some questions might include:

- **Why did you apply for this position or why are you back for a second interview?** Candidates should understand the job and be enthusiastic.
- **What were your accomplishments in your last job? What were your failures? What did you learn?** Candidates should show a record of success and learning.
- **What were your goals for the past three years, and did you meet them? Why or why not?** Candidates should have concrete goals and ways to measure their own success. Candidates should not use excuses for not meeting their goals.
- **Describe your typical day/week in your last job. What were the keys to success?** Look for scheduled key success behaviors as part of their typical week.
- **In what area could you be a superstar?** This question helps determine what they believe they are best at. Does that skill align with the position they are interviewing for?
- **What makes you unique?** Look for an understanding and confidence regarding what skills they can bring to the job.
- **We are not the "low-cost provider." Tell me about any experience you have selling on value, not on price.** Look for experience, confidence, and a quick answer.
- **You need six first appointments with a prospect decision maker each week. How will you achieve this number?** Candidates should demonstrate knowledge, energy, and logical prospecting steps. Also look for variety.
- **Who was your supervisor in your last position? What were their strengths and weaknesses? How did they hold you accountable?** Listen for a positive attitude—are they okay with being held accountable?

- **Ask why the candidate is leaving or has left a recent job.** Listen for excuse making or blame.
- **This job may require working remotely at times. What challenges do you think you'll face working remotely, and how will you deal with them?** Look for experience and an understanding of what it takes to be productive working remotely.
- **If we progress to a final interview, I will be asking you to arrange an interview with your past supervisors. What will they say regarding your strengths, weaknesses, and performance?** Listen for an eagerness to arrange the interview and a positive record of accomplishment.
- **"Please give me an example,"** says Tom Peters in his book *The Pursuit of WOW!* "These are the five most important words in the interviewer's arsenal."[11]

Hiring Mistake 7: Not Testing and/or Profiling

There are a variety of tests you can give potential employees to gauge natural gifts or identify particular skill sets, problem-solving abilities, or personality traits. These can be incredibly helpful, and by not using them, employers are turning their backs on a useful and often cost-effective tool. Remember the cost of bad hires. Some examples of testing and profiling tools are DISC, the Devine Group, Wonderlic, Objective Management Group, and many others. You can use tests and profiles for more than just hiring:

- **Team Understanding**—DISC is a behavior assessment tool, based on the DISC theory of psychologist William Moulton Marston, which centers on four different behavioral traits: **D—Director** (emphasis on ego and power, accomplishing results, the bottom line, confidence, and a fear of failure); **I—Influencer** (emphasis on social expression, influencing or persuading others, openness, relationships, and a fear of not being liked); **S—Steady Relator** (emphasis on peace and loyalty, cooperation, sincerity, dependability, and a fear of change); and **C—Critical Thinker** (emphasis on facts and figures, quality and accuracy, expertise, competency, and a fear of being wrong). There can be conflicts with the differing profiles. DISC can help teams work through some of those conflicts. Through better team understanding, people get why differing profiles act differently. I worked with a company that had four departmental executives that were all talented but as a team

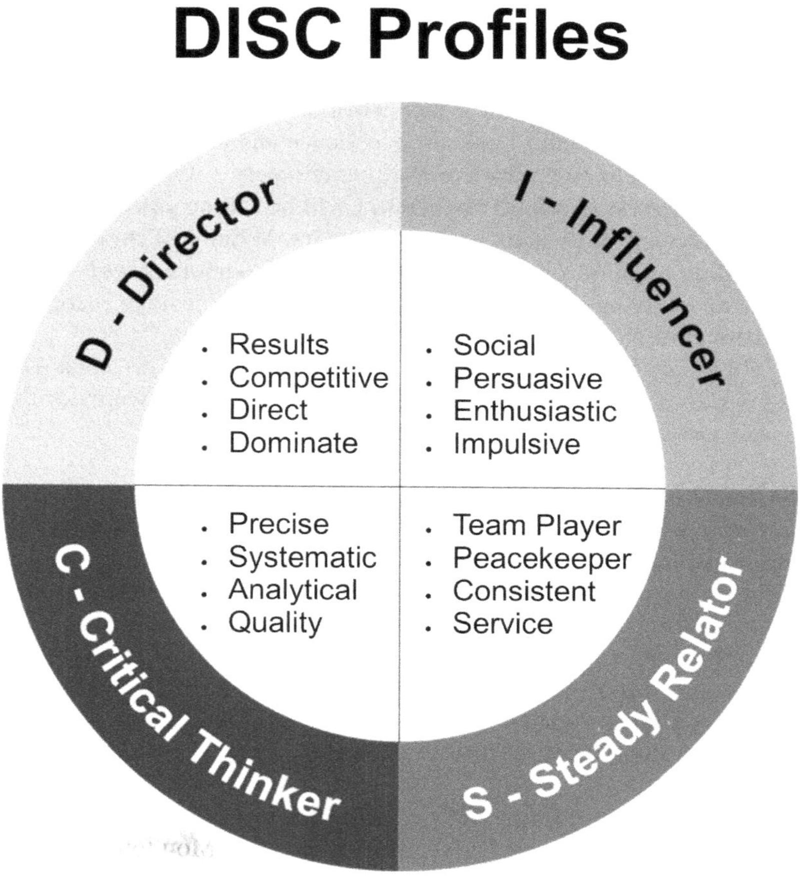

Figure 7.2. DISC Profiles

underperformed because they had profile conflict. The two DIs aligned in one camp, and the Two CSs aligned in the other camp. Had they worked well together they could have been an amazing team. Instead they chose to let their profile get in the way of their success and the success of the company. We used DISC to give them a better team understanding and improve teamwork, which soon showed up in their company results.

- **Qualifier/Disqualifier**—The Wonderlic test is a cognitive ability and problem-solving test used to assess the aptitude of prospective employees for learning and problem solving in a range of occupations. It consists of fifty multiple-choice questions to be answered in twelve minutes. The score is calculated as the number of correct answers given in the allotted time. Some companies require a minimum Wonderlic score for select positions. A score of twenty is typically considered average. Some companies use this test as a disqualifier for jobs that require a certain aptitude or problem-solving ability. Even the NFL uses the Wonderlic test.

- The DISC profile referenced above can also be used as a disqualifier. Let's assume we are looking for someone in a job that requires a substantial amount of detail and repetitiveness. Using DISC, I am going to look for someone with a high **C—Critical Thinker** and **S—Steady Relator**. If they are low for C and S, they are not likely to be happy or successful in this position. To be successful, the amount of energy they would need to expend would be enormous.
- **Natural Gifts (you and team)**—Profiles can help you understand strengths and weaknesses, so you not only get the right people but get people in the "Right Seats on the Bus." This is a critical step for your employees' success and, accordingly, your success. It is much easier to manage strengths than correct weaknesses.
- **Adjust Management Style**—We all tend to lead and manage in our core style, but sometimes we may be required to wear different hats to be an effective leader. If I have a low **D—Director**, but I am in a management position, I may need to wear my **D—Director** hat occasionally during accountability sessions. Conversely, if you are a high **D—Director** and low **I—Influencer**, you will still need to wear your **I—Influencer** hat occasionally to be more of a cheerleader. Surprisingly, one of the best leaders I know is a high **S—Steady Relator**, yet he knows how to wear all the hats and be an effective leader.
- **Tone for Every Meeting**—I like to go into meetings and think about what tone I want to set. I'm a high **D—Director**, and I've come to learn not all meetings can be **D—Director** meetings. Once again, I have learned to wear different hats for different meetings. If I am kicking off a new program and want people to buy in, I may want to wear my **I—Influencer** hat.
- **Prospect Insight and Customer Relations**—Although you won't give your prospects profile tests, once you become well versed using one of the profile tests, you can use your knowledge for prospect insight and customer relations. We all like to sell or service in our profile, but we should adapt and wear the hat for the customer or

prospect we are meeting with. If I am a high **D—Director** and want to move quickly to the result, that may not work well with a prospect that is a high **C—Critical Thinker** and wants all the details.

Hiring Mistake 8: Not Prequalifying

How do you prequalify? Require a detailed application and look at an applicant's career progression, their compensation progression, any lengthy time gaps, and, if gaps are present, the reason for them. How hard has someone worked to attain a goal? Did they pay for their own college? For some positions, it makes sense to schedule a telephone interview to see how well they handle themselves on the phone before bringing them in for an in-person interview. Another aspect of prequalifying may be a background check, testing, or profiling.

Although we call this item "prequalifying," what it actually provides are ways to disqualify applicants, so you can weed out people you know will not be a good fit with your company culture or the job. There are web-based tools where candidates can apply, submit their resume, fill out an application, complete a profile, and answer a series of questions. This will screen out candidates, so you only talk to those best suited to your position. Maybe the last resume on the stack, which we typical never get to, is your best candidate.

Hiring Mistake 9: Not Challenging Applicants

Don't be afraid to ask potential employees to do a little work to get the job—check with your labor attorney first. There is a great cartoon where a candidate walks into an IKEA job interview and is asked to take a seat and the chair is disassembled in front of the interviewer's desk. I once hired an individual to be a training and marketing director, and I knew the job was going to entail public speaking. Someone who had a more introverted personality was not going to be happy in the job. So, as part of her interview, I had the final candidates give me a one-hour presentation. I didn't care what the subject was; I just wanted to know that they were comfortable with public speaking and could put together an organized and interesting presentation. I also knew that anyone who balked at doing this was not the person for the job.

For a sales job that involves prospecting, have candidates bring in the business cards or contact information of twenty-five qualified prospects as their final test. If the job takes persistence, ask them to call you at 5:00 p.m. on Friday. When they call at 5:00 p.m. on Friday, say you're walking out the door and ask them to call you at 7:00 a.m. Monday. When they do that, tell them you're just walking into a meeting and ask them to call you Tuesday at noon. You get the picture. Will they do the basic things that the job requires?

Think of this step as a tryout, and your chance to prequalify the applicant. For telemarketers, consider a scripted telemarketing assignment. For route people, have them do a ride-along. Ask applicants to arrange an interview between you and their supervisor at their last job. The CEO of software developer Automatic, Matt Mullenweg, told the *Harvard Business Review* that he used to be too influenced by the interview, but now he gives candidates actual job responsibilities before he hires them. His experience? Tryouts are far better than interviews when predicting success.[12]

Hiring Mistake 10: Not Looking Inside the Company

Do you have a mechanism for growing talent from inside your company? Enterprise Car Rentals is amazing at this. Most of their executive hires come from inside the company, and they offer base-level employees mentorship opportunities and on-the-job and classroom training, all to fulfill their hiring motto, "The learning never stops." At Enterprise, the product may be a commodity (cars), but they differentiate through talent acquisition and development. The best screening tool on the planet is observing someone work inside your own company. Some of the best executives I've worked with as clients worked their way up from lower-level positions.

Hiring Mistake 11: Not Considering Cultural Fit

Whatever your culture, you'd better bring people in who fit that culture. People may comment that John Wooden, the winningest coach in college basketball history, has an amazing winning record of success because he had the best talent—people like Kareem Abdul-Jabbar and Bill Walton. But when he took over at UCLA, he was a relatively unknown coach and UCLA did not have a winning culture. He built a winning culture and a program that attracted the best talent. He identified and recruited the type of player he wanted, and the rest is history: ten NCAA basketball national championships in a twelve-year period as head coach at UCLA, including a record seven in a row. Prior to his arrival in Westwood, UCLA had only had two conference championship seasons in the previous eighteen years.

I recently talked to the CEO of a direct mail, catalog, and Internet marketing company, and he told me a great story. When he took over the company, he had a competitor whose culture and talent he envied. Fast-forward and that competitor was purchased by a large corporation that did not keep the same culture and lost much of that talent. He worked hard to build a company and culture that attracted the best talent and guess what? Many people from the talent pool he envied are now working for him. He said some of his people were so good that he wished he could build a wall around them. My hunch is that he has by creating a culture they don't want to leave.

Hiring Mistake 12: Not Factoring Growth

When working with companies that start growing at a faster pace than they have historically, it is *not* typically cash flow or operational capacity that stalls their growth; it is talent. Their acquisition of talent does not keep up with their growth. Many of my clients who used to grow 1 percent to 4 percent a year and then began growing 8 percent to 15 percent a year found that they quickly outran their talent.

That's because they were not used to hiring proactively and factoring in growth. My advice is to hire for where you're going to be in a year and plan for where you are going to be in five years. If I'm a $10 million company today, and I expect to be a $12 million company in a year, I need to hire as if I were a $12 million company *now*.

Advantage Challenge: Create a one-year organizational chart and a five-year organizational chart for your company.

Hiring Mistake 13: Not Aligning Compensation

Compensation should align company interest (Vital Goals), management interest (Make It Personal), and worker interest (Personal Goals). As much as I am a behaviorist, compensation should always be based on results. I was managing a group of sales representatives whose compensation package included a salary, benefits, and large commission incentives. Some of the top producers approached me about increasing their salary. At first, I was against it, but then I thought it through and decided to align everyone's interest. I adjusted their salary each quarter based on what they sold the prior quarter. It would adjust up and down accordingly. They loved the new plan, as did I, because they were very motivated every quarter to achieve their goals so their salary would stay the same or increase.

This was a great self-motivator and did not cost any more money relative to the better results. It aligned everyone's interest. The most expensive team is not the highest paid; it is one that does not produce.

Hiring Mistake 14: Vague or No Employment Agreement

It is critical to establish a Condition of Employment Agreement based on performance standards. Employees should know what success or failure looks like. It should never be a surprise. Don't just go through the motions. Make the agreement matter. It should spell out the job's duties; the company's core values and vision; behavior goals, both Baseline and Brass Ring; as well as results goals. It should also spell out learning expectations.

Hiring Mistake 15: No Blueprint for Success (Employee Retention)

There are no foolproof solutions to hiring well, but in my work with businesses, I have learned some lessons about talent. One of those lessons is that new hires are more successful when they are plugged in to a company that has a blueprint for success. It's interesting how successful a new hire can be when they are hired by a company that has good planning, effective strategies, a strong advantage, and proven systems. By all means, apply the principles in this chapter to upgrade your talent or solve a turnover issue, but to be consistently effective at finding and developing talent, apply the principles in the other chapters of this book as well.

Management is a critical component to staffing success. Marcus Buckingham and Curt Coffman, in their book *First, Break All the Rules*, said, "Employee retention and satisfaction: Overwhelmingly, based on their immediate manager!"[13] If you hire the right people and plug them into strong systems with strong management, they are more apt to stay with your company. Some success will breed departure; that is just the nature of business. I would prefer people leave because they are successful and have more opportunity versus leaving because they fail. The best employees will always be looking for new challenges and increased compensation.

Follow these steps and you will have a Talent Advantage. The ultimate throttle for building a Growth Advantage is the ability to get and keep enough of the right people.

Advantage Challenge: Are you committed to building a Talent Advantage? Good!
Identify the qualities and attributes of an ideal candidate.
How and where will you recruit ideal candidates?
What test(s) or profile(s) will you use to screen candidates? When?
What interview questions will you ask and what answers are you looking for?
What will be included in your Condition of Employment Agreement?
How will you measure results?
Reference the Talent Acquisition Advantage Challenge Application (Figure A.7) at the back of the book.

Chapter Summary

- Advantage Principle: Spend a Little More Time Recruiting and Developing Talent, and You Will Save a Lot of Time Managing Talent.
- Getting the right talent is a critical element of accomplishing anything you want to accomplish whether it be in business, sports, or life.
- Talent is everybody's "Job One!"
- Make obtaining talent an obsession. Whatever amount of time you are currently spending on finding and recruiting talent, increase it.
- I've found that with a good hiring strategy any size company can develop the talent they need to be a success.
- Twenty-five percent or less of new hires are Brass Ring performers.
- Know the attributes and qualities you want in your ideal candidate before you begin recruiting.
- ABH: Always Be Hiring.
- Ask interview questions for a reason. Know what you are looking for (or not looking for) before you even ask the question.
- Have a mechanism for growing talent from inside your company.
- Whatever your culture, bring people in who fit that culture.
- Compensation should align company interest (Vital Goals), management interest (Make It Personal), and worker interest (Personal Goals).
- It is critical to establish a Condition of Employment Agreement based on performance standards.
- It's amazing how successful a new hire can be when they are hired by a company that already has good planning, good strategy, a strong advantage, and good systems.

Chapter Eight

Training Advantage

Invest in Training and Learning

**ADVANTAGE PRINCIPLE:
TRAINING IS NOT AN EXPENSE; IT SHOULD ALWAYS BE AN INVESTMENT WITH A POSITIVE ROI (RETURN ON INVESTMENT).**

Competitive swimmer Michael Phelps said, "I think goals should never be easy, they should force you to work, even if they are uncomfortable at the time."[1] Phelps is the most decorated Olympian of all time, with twenty-eight medals, twenty-three of which are gold. Fans and sports commentators point to Phelps's six-foot-four-inch frame, his long torso, and his size fourteen feet as obvious reasons for his incredible success. It is true that these physical attributes are particularly well suited to swimming, and Phelps himself has said he feels grateful for his genetics. Yet there is something else that differentiated Phelps from his competitors and drove his success: his commitment to training.

While others trained five or six days per week, Michael Phelps was in the pool three to five hours a day, seven days a week: a huge Training Advantage. Imagine having the drive to get in the pool every day for five or six straight years. To maintain that workout schedule, Phelps slept eight hours a night and took a nap each afternoon. He also consumed twelve thousand calories each day.[2] While others might say they are interested in being the best, he was committed and devoted his whole life to it. Additionally, Phelps had a coach, Robert Bowman, who was as committed to his training and success as Phelps was. He also was at the pool seven days a week working, not just on making Phelps a better athlete but also on being a better coach. They both were focused on Disciplined Practice, practice that is focused and methodical with a process and a clear vision, practice that may not always be fun.

ADVANTAGE PRINCIPLE: DISCIPLINED PRACTICE IS PRACTICE THAT IS FOCUSED AND METHODICAL WITH A PROCESS AND A CLEAR VISION, PRACTICE THAT MAY NOT ALWAYS BE FUN.

Advantage Challenge: Ask yourself: what are you so committed to that you are willing to "get in the pool" every day for five straight years?

You are not competing in the Olympic games, but business too is a competition that requires a commitment to training and practice. As a leader, you owe it to yourself and your company to continually educate yourself and your team. The challenge is that too many people see training as a time waster and as an unnecessary expense—time and money that goes out but doesn't have a return. Training may not be a shiny piece of new equipment or the latest piece of new technology where it is easy to calculate your return on investment (ROI), but it should never cost you anything. In fact, if effective, it should provide your best ROI.

Let me give you an example. I consulted with a company that, over a multiyear period, increased revenue, operating profit, and the equity value of their company dramatically due to their hard work. However, after many years working together, they still saw my fees as an expense and would "jokingly" ask me if I would reduce them. I did not cut my price, but if you think about it, my price was cut because now it would be an even smaller percentage of their revenue and profit! After all that was accomplished, they still saw training and consulting as an expense—not factoring in any return. The people who led this company were great clients, very bright people, and their president was one of the best in their industry. They just had an all too typical mindset about devoting resources to training and learning; they saw it as an expense line on their profit and loss statement rather than focusing on the return. I tell clients, "If any consultant or trainer (including me) ever costs you anything, fire them immediately. If consulting, training, or any type of learning helps you obtain a small increase in annual growth and profit, the payback is typically manyfold."

Mark Twain said, "There is nothing training cannot do. Nothing above its reach. It can lift men to angelship."[3] Training has immense value that has been proven over and over again, and I'm a firm believer in the heights that training can take people and companies. Whatever you want to do—play a musical instrument, speak a new language fluently, run a marathon, be a scratch golfer, or be a better leader—training is paramount. Be it books, workshops, coaches, teachers, or consultants available to help you achieve your dream, or as Mark Twain says, achieve "angelship," if you are willing to train and put in the Disciplined Practice time, you can fulfill your dreams. I'm not sure there is an exact number of practice hours needed for all dreams to be realized, but Malcolm Gladwell, in his book *Outliers: The Story of Success*, calls it the "10,000 Hours Rule." Put in ten thousand hours of practice and you should be able to master most skills. However you look at it, that is not a bad start. In *Outliers*, Gladwell said, "Hard work is only a prison sentence when you lack motivation," and "Working really hard is what successful people do."[4]

Dan Gable is an amazing example of commitment to a Training Advantage. One of the greatest wrestlers of all time, he only lost one wrestling match in high school and college—an unbelievable record of 181–1. According to his logs, he hit the *Outliers* standard of mastery—ten thousand hours of practice—when he was a freshman in high school. But, according to him, it wasn't until he was training for the Olympics seven hours a day, seven days a week, when "I really got good." Gable went to the Munich Olympics and not only won the gold medal but didn't allow a single point to be scored against him. Not a single point! As a coach, he took that commitment with him. Being the University of Iowa's all-time winningest coach,[5] Gable won fifteen NCAA National Wrestling Team Titles while compiling a career record of 355–21–5. He coached 152 All-Americans, 45 national champions, 106 Big Ten champions, and 12 Olympians, including four gold, one silver, and three bronze medalists.[6]

Top performers are obsessed with training and practice. They don't just achieve greatness and then coast through the rest of their career. They stay out of their comfort zone, always striving to be the best. There is a great story about Tiger Woods that illustrates this principle.

The story goes: Tiger was walking through a clubhouse bar when John Daly asked Tiger to join him for a drink. John, although less disciplined and committed to practice, was also an accomplished professional golfer winning two major championships. Tiger's reply was, "If I had your talent I'd be doing the same thing you're doing."[7] Clearly, Tiger Woods is talented, but he knew he needed to practice and work hard to become great. People are not born great leaders or great golfers. It takes a commitment to Disciplined Practice if you want to become great at anything.

You may be saying, "I have such high turnover in my business; I'm not going to waste my money on training." I say, your logic is turned around. You should actually be doing just the opposite. If you have high turnover, you'd better have a system for getting people trained fast. Training will make them more successful in their jobs, and if they are more successful in their jobs, they'll be more apt to stay in their jobs. Although nothing will ever eliminate turnover, my experience in company after company is that employees who receive a lot of support, including training, are less likely to leave. On the other hand, if you have low turnover, even better. If people are going to be with your company for long periods of time, train them to be the very best. Zig Ziglar stated it well, "The only thing worse than training an employee and having them leave is to not train them and have them stay."[8]

Another positive aspect of training is the message it sends to employees that they are valued. I can't count the number of training events I've been involved with where I've met employees who are invigorated by the idea that the company they work for thought enough of them to send them to a multiday training boot camp. These may be new hires who already feel a sense of loyalty to the company or long-term employees who value your commitment to them and their craft.

"I think anything is possible as long as you put your mind to it and you put the work and time into it," Phelps has said.[9] Just like competitive swimming, for leadership, there are training Predictive Behaviors that lead to success.

Training Advantage—Predictive Behaviors:

Training Predictive Behavior 1: Identify Training Priorities.

You should always start by identifying your training priorities. Effective leaders know that training with a shotgun approach does not work; you've got to prioritize. What is it you're training this person or this group of people to learn, incorporate into their behavior, and accomplish? Consider these questions and develop a training program with intention instead of just winging it.

When I consider training priorities, I look beyond the baseline elements that everyone needs to know to be in a position (product knowledge, company knowledge, etc.); then I incorporate the training elements that will make them Brass Ring (planning skills, strategy competencies, etc.). *What are the top priorities for this employee now?* You should then incorporate tests—whether written, oral, role-plays, etc.—that confirm that learning and application has taken place.

Following is a list of training priorities I would pick for someone in an executive leadership position. I ask myself the question, "If they become proficient at these elements, are they likely to be successful?" In most cases I think you'll agree the answer is *yes*:

Executive Leader:

- **Company and Product Knowledge**—Baseline information that every leader should be an expert at.
- **Competitive Intelligence**—Do they understand the competitive landscape and threats?
- **Purpose**—Do they know the company purpose (i.e., why the company does what it does)?
- **Culture**—Do they understand and fit with the company culture and core values?
- **Planning**—Do they know the company's Vital Goals and understand how to develop a plan to accomplish goals (Vital Goal to Personal to Behavior to Metrics to Results)?
- **Strategy**—Do they understand the company's strategic plan and know how to develop strategy (how goals will be accomplished)?
- **Execution**—Do they know how to find, develop, motivate, and hold talent accountable?
- **Advantage**—Can they articulate the company's Value Advantage and Competitive Advantage? Do they understand the importance of investing in the company's advantage?
- **Opportunity**—Do they know what they are selling, to whom, where, and why?

Training Predictive Behavior 2: Teach Core Values and Predictive Behaviors.

A couple things that should always be factored into training for new employees are the company core values as well as the Predictive Behaviors you've determined are critical for success in their position. Instead of waiting for someone to be fully trained in all elements of their jobs, make sure they have adequate knowledge to start doing the Predictive Behaviors and living the company Core Values as soon as possible. There is nothing better than on-the-job training.

As an example, often companies will wait for an employee to be fully trained before they start requiring prospecting behavior. I like to get them engaged in doing the behavior as soon as possible, and by that, I mean the first or second week on the job. For me, those behaviors are part of the training. You've got classroom, video, and role-play training; then you've got real-life training where the new employee is actually doing the Predictive Behaviors required of the job. Why wait to see if they are willing and able to do behaviors that will make them a success in the job? Think of it this way: would it be better to take ninety days of golf lessons before playing a round of golf or play a few rounds after each lesson? Besides getting a new employee acquainted with their job right away, this helps to prime people for success. If they're unwilling to do the behavior or not a good fit for the company and position, better to know that on day five than on day ninety!

The whole point of training and management is to take an employee's right to fail away. We as leaders want to structure their days and weeks of training, just like we structure all other kinds of Predictive Behaviors, so they succeed.

Training Predictive Behavior 3: Make Training a Valuable Gift.

Albert Einstein said, "Teaching should be such that what is offered is perceived as a valuable gift and not as a hard duty."[10] When I conduct training seminars, I remind people all the time that I am there to help them and the company achieve their goals, be successful, and make more money. Although Brass Ringers are always hungry to learn, too often participants look at training as something they are being forced to do or as a correction of something they are doing wrong. I especially enjoy the debates regarding Predictive Behaviors where participants question what they are being asked to do. This is a great time to reinforce the why and ask if they have other ideas. Often when I ask that question I hear crickets, but sometimes I do get great ideas. Keep in mind: the person that typically learns the most in a training session is the trainer.

Alexander the Great and his father knew how valuable teaching could be. When he was born, he wasn't Alexander the Great; he was just Alexander. But his father, Phillip II, was a great leader and tactician, and Alexander had Aristotle for his teacher, a man who believed in focus and the virtue of practice. Aristotle taught Alexander in a disciplined, rigorous way. Back in Alexander's time, Gladwell's "10,000 Hours Rule" hadn't been discovered yet. But you can bet Alexander still put in those ten thousand hours studying in order to amass the largest empire of the ancient world before his thirtieth birthday.

Training Predictive Behavior 4: Training Must Be Scheduled.

Remember back in chapter 2 in the Vital Goals section where we talked about the quadrants and how important it was for the items inside the Leadership Quadrant (Quadrant L) to be scheduled? Training is a leadership activity, and leadership activities don't happen on their own; you have to schedule them, or they will get overrun by what's urgent at the moment. If you don't, weeks, months, and years will go by—time that you will never get back—without having any training in place.

An old logging aphorism often attributed to Abraham Lincoln says: "If I had six hours to chop down a tree, I'd spend the first four sharpening the axe." In business, too often people spend the six hours chopping on the tree and don't sharpen the axe (train) nearly enough. Training is a scheduled leadership activity that will sharpen your axes (employees), which will allow them to chop down more trees. It is common that after I do a training event and ask participants what they need to be successful in their job, their answer is more training. Ask your employees what they need to be more successful in their jobs.

Training Predictive Behavior 5: Training Must Be Repeated and Reinforced.

I have a style of consulting and teaching that sometimes drives people who are always looking for the next new thing crazy. I repeat and repeat and repeat the proven lessons, over and over and over again. Before I ever do anything new, I make sure that what I've already taught has been learned and incorporated. Once established, I review the planning and strategy process, as well as the plan, strategy, and outcomes, during every client visit.

Part of the reason for doing that is there are often new people in the sessions, but the more important part is that what gets reinforced becomes a part of the culture, and what does not get reinforced is rarely incorporated. Repetition gets results. That's why I recommend weekly training and reinforcement, role-plays, shared book reading, and so on. Anthony Robbins, author and speaker, understood this principle: "Any pattern of emotion or behavior that is continually reinforced will become an automatic and conditioned response. Anything we fail to reinforce will eventually dissipate."[11]

In terms of reinforcement, if you love a book, read it five times instead of reading five books one time. You'll get a lot more out of it. When I read a book, if I like it, first I'll read it multiple times, highlight it, paper clip it, and then I'll share it with my Executive Peer Groups—having them read the books. After all that, learning has taken place.

One activity I find uniquely helpful and that brings a group together quickly is to select a book to read as a team. Assign your training class or direct reports to read a section of the book for the next meeting. At the meeting, I'd draw a name out of my pocket and that person had to summarize that section of the book. That way, everybody read the book and had to be prepared to talk about that section. What we learned soon became a common language.

Training Predictive Behavior 6: Role-Play (practice).

Studies have shown that one factor, and only one factor, predicts student musical accomplishment: Disciplined Practice. Sure, some people have natural gifts in certain areas, but a substantial number of natural gifts have been wasted due to a lack of training and practice.

By his sixth birthday, Mozart had studied 3,500 hours of music with his father. Thomas Oppong reported in an article on CNBC.com, "In a letter to his sister penned in 1782, Mozart outlines a routine so intense that it left him a mere five hours of sleep a night."

> At six o'clock in the morning I have my hair dressed, and have finished my toilet by seven o'clock. I write till nine. From nine to one I give lessons. I then dine, unless I am invited out, when dinner is usually at two o'clock, sometimes at three, as it was to-day, and will be to-morrow at Countess Zichi's and Countess Thun's. I cannot begin to work before five or six o'clock in the evening, and I am often prevented doing so by some concert; otherwise I write till nine o'clock. I then go to my dear Constanze, though our pleasure in meeting is frequently embittered by

> the unkind speeches of her mother, which I will explain to my father in my next letter.
>
> Thence comes my wish to liberate and rescue her as soon as possible. At half-past ten or eleven I go home, but this depends on the mother's humor, or on my patience in bearing it. Owing to the number of concerts, and also the uncertainty whether I may not be summoned to one place or another, I cannot rely on my evening writing, so it is my custom (especially when I come home early) to write for a time before going to bed. I often sit up writing till one, and rise again at six.[12]

In a modern-day version of this kind of dedication, in the popular film *8 Mile*, based on the life of rapper Marshall Mathers, otherwise known as Eminem, a young Mathers has just won a competitive rap battle. His friends congratulate him outside the Detroit club where the battle has just been held and invite him to go out with them to celebrate. He declines, saying he has to go back to work.[13] He needs to practice. This principle applies to being the best at anything.

Coach John Wooden said, "How you practice is how you play."[14] As coach of the UCLA men's basketball team, Wooden won ten championships in twelve years, yet he rarely, if ever, talked about winning. He talked about—you guessed it—practice. Over a forty-year career, no matter how many games he'd won, his practices were always the same. He'd have his index cards and put his team through his drills. He had practice down to a science, and he got results. Wooden's philosophy was you practiced how you were going to win a game. His results speak for themselves.

Lao-Tse, Chinese philosopher, said, "If you tell me, I will listen. If you show me, I will see. But if you let me experience, I will learn." In business training, make sure people experience (role-play or live) what it is we're trying to teach them.

Training Predictive Behavior 7: Give Constant Feedback.

Ken Blanchard said, "Feedback is the breakfast of champions."[15] Doing training without feedback is like going bowling without seeing the pins. You're not going to get better because you don't know how you are doing. Imagine hitting a golf ball and not seeing its flight or shooting an arrow and not seeing the target. Think of a comedian. They hone their act with feedback from an audience. If the audience laughs, the joke is probably good and gets included in their act. If they don't, next. Lenny Bruce said, "The audience is a genius," and Jimmy Carr adds, "The audience knows funny better than any comedian."[16]

Often, managers are afraid to give feedback and employees are reluctant to receive it with an open mind. They really shouldn't be. Feedback is an absolute necessity for improvement. Mozart became Mozart because his father, a famous composer and performer, gave him constant feedback. Tiger became Tiger because his father, a teacher and golf addict, had him playing and practicing at age two with constant feedback. Father and son gave the same reason for his success: hard work.

Training Predictive Behavior 8: Demanding (Not Always Fun).

Training is not about having fun. It is about improvement at whatever skill you are trying to master, and that may take getting out of your comfort zone. Michael Phelps said, "If you want to be the best, you have to do things that other people aren't willing to do." In business, if you're willing to sacrifice and do things regarding training that your competition isn't, your company will have more success.

Muhammad Ali said, "I hated every minute of training, but I said, don't quit. Suffer now and live the rest of your life as a champion."[17] Training is hard work and demanding. At times, it may seem grueling. I'm not suggesting that training should *never* be fun, but the focus of training should be to get better. The pro golfer at the driving range isn't there to have fun. She's there to work. I go to the driving range and like to hit the club I hit the best; a pro goes to the range and works on all parts of their game but also focuses on the area they are struggling.

Wolfgang Amadeus Mozart's description of practice: "It is a mistake to think that the practice of my art has become easy to me. I assure you, dear friend, no one has given so much care to the study of composition as I. There is scarcely a famous master's in music whose works I have not frequently and diligently studied."[18]

Training Predictive Behavior 9: Make Training an Integral Part of Your Culture.

Make learning an integral part of your culture, and you will attract and retain talent at a better pace than your competition, which will help build on your Talent Advantage. A training culture builds on itself. As well-trained people have success, they stay with your company, and they, and others around them, will begin to see training as a valuable gift. A wonderful Chinese proverb sums training up well: "When planning for a year, plant corn. When planning for a decade, plant trees. When planning for life, train and educate people."[19]

Advantage Challenge: Time to work on your Training Advantage.
Pick a position that reports to you and determine your training priorities.
List five to six training priorities:
How will you train?
How will you reinforce?
How will you determine learning and application has occurred?
Reference the Training Advantage Challenge Application (Figure A.8) at the back of the book.

Chapter Summary

- Training is a leadership activity.
- Advantage Principle: Training Is Not an Expense; It Should Always Be an Investment with a Positive ROI (Return on Investment).
- Advantage Principle: Disciplined Practice Is Practice That Is Focused and Methodical with a Process and a Clear Vision, Practice That May Not Always Be Fun.
- Top performers are obsessed with training and practice. They don't just achieve greatness and then coast through the rest of their career. They keep striving to be the best.
- Training sends a message to the employee that they are valued.
- Effective leaders know that training with a shotgun approach does not work; you've got to prioritize.
- The point of training and management is to take an employee's right to fail away.
- What gets reinforced becomes a part of the culture, and what does not get reinforced dissipates.
- How you practice is how you will play.
- Training without feedback is like bowling without seeing the pins.
- Training is not about having fun. It is about improvement.
- Make learning an integral part of your culture, and you will attract and retain talent.

Chapter Nine

Motivation Advantage

Master the Four Magic Motivation Questions

ADVANTAGE PRINCIPLE: MOTIVATION IS THE ART OF GETTING YOURSELF OR SOMEONE ELSE TO CONSISTENTLY DO THE RIGHT ACTIONS, EVEN WHEN IT IS NOT CONVENIENT OR EASY.

Dwight D. Eisenhower, thirty-fourth president of the United States, five-star general in the Army, and supreme commander of the Allied Expeditionary Force in Europe during WWII, said, "Motivation is that art of getting people to do what you want them to do because they want to do it."[1] Early in my career, I was the general manager of a company. It was November, and the employees at the production plant knew they would be getting the day off on Thanksgiving, but they wanted Friday off, too. Typically, this company would not give production people the Friday after that holiday off because it was already a short workweek. Because of Thanksgiving, we had to get five days of work done in four. I found out they wanted that day off when one of the lead people from the plant came to see me. "You know, Bob," she said, "the team would really like to have Friday off." I didn't say *no*; I didn't say *yes*. I said I'd think about it, and I did. What I decided was that if they wanted their goal, the company had to accomplish its goals. As we serviced our customers weekly, our goal was simply to get a week's worth of work completed. If the employees could do that, then maybe they actually *could* have the four-day Thanksgiving weekend to spend with their families.

Keep in mind: this was a well-run plant. I had a production consultant, I had production standards, I had metrics, and we had incentives. As a matter of fact, I was in a peer group with other companies from the same industry, and we had the best production metrics in the entire group. So I went back to the lead people in the plant and told them, "Okay, here's the deal. If the production team wants Friday off, here's what we have to do. By Wednesday we need to have this amount of work done." At that point, I went through each area of the plant, set the production goals, and identified what we needed to accomplish in each area. Let me just say, the numbers I was giving them were a real challenge to accomplish. I'm not sure I thought we could do it. But on Wednesday when I looked at the results, I saw that those three days had been the most productive week this plant had ever had. The production team never seemed happier. They blew the doors off the goals, and it seemed to happen with ease. And you know why? Because it was something the production workers really wanted. They were self-managed and self-motivated, and they never worked harder or more efficiently.

Now, of course, I wondered to myself, *Why can't we do this every week?* For the answer, I talked to the lead people in the plant and asked them, "What's something you all would really like?" They told me they'd like to be able to get out of work early on Fridays. So I put an incentive together where the whole plant had to accomplish the goal or nobody was rewarded. I don't always like to tie incentives to such a large group, but for this production team, it worked. If each area of the plant achieved their goals for the week by Friday at a set time, they could go home a predetermined number of hours early and be paid for the entire forty-hour week. It was amazing how motivated they were and how well the incentive worked. They were motivated to do what I wanted them to do because they wanted to do it, too. Besides increasing productivity, this type of incentive should also make management easier.

Of course, some people (Brass Ringers) just naturally operate at a higher level. That's because they have a lot of personal motivation, but try as we might, Brass Ringers are never going to be your whole workforce. This chapter is about building a Motivation Advantage with your entire team.

Personal Motivation

What's the first motivator? That's easy: someone's personal sense of accomplishment; how they want to be viewed along with the things they want to accomplish in life. But even for that, there are different levels for different people. Someone who just wants to float by and do the minimal amount is a different management challenge than someone who wants to eventually get your job. Most people need some form of external motivation. That's just reality. They consciously or unconsciously want to be motivated to do and accomplish more, which means you, as their manager, can enhance whatever level of motivation they already have.

ADVANTAGE PRINCIPLE: YOUR PERSONAL MOTIVATION LEVEL IS A CHOICE.

Levels of personal motivation:

Brass Ring Motivation—These individuals are highly self-motivated. You will know these people when you have them because they'll be your best producers without a lot of nudging. Brass Ringers are the people that may even push you to be a better leader. Of course, you'd like everyone in your company to be in this category, and others might tell you to have all Brass Ringers on your team, but I've yet to see a company accomplish that feat. It isn't realistic unless you have unlimited funds, and even then, I doubt it is achievable. Remember, your top producers—Brass Ringers—are not lucky; they work harder, are incredibly motivated, and keep striving to be better. Whether in music, sports, chess, writing, sales, or leadership, Brass Ringers put in the Disciplined Practice and effort to be among the best at what they do.

Baseline Motivation—Baseliners will typically achieve the basic standards of their job but without strong leadership aren't always consistent and don't often strive for more. As we've discussed in prior chapters, with the exception of executive management, I'll take all the Above Baseline producers I can get. That's because their production is vital, and it is my job as a manager to always work to motivate these people to desire to accomplish more. Great leaders should not just maintain but should nudge Baseline performers toward Brass Ring. Management is key to the direction a Baseline worker's performance goes. Enhance their motivation and you will enhance their results.

SLUG (Seriously Lazy, Undisciplined Grown-up)—There are just some people you are not going to motivate, no matter what you do. They avoid hard work and success, plus believe that avoidance is an accomplishment. They have little self-motivation and are virtually impossible to motivate externally. Now, the people you and I work with are, for the most part, hardworking. So, in my experience, luckily, these undisciplined employees are a small percentage of the workforce. But if a company is like a farm, SLUGs are a drain on how much that farm produces.

ADVANTAGE PRINCIPLE: PROTECT YOUR CROPS FROM SLUGs (SERIOUSLY LAZY, UNDISCIPLINED GROWN-UPS).

Imagine that you are a farmer who has one hundred seeded acres. You and your family depend on the harvest of those one hundred acres for your livelihood. Can you afford to have fifty acres that produce only a small fraction of what they could be producing or perhaps don't produce anything at all? Of course not—you'd starve!

Well, it's the same for any business team. If you have a team of one hundred people, too often 20 percent are doing most of the production. A business team isn't a farm, so you'll never get even production out of all one hundred people, but you still must try to change that formula and get more production out of more of your acres. Do this and your company will experience unprecedented success. When Growth Advantage works with companies, we encourage them to expand the elements that produce growth. This, in turn, expands the number of producers, and if we can get 75 percent or more of the contributors to achieve Above Baseline or Brass Ring status, those companies will grow at unprecedented rates above their historic standards.

Advantage Challenge: Rate your direct reports. Is their motivation level Brass Ring, Baseline, or are they a SLUG (Seriously Lazy, Undisciplined Grown-up)?

It is important that people understand this principle; they are 100 percent in control of their motivation level, which puts them 100 percent in control of what they accomplish in life. Master Yoda said it best: "Do or do not; there is no try." If you have a dream, don't try—do. You may do and fail but you will learn from your failure. Use what you learn to adjust, and if you keep doing and learning, you will eventually succeed. Often the difference between success and failure is perseverance.

ADVANTAGE PRINCIPLE: DON'T JUST FOCUS ON MOTIVATING PEOPLE; FOCUS ON HIRING MOTIVATED PEOPLE!

If a person's motivation level is such a critical element of success, then I don't care if you are talking about athletes, musicians, salespeople, teachers, coaches, or anyone else, screening for motivation should be part of your hiring process. I once ran an organization where the first three hires came from families that had dairy farms—the hardest-working people on the planet. They were so self-motivated that even when they were overworked, they discouraged me from hiring more people. They made me a better leader and made the organization look good. Motivated employees can make you look good as well.

This being said, hiring is never an exact science, so managers must be good at both hiring and motivating, which leads us to the "Four Magic Motivation Questions."

The Four Magic Motivation Questions:

1. **What**—What do you want me to accomplish?
2. **Can**—Can I do it?
3. **Worth**—Is it worth doing?
4. **Why**—Why are you asking me to do it?

The Four Magic Motivation Questions are a tool that should be used to gauge and enhance the motivation levels of your team. They are applicable to all employees but are especially beneficial to use with underperforming employees to determine why they are not achieving the requirements of their job. Ask these questions and you can determine if the employee knows what they are supposed to be doing, if they believe they are capable of doing the job, if they believe the job is worth doing, and, finally, if they know why they are being asked to perform the duties of the job. These questions may look simple, but by asking them, you can glean a lot of valuable information. If an employee answers *yes* to these four questions and they are still not fulfilling the requirements of their job, you may have a SLUG on your hands. If they can't answer *yes* to the four questions, then as their leader you should find out why and address the situation.

Let's take an in-depth look at these questions one at a time. Work at it until everyone on your team can answer *yes* to all four questions. Although building a Motivation Advantage is important for all employees, with accelerated trends in remote work, eCommerce, and automation, being able to answer *yes* to these four questions becomes even more crucial.

Question 1: What—What do you want me to accomplish?

- Vital Company Goals
- Vital Departmental Goals
- Individual Goals (make it personal)
- Predictive Behaviors
- Accountability Metrics

Do all your employees know exactly what they are expected to do and accomplish? Do they know the Vital Goals? Do they know the details and their personal aspect of what you are asking them to accomplish? Do they know the Predictive Behaviors and metrics involved? In order to answer *yes* to this question, the employee needs to have an understanding of specifically what is required of them day in and day out, as well as what the bull's-eye looks like. This is the essence of what we covered in Part I, "The Planning Advantage." To develop a culture of engagement, you must have clear expectations and effectively communicate those expectations to your team.

Let me give you an example from my own experience. It was early in my career, and I had just been hired as a vice president/general manager of a company. I was a young manager, younger than the managers that reported to me. I had a service executive that had been with the company for many years and was a good guy but wasn't doing what I needed him to do for the company to accomplish its Vital Goals. Now, it wasn't my way—and still isn't my way—to jump in and immediately start critiquing everything and everyone. I like to spend some time watching and learning what people are doing and then see how I can evolve the company culture to enhance performance. With this service executive, after a few months, I sat him down and basically just told him, "You're failing." He was shocked!

I didn't think he had a chance to succeed in the position. He did not seem to have the right natural gifts (profile), he wasn't getting things done on a consistent basis, and I even questioned whether he would be willing to make the changes required of him and his team to be successful in his job. To his credit, when I told him he was failing, he didn't go on the defensive like I expected; he went on the offensive and asked me, "What is it you want me to accomplish?" Now I was the one who was shocked. I started being very clear about my expectations, and this service executive became, much to my surprise, a Brass Ring producer. I never would have guessed he had it in him. As it turned out, he was very self-motivated; he wanted to be successful and was willing to do what it took to achieve success. He just didn't have a clear **WHAT**. No one had ever given him that before, including me. It is imperative that everyone on your team has a clear WHAT.

Advantage Challenge: As a leader, ask yourself: Am I giving people a clear WHAT for what I need them to accomplish?

Question 2: Can—Can I do it?

- Do I have the natural gifts?
- Do I have the skills/training?
- Do I have the right tools?
- Do I have hope?

Does everyone on your team believe they are capable of completing the tasks they are expected to accomplish? What I mean by that is, what would my response be if somebody came to me and said, "Hey, Bob, if you can complete an Ironman Triathlon in ten hours, I'll give you $10 million"? Now, I'm a motivated person, and I'd certainly be motivated by the $10 million, but that amount of money wouldn't matter because I am not physically capable of completing a triathlon at all, let alone in ten hours. To be motivated, your people must believe they have the innate ability to do the job.

Well, for some people, certain activities in a company are like that triathlon. Many factors are in play here. They may not have the right natural gifts (either behaviorally, physically, intellectually, or emotionally), the right skills or training, the right tools, or hope that the job can be done. When it comes to completing a triathlon, I would answer *no* to all four questions.

Natural Gifts—Does the employee have the makeup or natural gifts for the job? When you don't have the natural gifts, you are either not capable of doing the job or it takes excess energy for you to complete the job on an ongoing basis. If doing a certain task is only a small part of your job/day and you don't have the natural gifts, that's okay. We all have some parts of our job that we don't have the makeup for, and it is okay to expend the extra energy in bursts. Or, although I would not recommend it, some people can maintain the required energy on an ongoing basis if they are fulfilling a dream.

Johnny Carson, the consummate talk show host, was an example of this. It has been reported that offstage, he was a classic introvert—the kind of person who recharged by being alone and was depleted by being among people. After a show in front of millions, he'd get into his car with a palpable sense of relief, as in, that was a good show; now I'd like to be alone in the dark listening to jazz. He didn't socialize much. He saved his energy for performance.[2] Now, unless it's your dream career, I would suggest finding a job that is better suited to your natural gifts.

Some people are very accurate and detailed, and others are not. I call that the "sheriff" profile. If somebody does not have detail in their profile, meaning detailed tasks are challenging for them, and they are a people person who likes to socialize, it would not make sense to put this person in a data entry position that requires them to be perfect and doesn't offer much human contact. They would lose motivation for the job quickly, even if they were self-motivated. Conversely, if someone is introverted and loves detailed and accurate work, putting them in a job that requires constant social interaction would be a real challenge.

In both these examples, a lack of motivation isn't the issue. These employees are not a good fit for the requirements of the job done. They just don't have the natural gifts, which is a demotivator. Effective leaders match natural gifts and job duties.

Now, I think it would be helpful to take a minute here to review the DISC behavior profiles we introduced in chapter 7, "Talent Advantage." Such behavior profiles can help you understand the strengths and weaknesses, so you not only get the right people in your company, but you put them in the right positions. DISC (and other profiling tools) help identify and underscore how important natural gifts are to success.

ADVANTAGE PRINCIPLE: FOCUS ON STRENGTHS, NOT WEAKNESSES.

The four basic DISC behavior profiles are D—Director (driven—motivated by results), I—Influencer (social—needs to be liked), S—Steady Relator (consistent—seeks stability), and C—Critical Thinker (systematic—needs to be right). So you're not going to have success by putting a people-person with a high "I" in a job that requires intense detail/accuracy and never interacts with another soul. You aren't going to want someone with low "C" and "S" in their profile to manage your database, nor are you going to like the results of putting a "D" in a job where they have underling responsibilities that can't be quantified and they are not in control of achieving. Make sure you have the right natural gifts in the right positions.

Training and Reinforcement—I agree with the book *Influencer: The Power to Change Anything*, which stated, "The persistent problems we face stem more from a lack of skill—which stems from a lack of deliberate practice—than from a genetic curse, a lack of courage, or a character flaw."[3] Do all your employees have the skill set to be successful in their job? People that don't have the proper skills feel like they are incapable of doing the job and, accordingly, lose motivation. The best way to enhance the skill set is through professional training and continued reinforcement. Most people don't fail because they don't have the desire to succeed. Too often, people fail because they don't have the right skills, training, and reinforcement.

I worked with a sales representative who had one foot out the door because she did not believe she could do the job. She was not properly trained. Training and reinforcement were a critical element of giving her the confidence in herself that she could succeed. Once she had belief, she took off like a rocket and became a top performer. I've seen training have this type of impact on people repeatedly throughout my career.

Training and reinforcement are critical Quadrant L—Leadership activities that too often get neglected. You simply cannot give people too much training. Employees want training, and, as we just discussed in chapter 8, "Training Advantage," training is not an expense; it is one of the best investments a company can make, not just in performance but in the future of their organization, as well as in strengthening the advantage a company has in the marketplace.

ADVANTAGE PRINCIPLE: WHAT GETS REINFORCED GETS APPLIED.

Developing skills does not just require training but also needs never-ending reinforcement. Without training reinforcement, skills will eventually dissipate. The best athletes, musicians, and performers practice their craft incessantly. So should business executives, managers, sales representatives, customer service representatives, engineers, and so on. Aly Raisman, an American gymnast, two time Olympian, and gold medalist, summed up training in this quote: "That's when I'm most comfortable: sweating in a gym, covered in chalk."[4] She was not born a natural gymnast. Her coach, Mihai Brestyan, teased her about being the most uncoordinated gymnast on the floor. She trained six to eight hours per day repeating the same tasks over and over again to achieve Olympic gold.

Tools—On February 9, 1941, Prime Minister Winston Churchill talked to the citizens of Britain in a now famous radio broadcast praising his countrymen for their courage and capability in a time of war and, also, to stress the need for cooperation between America and the European allies in the form of financial and economic support. Winston Churchill said, "We shall not fail or falter; we shall not weaken or tire. Neither the sudden shock of battle, nor the long-drawn trials of vigilance and exertion will wear us down. Give us the tools, and we will finish the job."[5] Of course, we now know how the war turned out, thank heaven. Many have said, "Business is war." Now, doing a job is not the same as being a soldier in wartime, and yet having tools is crucial for business success, too. In our careers as leaders, if our employees are given the tools they need, they should be able to finish the job.

Think of a carpenter, a mechanic, or a plumber without the proper tools; they can't be effective at completing their jobs. Well, I can tell you from experience that being an executive, a manager, a sales professional, or a service representative requires having the proper tools as well. An executive may require a tool for tracking and reporting key metrics, a plant manager needs the proper equipment to maximize the efficiency of their plant, a professional sales representative may require a prospect database and the tools for giving a professional presentation, and a service team may require customer relationship management software as well as routing software for route drivers to make effective deliveries. A Lyft driver needs a quality vehicle and a mobile phone with mapping software. A key leadership activity is to make sure your company and your team have the tools to succeed and win in the marketplace.

Hope—Without hope, motivation dies. With hope, anything can be accomplished. If you don't have hope that you can accomplish the dream, your lack of it will be a self-fulfilling prophecy. Business leaders can learn a lot from history's successful military leaders who are experts in inspiring hope. Napoleon Bonaparte stated, "The only way to lead people is to show them a future; a leader is a dealer in hope."

One of the greatest conquerors in history, Napoleon conquered almost the whole continent of Europe. Napoleon, as a leader, clearly understood the importance of hope. In 1795, the governors of France suggested to Napoleon that he lead the charge to invade England. Napoleon gave the idea some thought but determined France's naval forces were inferior to Britain's and the invasion idea was premature. He proposed an alternative: let him take his cavalry to Egypt, where he would wipe out British trade routes. The governors agreed, and in 1798, he scored an important victory at the Battle of the Pyramids[6]—a step toward building hope. Napoleon used these types of hope-building strategies throughout his career.

When I started in sales, I was right out of college, young, shy, with no business or sales experience. I was unsure of how successful I'd be in my new job, and at that point, I did not have a lot of hope. Though I didn't know it yet, I did have some natural gifts to be successful in sales. I had an excellent manager who trained us continually (every Monday and every Friday), so when he finally let us loose, we were ready to go. He gave us the roadmap to success by emphasizing the importance of doing the desired behavior (Predictive Behaviors), instilled the proper skills, and reinforced everything. I was lucky to have this manager as my first real boss out of college. The success I achieved with his help was a great motivator that has continued throughout my life. I was well trained, and I had access to wonderful sales tools.

Those things all poised me for success, and yet perhaps most important to my future was the guy my manager assigned me to ride with after training in order to experience sales firsthand. He was a veteran and had been with the company for forty years. Together, we made a cold call with him doing the talking and me observing. I did not know this was not typical, but during the cold call, he got through to a decision maker, found out the prospect was not happy with his present supplier, gave a proposal, and made a big sale. Since I was so inexperienced, I did not know this kind of thing didn't happen every day. I calculated the commission he just made, and guess what? I did not want to ride with him anymore! I was extremely motivated to start knocking on doors for myself. Although I am still waiting for the original cold call to turn into a big sale, within a short period of time, and with the help of my boss, I "tasted blood" for myself, which drove my motivation even more. Getting your team members to taste success is a huge part of being an effective leader. Give them help in the beginning, and it will be much more likely to pay off later—simple but important.

Imagine the alternative: an employee starts in a new job and weeks or months go by with no success. Even the best-intended employees will eventually lose their motivation.

Question 3: Worth—Is it worth doing?

- Having a job
- Compensation
- Incentives (intrinsic and extrinsic)
- Culture: Positive work environment

Having a Job—It is critical that employees believe what you are asking them to do is worth doing for the company, their department, and, yes, especially for themselves.

Sometimes the answer to this question is *yes* simply because you've given someone a job. That is a factor that ebbs and flows and will obviously be a more powerful influencer in a market where jobs are scarce than in a market where jobs are plentiful. Regardless, I feel that providing someone a job is a valuable gift. Now, do everything you can do to enhance the value of a job by building a magnetic culture. If someone does not value their job, it is unlikely they will be motivated to do their best.

Compensation—Compensation is often underestimated as a motivator. It is, for most people, the primary reason they get out of bed in the morning and go to work. The level of compensation, like the job itself, is driven by the job market. As the market for talent gets more competitive, you may have to pay more to attract and keep motivated people.

I've done management compensation surveys with my Peer Groups, and the results were interesting and, for some, a little surprising. Companies that were properly staffed with the highest management compensation were often the most profitable companies. How could companies in the same industries paying more people more compensation possibly be more profitable? These companies are getting a payback on their Talent Advantage. Conversely, companies that are too lean are often the least profitable and, accordingly, think they can't afford to hire quality managers and executives. It is a mindset that creates a downward spiral, a self-fulfilling prophecy.

Incentives (Intrinsic and Extrinsic)—Extrinsic and intrinsic incentives are additive and not an "either-or" proposition. Both should be utilized to maximize motivation.

ADVANTAGE PRINCIPLE: TURNOVER IS EXPENSIVE; APPRECIATION ISN'T.

Intrinsic motivation involves completing tasks simply for the satisfaction that the task provides. Intrinsic incentives include giving people a sense of purpose with their job, along with other rewarding elements like respect, appreciation, a sense of achievement, and being recognized publicly for their hard work. These are all the things that aren't a paycheck, a trip, or a prize. Employees internalize these incentives, and leaders ignore them at their own peril. Not only are they inexpensive or even free to bestow; they can be the difference between retaining a motivated employee or watching them leave to go work for your competition.

Adrian Gostick and Chester Elton in their book *The Carrot Principle* note, "Of the people who report the highest morale at work, 94.4 percent agree that their managers are effective at recognition."[7] Yet most managers don't know how to do recognition well, and if they do, they don't do it often enough. Simply said, recognition motivates workers. I once worked with a team, and during the weekly staff meeting, the first thing the leader and fellow team members did was to recognize another's accomplishments. It started the meeting off on a positive note and helped to build a positive culture. The key is to make sure the recognition is for true progress and accomplishment, not hollow praise.

One of the top reasons motivated employees quit their jobs is because of a lack of intrinsic rewards. Brass Ring producers who don't feel appreciated will start looking for a better job, and I can assure you, there are plenty of companies that will be happy to recognize and appreciate your top producers. Progress leads to achievement, which leads to recognition, appreciation, and respect. This, in return, leads to a loyal employee; loyal employees lead to loyal customers, and loyal customers lead to higher customer retention, resulting in increased growth and profit. In fact, studies by Bain & Company, along with Earl Sasser of the Harvard Business School, have shown that even a 5 percent increase in customer retention can lead to an increase in profits of between 25 and 95 percent.[8]

ADVANTAGE PRINCIPLE: YOU WILL GET WHAT YOU REWARD. BE CLEAR ABOUT WHAT YOU WANT AND REWARD IT.

Extrinsic motivation deals with motivations that are outside of your passions and personal self-esteem. Extrinsic incentives include more tangible incentives like salary increases, benefits, commissions, prizes, time off, and bonuses. These incentives are great motivators. The key is to make sure they are aimed at contributions as they relate to your Vital Goals.

Whatever extrinsic incentives or rewards you are using, make sure to pay the incentive as close to the action and/or result as possible. The closer the reward to the result, the more motivating the incentive will be. The reverse is also true. If I accomplish something today, but don't get the reward for months or a year, the incentive will be less effective. Or, as the comedian Steven Wright said, "Hard work pays off in the future. Laziness pays off now."[9] That's because the longer it takes in the mind of an employee to tie together the outcome and the incentive, the less powerful the connection will be. As an example, when a sales representative makes a sale, except in the case of very large accounts, give them the commission check as soon as possible. You can always make adjustments later. Nothing works better to reinforce success than an instantaneous, or near instantaneous, reward.

Weight loss is something a large percentage of the population is trying to accomplish but too often fail and give up. The problem is that the reward for eating well and exercising is not instantaneous. If I skipped that pizza and beer tonight and woke up two pounds lighter tomorrow, it would be easy to stay motivated and lose the weight. But that is just not how it works, and accordingly, people lose their motivation. We can't control the timeliness of the incentive for weight loss, but we can control the timeliness of the incentives we provide our teams.

Be aware of what motivates people. As discussed in chapter 7, "Talent Advantage," I had a very successful sales team, and a large percentage of their pay was commission and bonuses. Even though the more they sold the more they made, and their commissions were unlimited, they kept approaching me for a larger salary. Instead of saying *no*, I developed a system where the salary was adjusted each quarter based on what they sold the prior quarter. It was the same total compensation, but they were more motivated by increasing their salary than they were by increasing their commission. This turned out to be a great incentive because once they hit a salary level, they would do anything within their power not to drop back to a lower salary. As stated by Richard H. Thaler and Cass R. Sunstein, "Roughly speaking, losing something makes you twice as miserable as gaining the same thing makes you happy,"[10] making it a great motivator.

Positive Work Environment—Another tangible incentive is a positive work environment. Especially for the younger generations, this is a great motivator. We spend the majority of our waking life at work; it would be crazy to not make it positive and rewarding. A great example of this is the fish stand at Pike Place Market in Seattle as discussed in the book *Fish! A Proven Way to Boost Morale and Improve Results* by Stephen C. Lundin, Harry Paul, and John Christensen. The lessons imparted in *Fish!* are very straightforward and inspiring. The authors assert that employees have the power to change their own attitudes in the workplace, creating an environment that will not only be more positive and productive but also make them happier. What is impactful is that *Fish!* uses the Pike Place Market in Seattle, which has lively fishmongers tossing fish to and fro. The idea is that if these workers—who have very difficult jobs—can maintain an amazingly motivated attitude about their work, then so can anyone. Attitude is a choice. The authors state, "There is always a choice about the way you do your work, even if there is not a choice about the work itself."[11]

A positive work environment may not be a financial incentive, but it is something workers can feel and experience. This does not mean that, as a manager, you don't deal directly with negatives, but it does mean we should avoid the natural tendency to be negative and instead work to pick up on and acknowledge the good things that are being accomplished as well. How many kids have a story of coming home with a school report card that has five As and one D, and all the parents want to talk about is the D? Yes, the D needs to be addressed, but not at the price of completely ignoring all of those As.

A positive culture and a cohesive team are things people *want* to be a part of. The need to be accepted and respected can be a powerful motivator.

Question 4: Why—Why are you asking me to do it?

- Inertia
- Ask
- Accountability
- Condition of the job

If your employees do not understand why you are asking them to accomplish specific tasks, you have not done your job as a leader. The Why question is critical to motivation. It is imperative that you educate your team regarding why you want them to do something new, something better, or more of something they are already doing. I always focus on the Why in my training, and so should you.

I was doing a full-day training program with a group of long-tenured, union route-delivery drivers. We were asking them to have a bigger role in growing the company. Typically, when I do these types of sessions, they are one or two hours long, but because the CEO wanted to make the most of my visit, he asked me to do a full-day session. I also knew that this team, like most, was not enthusiastic about change or training sessions, so I thought I was going to be "eaten alive." Well, I decided to spend more time than usual on the Why and showed the impact this team's efforts would have on the company's growth and profit. To my surprise, it clicked. It turned out to be one of the most enjoyable and effective training sessions I've ever conducted. After the session, I actually had a couple participants come up and thank me. They said, "I never knew my contribution meant so much to the company's growth." Mission accomplished!

ADVANTAGE PRINCIPLE: IT IS CRITICAL THAT ONCE YOU ESTABLISH A VITAL GOAL, YOU IMMEDIATELY WORK TO CREATE MOMENTUM (PROGRESS).

Inertia—There are a number of elements to be an effective manager. One critical element to the formula comes down to being a tenacious nudge, someone who is willing to persistently draw a worker's attention to something important and then gently, or sometimes not so gently, prod them toward productivity and success. Being a nudge means not allowing complacent inertia to set in. In physics, inertia means the tendency for objects at rest to remain at rest and for objects in uniform motion to continue in motion in a straight line unless acted on by an outside force. As a manager, you're the outside force! Once result and behavior goals are established, as managers, we need to get people in motion and moving in the right direction. The number one motivator of people is progress, and it is important that people experience progress as soon as possible. Enough progress and you will create a flywheel effect, which is a wonderful experience that builds off itself.

Ask—Behavior Intention Questions—Asking Behavior Intention Questions increases the likelihood the desired behaviors will occur manyfold. I always meet with my direct reports weekly or even daily in some instances. One of the most important parts of that meeting is to ask Behavior Intention Questions and then follow up the following week to confirm the discussed behaviors and outcomes were accomplished. I ask, "What are the priorities for the week and when, where, and how will they be performed?" If I ask each week what's been done and what they plan to do the upcoming week, hiding places are removed. I find out fast whether I have a Brass Ringer, a Baseliner, or a SLUG on my hands. If someone is able week in and week out to tell you they have not done their job, their level of motivation is fairly obvious.

It isn't just the act of asking Behavior Intention Questions that will affect outcomes. You need to hold your people accountable for their answers. Trust me on this. If you consistently employ this model, your people will get more done. It really is just that simple. For example, you could simply ask, "Hey, Joe, you were a little short on your prospecting behavior this week. Tell me what happened." "Okay, well, that's not going to happen next week, is it?" "What are we going to do if it does?" "When are you going to prospect this week?" Make the questions as specific as possible. That way, the answers will be specific, too.

The odds of something positive being done go up exponentially when you ask Behavior Intention Questions weekly.

Accountability—Accountability is the management pixie dust that makes the other elements of this chapter and this book work. Without accountability, strategy and planning are not as effective. Although we sometimes think of accountability as a negative or even a punishment, it is actually a great gift. In order for accountability to be present, there need to be specific goals, not just for workers but also for managers and executives. Accountability, like death and taxes, is something no one can escape. The difference is accountability is a good thing.

Accountability includes standards for Brass Ring and Baseline performance, weekly meetings, regular feedback, and interacting with your team and with your direct reports one-on-one. The only people who worry or are anxious about this concept are the ones who are not doing the required activity.

If you go through the entire process in this chapter and your team members are still not motivated to do what you expect them to do, there need to be consequences. One of those consequences might be termination. At some point, it must be up to the employee and not the manager—provided the manager has done their job. Or as Lou Holtz said, "Motivation is simple. You eliminate those who are not motivated."[12] I've had CEOs in my Executive Peer Groups talk about how they finally let an underperforming or disruptive employee (SLUG) go after years or even decades and how positive the impact was on the culture of their company. Once a SLUG is terminated, managers seldom ask themselves why they did it but wonder instead why they did not act sooner.

Get ready, because in chapter 10 we will take a deeper dive into accountability.

Advantage Challenge: Are you motivated to create a Motivation Advantage? Pick one employee position and an outcome that you would like to influence with motivational activities. List two or three motivational ideas for each of the magic motivation questions (What, Can, Worth, and Why) that will influence outcomes.

Reference the Motivation Advantage Challenge Application (Figure A.9) at the back of the book.

Chapter Summary

- Advantage Principle: Motivation Is the Art of Getting Yourself or Someone Else to Consistently Do the Right Actions, Even When It Is Not Convenient or Easy.
- The biggest motivator is a person's evaluation of their own behavior and accomplishment.

- Advantage Principle: Your Personal Motivation Level Is a Choice.
- Most people need some form of external motivation; that's just reality.
- Levels of personal motivation: Brass Ring, Baseline, and SLUG (Seriously Lazy, Undisciplined Grown-ups).
- Advantage Principle: Protect Your Crops from SLUGs (Seriously Lazy, Undisciplined Grown-ups).
- The Four Magic Motivation Questions: Does the person know *What* they are expected to do? *Can* they do it? Is it *Worth* it? Do they know *Why* they are expected to do it?
- Advantage Principle: Don't Just Focus on Motivating People; Focus on Hiring Motivated People!
- Advantage Principle: Focus on Strengths, Not Weaknesses.
- Advantage Principle: What Gets Reinforced Gets Applied.
- Without hope, motivation dies. With hope, anything can be accomplished.
- Extrinsic and intrinsic incentives are additive and not an "either-or" proposition. Both should be utilized to maximize motivation.
- Advantage Principle: Turnover Is Expensive; Appreciation Isn't.
- Advantage Principle: You Will Get What You Reward. Be Clear about What You Want and Reward It.
- We spend the majority of our waking life at work; it would be crazy to not make it positive and rewarding.
- Advantage Principle: It Is Critical That Once You Establish a Vital Goal, You Immediately Work to Create Momentum (Progress).
- As a manager, you're the outside force! Once result and behavior goals are established, as managers, we need to get people in motion and moving in the right direction.
- The odds of something being done go up exponentially when you ask Behavior Intention Questions weekly.

Chapter Ten

Accountability Advantage

Be Accountable to Accountability

ADVANTAGE PRINCIPLE: THE KEY TO EXECUTING PLANS IS HOLDING YOURSELF AND TEAM MEMBERS ACCOUNTABLE.

Bob Proctor, author and speaker, said, "Accountability is the glue that ties commitment to the result."[1] Accountability is a critical success component in business and in life because everything else we talk about in this book will never be maximized without efficacious accountability. If planning is "what," strategy is "how," and execution is "now"—then accountability is a key element of execution that ties everything together and produces Brass Ring results. Yes, having a strategy will have an impact on success. Yes, planning will impact success. Yes, hiring the right people, and giving them the right training, within the right culture, will all have a positive impact on your company's success. However, you can multiply that positive impact exponentially if you and your team develop an Accountability Advantage.

Although critical, accountability is not just about leaders holding team members accountable. When you have truly built an Accountability Culture, team members will hold other team members accountable. When I consult with companies, it is often a challenge to get managers to hold subordinates accountable on a consistent basis, but when they do, you see the culture of companies change for the better. Now fast-forward to a company where peers are willing to hold each other accountable; well, that's a game changer that truly creates an Accountability Advantage that your competitors can't touch. This is a tough skill to master, but when this leadership behavior is committed to, taught, and modeled, the outcomes will be magic.

Great athletes, like Michael Jordan, are excellent examples of team member accountability. In the documentary *The Last Dance*, he said, "My mentality is to go out and win at any costs—if you don't want to live that regimented mentality then you don't need to be alongside of me—I'm going to ridicule you if you don't get on the same level with me, and if you don't get on the same level, it's going to be hell for you."[2] This is an extreme, but effective, example. Michael Jordan's and his team's results speak for themselves. This is one of the challenges faced with remote workers. Often there is no peer support or accountability. The manager may need to be extra diligent at setting clear rules and expectations, utilize project management or tracking software, and limit flexibility. They may also want to assign peer-to-peer accountability partners.

Everyone should have an accountability coach in business and in life. One peer-to-peer accountability exercise that can be effective is to assign peers as accountability partners, partners that meet weekly and hold each other accountable for completing assignments as well as doing the required Predictive Behaviors toward achieving Vital Goals. Mentoring increases learning, productivity, and success. Find someone who will tell it like it is, someone who will call your bluff and give you a new perspective. Make it someone who has more experience—someone who has done it before. Accountability partners will accelerate you forward. The surest way to achieve success is to model your work after someone who is already successful.

This is why many people use a personal trainer to achieve their fitness goals. The benefit of a personal trainer is that they will listen to what you want to achieve and then help to devise a plan to get there. More important, they will help to keep you challenged, motivated, and accountable.

ADVANTAGE PRINCIPLE: VAGUENESS IS THE ADVERSARY OF ACCOUNTABILITY.

Leadership = Making Sure We Aim at the Right Bull's-eyes (Results)

Whether in the military, a team sport, or business, leadership is about aiming at the right bull's-eyes. Leaders always make sure their teams understand the purpose (the Why), the vision (the future), the Vital Goals (the What), as well as the strategy (the How) before they get started. Employees can't hit the bull's-eye if they don't know where the target is or what the bull's-eye looks like.

Yet I find most people are confused about what they are supposed to accomplish, in business and in life, which makes accountability almost impossible. When I'm newly hired as a consultant by a company, I go in and ask, "What are your top goals? What are your department goals? What are your individual goals?" I have yet to start working with a company where the employees knew the answers!

This tells me their goals are nonexistent or are too vague. If people are vague on what needs to be done, how are we ever going to be clear about holding each other accountable? World-class businesses, championship sports teams, Olympic athletes, and Brass Ringers are never confused about what they are trying to accomplish. They know what the bull's-eyes look like, and they know the path to hit them—as well as how to hold each other accountable. The Dalai Lama said it well: "I believe that constant effort, tireless effort, pursuing clear goals with sincere effort is the only way."[3]

Management = Making Sure We Consistently Hit the Bull's-eyes (Systems)

Michael Gerber, the author of the *E-Myth* books, said, "Organize around business functions, not people. Build systems within each business function. Let systems run the business and people run the systems. People come and go but the systems remain constant."[4] As managers we need to ask ourselves, Have we instituted the right systems, the right training, the proper tools, and all the elements required so that people have what they need to consistently hit their targets and be successful? I've seen this happen in every element of success. If you want to see team members get better at anything, create better systems, and you will see the success of both your new hires and your veteran employees rise dramatically. Another benefit of systems is that a large percentage of a company's day-to-day operations can be run by processes and procedures, allowing leaders to manage by exception and spend more time on leadership activities.

This idea of putting good people into bad systems is one of the "aha" moments I've experienced as a consultant. I'd always thought, "I'm going to find a better preemployment screening profile, a better hiring tool, so we can hire better talent." What I've found is that if you put people in better systems, we become better recruiters and selectors of talent because more of our people automatically succeed. This doesn't mean that hiring isn't an important factor of growth, as we detailed in chapter 7, "Talent Advantage," but companies that have constant turnover (above industry standards) probably don't have a hiring problem; they more than likely have a "Hit the Bull's-eyes" problem, meaning a systems problem. In these instances, a systems correction is needed before you make a people correction. Carrie Wilkerson, the author of *The Barefoot Executive*, made it clear when she said, "Systems are not sexy—but they really DO drive everything we do!"[5]

Accountability = Making Sure We Take Enough Shots (Predictive Behaviors)

Accountability is about making sure that the correct number of shots (Predictive Behaviors) established to hit the bull's-eyes (Vital Goals, major initiatives, and projects) get taken and completed on a timely and consistent basis. Holding people accountable is a wonderful gift that leads to enhanced success for the individual, the department, and the company. This book is all about building a Growth Advantage in the marketplace, and building an Accountability Culture is a critical step toward getting there. An important concept from Patrick Lencioni in *The Five Dysfunctions of a Team* is, "If teammates are not being held accountable for their contributions, they will be more likely to turn their attention to their own needs."[6] Employees focusing on their own needs will not drive team success.

What Will an Accountability Culture Do for Your Company?

Promotes responsibility—When people go into a situation knowing they are going to be held accountable for their well-defined Predictive

Behaviors, goal achievement, and project completion, they realize there are no hiding places and become more responsible on their own. The positive effect this has on results is astonishing.

Encourages setting higher goals—Developing strategies, creating plans, and holding people accountable promotes better results, which in return raises expectations and encourages higher goals setting. I've worked with many companies whose owners and managers were happy with mediocre results until they proved to themselves that they could achieve more. Then their expectations for the future went through the roof. This becomes the "new normal."

Motivates Predictive Behaviors—In the last chapter, we did a deep dive on motivation. Accountability produces results and progress toward desired results, which in return is a great motivator. Everything ties together, but only if your team knows they are going to be held accountable by leaders and fellow team members on a daily and weekly basis. That's when motivation levels increase. It's that simple.

Retains top talent—Brass Ringers want to be on a winning team. They want to be on a team where the people who aren't doing what they are supposed to be doing are held accountable. Accordingly, Accountability Cultures are a great attractor of Brass Ring talent.

Eliminates underperformers—Conversely, Below Baseline underperformers will either step up or move on in a culture of accountability. If we are managing effectively, the consequences for Below Baseline performance should never be a surprise. John Rossman, author of *The Amazon Way*, noted, "Strong processes with measurable outcomes eliminate bureaucracy and expose underperformers."[7]

Takes control of outcomes (Vital Goals)—Too often companies are not in control of their outcomes. They are wishing versus planning for the outcomes they desire. Accountability to detailed plans and strategies changes all of this and puts people in control of their outcomes. This is empowering and builds on itself. This is straightforward leadership. Plans plus accountability equal results, and results build team trust.

Advantage Challenge: Ask yourself: Do I have an accountability culture at my company? Are managers consistently holding subordinates accountable and are peers holding peers accountable?

There are specific steps companies can take to develop an Accountability Advantage. This section explores six key components of accountability:

1. Foster Accountability Culture principles.
2. Develop performance standards.
3. Have effective meetings.
4. Work efficiently.
5. Gauge effectiveness.
6. Demand positive attitudes.

ADVANTAGE PRINCIPLE: BUILD AN ACCOUNTABILITY CULTURE AND YOU WILL HAVE A RESULTS CULTURE.

Accountability Component 1: Foster Accountability Culture Principles.

If you had to provide a list of three to five words or phrases that define your company's Accountability Culture now, what would they be? Include both positive and negative examples. Now, create a list of three to five words or phrases that describe the Accountability Culture you want. As with your company culture, you are in control of creating your Accountability Culture. You will need to identify the principles that will foster the culture you want to build. Here are examples of leadership principles that help companies transition to a culture of accountability: trust, keeping commitments, empowerment, honoring the absent, modeling behavior, honesty and ethics, consistency and fairness, getting results, taking ownership, positive accountability, focusing on strengths, choosing responses, and failing forward. You will need to determine the principles that drive your Accountability Culture.

Accountability Culture Builder: Trust—Peter Drucker wrote, "In military training, the first rule is to instill soldiers with trust in their officers, because without trust, they won't fight."[8] The same is true in business. If employees don't trust their managers or peers, it is virtually impossible to build a productive culture of accountability. Without trust, you are more likely to build a culture of disfunction. I've seen too many companies where the executive team members don't trust each other. This is an accountability Culture Killer. In these situations, you have to work on the trust issues first, and if the issues can't be resolved, you may need to make personnel changes. I once worked for an owner who called me in his office and said, "Bob, I like how you are, but not with me." Basically, he was telling me that he liked that I was holding people accountable, but that I worked for him—not him for me. This was a memorable moment for me. It taught me a lot about how my leadership style was perceived and to buffer my "D" profile at times. If the owner and I had not built a relationship of trust, this conversation may never have happened. Following are some trust-building Predictive Behaviors that should be modeled by all leaders, managers, and fellow team members:

- **Keep your promises and your commitments.** If you say you're going to do something, you need to follow through and do it. If you don't, your team will stop taking you seriously. Don't flip-flop and have a new initiative of the week.
- **Promote empowerment.** Just because you are managing outcomes and Predictive Behaviors does not mean you are not empowering your people. In fact, it's just the opposite! When people know what they are supposed to do and they do it, they have all the freedom and empowerment in the world. It is only micromanagement when people are not doing what they are supposed to do.
- **Honor the absent.** Don't talk negatively about somebody if they're not in the room. For example, if Pete sticks his head in your office and wants to talk to you about Jim, unless it's something illegal or involves some type of harassment, that conversation should not take place until Jim is invited to participate in it.
- **Model the behavior you expect.** If there are specific Predictive Behaviors and Core Values you expect your employees to perform as representatives of your company—and there should be—make sure you are modeling those behaviors and values, too. Otherwise, you are derailing the culture you are trying to build. When they see you model the behaviors and values, team members will understand your commitment level to the team.
- **Never compromise your honesty or ethics.** Or as Mark Twain said, "If you tell the truth, you don't have to remember anything."[9] If you want trust to be a part of your Accountability Culture, you cannot compromise here. I was a young manager working for a large company at a meeting being conducted with a top executive. After the presentation, I said to the executive, "That's not ethical." The executive said, "There is no room for ethics in this industry." At that

moment, my trust for that executive was gone. And I'm sure I was not the only one in the room who felt that way.

- **Be quick, be consistent, and be fair.** Accountability needs to be applied quickly, consistently, and fairly. It can't be applied capriciously when it is convenient. The closer the feedback is to the action (or lack thereof) the more impact it will have. Consistent accountability will have a huge impact on success. This does not mean you can't make exceptions for Brass Ring performance. Brass Ring performers can earn "get out of jail free cards." I once was hired by a company and was told right out of the gate that Jean would not consistently do the Predictive Behaviors but would produce Brass Ring results. This kind of employee is rare, but they do exist. In this case, I still positively nudged Jean but did not want to apply any consequences that would cause her to leave the company. Jimmy Johnson, the first and one of only three football coaches to lead teams to both a major college football championship and a Super Bowl victory, lived this principle. He said,

> It's been misconstrued a little bit as far as my approach to players. I always said there's a different standard for all the players. Every year I told the guys, I said, 'Listen, I'm going to be very consistent. I'm going to treat every one of you differently. And how I treat you is: Do you abide by the rules and regulations? Do you do what we ask you to do? And are you a good player?' For instance, I said maybe I might cut a certain player for sleeping in a meeting because he was not a good player, he was late to a lot of meetings, and he did things that we didn't want him to. Whereas if Troy Aikman [star quarterback] would have done it—and he wouldn't have done it—but if Troy Aikman would've fell asleep in a meeting, I would've disciplined him, but I wouldn't have cut him.[10]

- **Get results.** This is the biggest trust builder there is. Get results and your people will trust you and your process. If a company hires Growth Advantage and follows the process perfectly without seeing improved results, they will lose trust in the process. The key is to always follow a process perfectly before that determination is made. If I say I am on a calorie deficit diet and have a pizza and six-pack of beer for dinner, chances are my failure is not the diet's fault.

Accountability Culture Builder: Take ownership.—Benjamin Franklin said, "Drive thy business, or it will drive thee."[11] Leaders take ownership of the outcomes of their team. In fact, when things are going well, effective leaders pass the credit down. And when things don't go well, they take the blame. Performance is the responsibility of the leader. It is not the economy's fault, it's not your competitor's fault, and it should not be your subordinates' fault. You are responsible for their performance. When you take ownership, you will see your team members step up and take ownership too. This does not mean that you don't hold them accountable. Just the opposite: when team members see a leader take responsibility, they become more receptive to accountability and will hold themselves accountable as well.

Accountability Culture Builder: It is not a democracy or a popularity contest.—Most managers want to be liked. I certainly do. But at the end of the day, if you have a strong need to be liked by your subordinates, don't be a manager. Managers take ownership and make hard decisions for the good of the company and the team. Some decisions that need to be made won't please everyone. I'm not suggesting you be unpleasant with your coworkers; I'm saying you need to be willing to be unpopular. You've got to be prepared to hold people accountable. Maintaining a culture of accountability is something that needs to be managed. If people slip into bad habits, you can't simply fix it and never look at it again. You need to continue to monitor so you're quick to react if correction is needed.

As an example, one of my clients used to tell me, "Bob, I like it when you get here, but I like it even more when you leave." I took that as a compliment. Part of my job is to be an accountability nudge, and we all worked hard during my visits. This had been a difficult session when he said that, but we'd gotten through it successfully. Remember, as a leader your number one job is to accomplish well-defined results.

Accountability Culture Builder: Positive Accountability—John F. Kennedy said, "When written in Chinese, the word 'crisis' is composed of two characters. One represents danger, the other represents opportunity."[12] Focus on opportunities, not just problems. This does not mean that as managers and owners we don't deal with whatever issues the company might be encountering; it just means accomplishments should be celebrated louder. It's human nature; 99 percent of what we worry about and stress about never happens, but that doesn't mean we don't worry and stress! We can't ignore problems, but we also don't have to focus solely on them. If we are always negative, our accountability sessions will zap the energy out of the team. As your team begins to learn that accountability is a positive Culture Builder that drives company performance and individual growth, makes the company a more enjoyable place to work, and is not a monster in a scary mask, they'll warm up to the word.

Accountability Culture Builder: Focus on strengths, not just weaknesses.—Understand the natural gifts of your direct reports. Is the person well-suited for the job they have? It is your responsibility to put people in the right positions to be successful. Coach John Wooden said, "Do not let what you cannot do interfere with what you can do."[13] Testing and profiling should be used as much for management as it is for hiring. For a quick refresher on how effective this can be, see chapter 7, "Talent Advantage," on using DISC and other tools for testing and profiling.

Accountability Culture Builder: Choose your response.—Let's say you have a team member named Joe, and Joe is generally a pretty good employee, but then something goes wrong. Maybe he skips behavior for a few days or misses a meeting. And, at the same time, the day you realize this, you're already in a bad mood. You are visiting Bad Attitude Village. Maybe traffic was heavy on the way to work, or you got into an argument at home. Whatever the reason, you show up to work not your usual, positive self. This day might not be the best time to schedule an accountability session with Joe.

Remember: you can't always choose what happens. You can't choose how much traffic is on the road, you can't choose the weather, you can't choose the price of oil, but you can choose your response to any situation. We have an "Event," we have a "Decision" to make about that event, and we have a "Response." We don't want to jump from "Event" to "Response." We always want to stay coolheaded enough to make a rational decision about what response we are going to have. That's the leadership difference—controlling the situation versus the situation controlling you. As managers, we have to be able to do the right things to make our people productive, so that departments are productive, and so that companies are productive. Or as Viktor Frankl, Holocaust survivor and author of *Man's Search for Meaning*, said, "The last of the human freedoms is to choose one's attitude in any given set of circumstances."[14]

Years ago, when the price of oil climbed to $140 a barrel and gas went above $5 a gallon, people were panicking. Well, imagine if your business depended on driving long miles! I had one client who had trucks on the road every day. I called him up and we were shooting the breeze and I said, "Man, can you believe the price of gas?" He shocked me by saying, "I love it!" And I said, "What do you mean you love it? How can you love it? You're in the delivery business." He said, "Bob, we're in such better financial shape than our competitors. This won't hurt me." What he said was so interesting to me. He was choosing his response and looking at a crisis as an opportunity. Now, I'm sure he didn't want gas prices to stay that high forever, but he was taking advantage of a situation others saw as a negative. He didn't put the panic on. He knew his company was financially strong and would get through it. His positive response had to have a positive impact on his employees.

Accountability Culture Builder: Fail forward.—John C. Maxwell, in his book *Failing Forward*, asked a life-changing question: "If the possibility of failure were erased, what would you attempt to achieve?"[15] Although our ultimate goal is success for each team member and the company, we don't want to be afraid of failure. Often, failure is a stepping-stone to achieving our success. The key is, if someone fails, I want them to fail doing something within their level of authority, versus failing by not doing something or by neglect. Accountability should apply accordingly. Don't have negative consequences if someone fails with the best intention and effort. If you do, team members will fear failure and that can be a Culture Killer. As Robert F. Kennedy said, "Only those that dare to fail greatly can ever achieve greatly."[16] Abraham Lincoln was an impressive example of failing forward; here is his list of "failures":[17]

1831—Lost his job
1832—Defeated for a seat in the Illinois state legislature
1833—Failed in business
1834—Elected to Illinois state legislature (success!)
1835—His sweetheart died
1836—Had a nervous breakdown
1838—Defeated in seeking to be Illinois House Speaker
1843—Defeated in his nomination to the US Congress
1846—Elected to Congress (success!)
1848—Lost renomination
1849—Rejected for a job as land officer
1854—Defeated for US Senate
1856—Defeated in nomination for vice president
1858—Again defeated for US Senate
1860—Elected president

Thomas Edison said, "Many of life's failures are people that did not realize how close to success they were when they gave up."[18] Lincoln never gave up. Don't be afraid of making mistakes. If you're not making mistakes, you're not taking risks, you're not learning, and that means you're not progressing. The key is to make small mistakes faster than the competition, so you have more chances to learn and win. Jim Collins, in his book *Great by Choice*, says this about failure: "First, you fire bullets (low-cost, low-risk, low-distraction experiments) to figure out what will work—calibrating your line of sight by taking small shots. Then, once you have empirical validation, you fire a cannonball (concentrating resources into a big bet) on the calibrated line of sight."[19] Firing uncalibrated cannonballs can lead to disaster.

Accountability Component 2: Develop Performance Standards.

As noted in chapters 1–6, it is critical that specific performance standards are established for every position and for every team member. We like using the concept of Baseline and Brass Ring goals and metrics for Vital Goals, Predictive Behaviors, and project completion timelines. Brass Ring standards are stretch goals that are achievable but require a superior level of performance. Baseline Standards represent the minimum acceptable standard and should be reasonably achievable for everyone on the team. Below Baseline Standards represent an unacceptable standard of performance. Think of it this way: Brass Ringers get an A, Baseline performers get a B, and everyone else gets an F. There is no C or D in business. You can't survive with C and D performance in the business world.

The problem with performance standards is twofold. One, too many companies don't have established standards (goals, metrics, and timelines), and two, those that do don't consistently hold team members accountable to the standards they establish. A standard established without accountability is a wish. Conversely, a team that holds itself accountable to established standards removes "hiding places" and then, "like magic," will achieve their dreams.

This is one of the reasons we have our clients submit monthly numbers based on their established Growth Advantage goals. It is not because I like the extra work! It is because we become part of the team, as well as an extra accountability nudge. We then review the metrics during each visit to the client, which helps the client's team members learn the importance of holding each other accountable.

No one wants to see a presentation to their team where they or their team members are Below Baseline. Leaders owe it to the organizations they represent not to tolerate perpetually Below Baseline performers in important jobs, or, for that matter, in any job.

When setting performance standards, always **Dream Big**! What you plant in your mind is what will grow. Earl Nightingale explained this in an audio recording, *The Strangest Secret*, a 1957 record that sold more than one million copies, received the first Gold Record for the spoken word, and helped launch the business motivation and audio publishing industries. He said, "We live today in a golden age. We are fortunate to live in the richest era that ever existed on the face of the earth. Let's take one hundred individuals who start even at the age of twenty-five. Do you have any idea what will happen to those men and women by the time they are sixty-five? These one hundred people, who all state even at the age of twenty-five, all believe they're going to be successful." But by the time they are sixty-five, only five out of the one hundred define themselves as being successful. Nightingale continues, "A success is anyone who is doing/pursuing deliberately a predetermined goal/job because that's what he or she decided to do . . . deliberately. But only one out of twenty does that. 'Success is the progressive realization of a worthy ideal.'"[20] This principle was true in 1957, it's true now, and it will be true fifty years from now.

What's the difference? The difference is goals. Successful people establish goals. Our minds are like a farmer's field. What we plant in our mind, be it positive or negative, is what grows. Don't plant weeds! Plant big goals!

The power of suggestion and accomplishment is formidable. An example of this is the four-minute mile. Until 1954, this feat was thought to be physiologically impossible. Then Roger Bannister broke that physiological barrier and ran a four-minute mile. Forty-six days later, another runner did it. By the end of 1955, three hundred runners had done it.[21] Today, high school runners regularly break a four-minute mile.

As owners and managers of companies, we need to ask ourselves, What is our four-minute mile? And then we need to break through it. And once we break through, our potential increases. As A. G. Lafley said in his book *Playing to Win*, "Too many companies eventually die a death of modest aspirations."[22]

Accountability Component 3: Have Effective Meetings.

Meetings often get a bad rap as time wasters, and that is true of unneeded or poorly designed meetings. That said, I've found that meetings (especially weekly team and one-on-one meetings) are one of the most effective times for holding subordinates and fellow team members accountable. Meetings are a tool, and effective meetings don't happen by accident. They happen by design. Here are some ways to ensure that you are running effective meetings.

Meet with a purpose (specific outcomes). Make sure your meetings are focused on specific tasks, outcomes, and accomplishments:

- Plan; set the agenda, objectives, and priorities beforehand. Don't wing it and waste your fellow team members' time.
- Provide the agenda beforehand and stick to it. Regularly scheduled meetings may have a recurring set agenda.
- Assign pre-work and participants' expectations.
- Focus on Vital Goals, Predictive Behaviors, as well as major projects.
- Invite people who can impact the outcomes.
- Budget your time; then start and end on time.
- Solve problems, make decisions, and move on. Don't continually dwell on the same issues.
- Don't allow meetings to be complaint sessions. Meetings should build on a positive culture.
- No "meeting after the meeting." If you disagree with something, bring it up during the meeting, not in the parking lot afterward.
- Always get commitments before moving on.

ADVANTAGE PRINCIPLE: HOLD WEEKLY ACCOUNTABILITY MEETINGS WITH DIRECT REPORTS (TEAM AND INDIVIDUAL) AND EXPECT YOUR DIRECT REPORTS TO HOLD WEEKLY ACCOUNTABILITY MEETINGS WITH THEIR DIRECT REPORTS.

Here is a meeting schedule that has worked well for me:

Daily Check-in (especially for Below Baseline performers): This is not feasible for all teams, but I like brief daily check-in meetings where everyone gives a quick update regarding their progress and priorities. In order to ensure they are brief, you can do these meetings standing up. I found that this type of meeting does not cost time but rather saves time by getting critical discussions out of the way all at once.

Even if it does not make sense to have a daily meeting with the entire team, I recommend having a daily nudge meeting with anyone Below Baseline until they are Above Baseline or Brass Ring. These meetings can be done in person or on the phone. The Blue Angels, the US Navy's flight demonstration squadron, are a great example of this concept. They do a briefing before and a debrief after each air show to address issues that came up during the show.[23] Their ultimate goal is elevating performance, and they don't wait to meet once each month to have these discussions.

Weekly Meetings (team and one-on-ones): Managers should always have weekly meetings with their subordinates as a team and a one-on-one with each team member individually. No exceptions. These are critical accountability sessions. Having these types of meetings less frequently or not at all allows team members to stay off course for too long. When people have to report outcomes to a peer group, it helps build on the Accountability Culture. Additionally, when they tell the team what they are planning to accomplish in the upcoming week and then report back the following week, it is more likely to get done. During these meetings you should:

- Leader kickoff—Review the week.
- Make positive deposits by acknowledging positive outcomes from the prior week.
- Each direct report presents outcomes, metrics, and updates on key outcomes and projects within their area of responsibility.
- Each direct report shares their plans and their priorities for the upcoming week.
- If needed, address one major topic. These can also be set aside for special meetings.

Monthly Executive and Vital Goal Team Meetings: Building teams around Vital Goals and major initiatives helps to create focus and maintain sustained results. People can overlap and be on multiple teams. As an example, when I work with companies, we typically form an Executive Strategy Team whose focus is strategic planning and a Growth Team whose focus is growth planning and execution. I like these types of teams to meet monthly in order to review outcomes, recommit, and make needed adjustments.

Quarterly Off-site: These are essential meetings that should focus on planning, strategy, major projects, outcomes, and adjustments. When I work with companies, I typically visit the client two to four times each year to reinforce concepts, review progress, and keep the focus. People get busy and need these realignments. Clients often comment to me that they get more done right before and right after my visit because they refocus and recommit.

Annual Strategic and Growth Planning: These are high-level meetings where plans and strategies are developed. Most executive leadership teams spend little to no time planning or discussing strategy. The Growth Advantage Blueprint is a leadership strategy for growth, and when we work with companies, we conduct a strategy and a planning session to kick off each year. The key to these sessions is to establish Vital Goals, Predictive Behaviors, Key Metrics, and Top Strategic Initiatives and decide how to allocate the company's limited resources into a systemized action plan designed to achieve Vital Goals and objectives.

Accountability Component 4: Work Efficiently.

ADVANTAGE PRINCIPLE: GIVE YOURSELF PERMISSION TO USE YOUR TIME EFFICIENTLY.

It is a leader's job to hold everyone accountable regarding how they are spending their time. Are they efficient? Are they and their team spending the majority of their time on the things that will impact success? More people doing the most important things more often. Consider your typical workweek. Yes, I know, if there can even be such a thing! How much time do you spend Doing (In the Game), Managing (Nudging—Accountability), Creating (Branding), Leading (Planning and Strategy), and Training (Coaching)? And how much of your time is wasted or spent on items you should have delegated?

Once you have a good idea of how much time you and your team spend on each activity, consider: what would be the ideal division of your professional time? The answers to this question can be startling. If you want to be effective, hold yourself and your team accountable to spending the maximum amount of time on the behaviors and outcomes that will allow you to accomplish your Vital Goals and give your company an advantage in the market.

As Blaine Lee, author of *The Power Principle*, said, "The leader who exercises power with honor will work from the inside out, starting with himself."[24] He suggested you should ask yourself, If you want to change the amount of time you spend on any activity, whose permission do you need? The answer is your own! Give yourself permission to use your time efficiently. It is crazy that we are in control of how we spend our time, yet we don't use it efficiently. If you are a leader, spend your time on leadership activities.

Accountability Component 5: Gauge Effectiveness.

Paul "Bear" Bryant said, "It is not the will to win that matters, everyone has that. It is the will to prepare that matters."[25] To be effective and produce the desired results, you need sufficient energy, the right skill set, the right tool set, and the right mindset. If someone is not producing, which of these items are lacking? It is your job as a leader to come up with the answer. If your people have everything they need—energy, the right skills, the right tools, the right mindset—and they're doing the Predictive Behaviors, the results will follow. A leader takes the time to prepare to win in business. In order to maximize effectiveness, it is a leader's job to evaluate themselves and their team and develop an action plan for each team member.

The Prepare Your Team to Win! Grid depicts the critical items an employee must master to be effective and achieve success. I suggest using this model as a guide when doing employee performance reviews to determine what you as a manager and the employee need to work on to maximize success. If the employee is Brass Ring, my ultimate

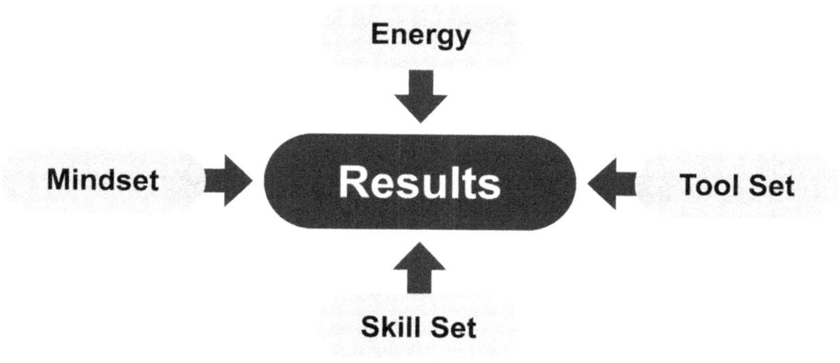

Figure 10.1. Energy + Mindset + Skill Set + Tool Set = Results

goals are to maintain that performance and retain them as an employee. If the employee is Above Baseline, I am trying to work with them on whatever is keeping them from achieving Brass Ring and positively nudge them toward that objective. If they are Below Baseline, there need to be accountability consequences and we work with them to get to Baseline and Above.

Mindset—This should be easy because it is a *choice*, but too often, employees choose to have a bad mindset. If an attitude is Below Baseline, it is a leader's responsibility to hold team members accountable and require an adjustment. Recall "Bad Attitude Village." All of us can make a visit there from time to time. That's okay. Just don't become a resident! Residents start thinking that every day is a bad day, and it shows in their attitude. The true problem occurs when people become the mayor of Bad Attitude Village and start recruiting other people to move in with them. Residents and mayors are Culture Killers who must either change their mindset or be removed from the team.

When doing an employee review, if the employee has a bad mindset, be direct, give them examples, and emphasize their attitude is a choice

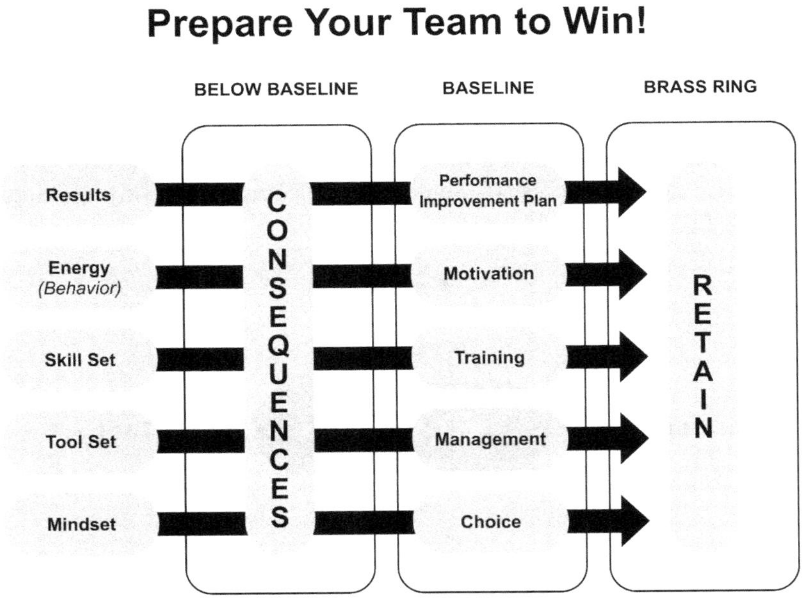

Figure 10.2. Prepare Your Team to Win!

and if they want to be a part of the team, they need to make better choices. Until they improve their attitude, don't include them in team meetings or other team activities.

Tool Set—It is management's responsibility to make sure employees have the required tools to do the job. Key questions here are: Do employees have the proper tools and are they using them effectively? You've already made the investment in talent by hiring the right person; it absolutely makes sense to make the *investment in essential tools.* If it is a utilization issue, that option needs to be taken off the table and the employee needs to understand that fully utilizing provided tools is a condition of the job. If tools are not used dutifully, there is no way to know if they are effective. Too often, companies invest in tools and allow employees to choose not to use them. Stop doing that!

Skill Set—It is both management's and each employee's responsibility to make sure they have the skill set to do the job effectively. As we discussed in chapter 8, "Training Advantage," proper *training and reinforcement* are a critical component of success and a differentiator in the marketplace. Simply put, if your team members are better trained and have better knowledge and skills, they will outperform their competitive peers. The best in the world at anything (in and out of business) always work to improve their skill set with a hunger for training and Disciplined Practice.

Energy/Behavior—By this point in the book, we should all be aware of the importance of employees demonstrating the energy to complete their Predictive Behaviors dutifully. I think of behavior two ways in this section: (1) Are they completing their Predictive Behaviors consistently? (2) Does their behavior with fellow team members, as well as with customers and prospects, model the Core Values we want as a company? If not, this is an energy issue and motivation must be addressed.

Results—The ultimate goal for leaders and the ultimate gauge of effectiveness is producing consistent results, results for the individual, the team, and the company. Typically, if someone is not producing consistent results, it is because they are lacking in one of the areas noted above. It is rare that I find somebody who has a good attitude, is well trained, has and utilizes the needed tools, consistently completes their Predictive Behaviors, models the company's values, and still does not achieve Above Baseline or Brass Ring results. If results are not being achieved, a *performance improvement plan* needs to be established and committed to with well-defined outcomes and timetables.

Accountability Component 6: Demand Positive Attitudes

ADVANTAGE PRINCIPLE:
POSITIVE ATTITUDES ARE CONTAGIOUS.
SO ARE NEGATIVE ATTITUDES.

Of all the factors related to accountability, managers often have a hard time holding team members accountable to maintaining a positive attitude. This is partly because attitude is subjective, partly because it is difficult to measure, and partly because it takes leadership courage to sit someone down and address a bad attitude head-on. I consulted with a company whose service team had both residents and mayors of Bad Attitude Village. Shockingly, they allowed it, and their excuse was that these employees were good with the customers; they just conveyed bad attitudes with fellow team members. I could feel it fifteen minutes into our first meeting. Once they viewed it honestly and realized the negative effect it was having on the company culture, they addressed it head-on, and it changed. Some negative team members needed a discussion or two, some took more work, and a couple mayors needed to go. It did not happen overnight, but the positive shift could be felt throughout the company. Remember, a bad attitude can only exist if it is allowed. If you have bad attitudes on your team, it is critical that you address them immediately.

I aspire to a culture with little to no excuses, blaming, or complaining. Complain and that is what you will focus on. All blame is a waste of time. And, in the words of George Washington Carver, "99 percent of all failure comes from people who have the habit of making excuses."[26] Think of it this way: every negative event contains within it an equal or greater positive opportunity. If someone who reports to me has an issue, I don't want them talking about it in a negative way to other people; I want them talking to me about it. On the other hand, positive observations should always be shared with your direct reports. I call this "negatives up, positives down."

Incorporate these six components and you will create an Accountability Culture. It takes consistent hard work, but the rewards are worth it.

Advantage Challenge: Be accountable to achieving an Accountability Culture. List three to five words or phrases that define your company's Accountability Culture now. Make a list of both positive and negative examples. Now, list three to five words or phrases that describe the Accountability Culture you want to achieve. Hold yourself and your team accountable to the new culture.

Reference the Accountability Culture Advantage Challenge Application (Figure A.10) at the back of the book.

Chapter Summary

- Advantage Principle: The Key to Executing Plan Is Holding Yourself and Team Members Accountable.
- Accountability is a critical success component in business and in life.
- If planning is "what," strategy is "how," and execution is "now"—then accountability is a key element of execution that ties everything together and produces Brass Ring results.
- Advantage Principle: Vagueness Is the Adversary of Accountability.
- Leadership = Making Sure We Aim at the Right Bull's-eyes (Results); Management = Making Sure We Consistently Hit the Bull's-eyes (Systems); Accountability = Making Sure We Take Enough Shots (Predictive Behaviors).
- If you put people in better systems, we become better hirers because more people automatically succeed.
- Advantage Principle: Build an Accountability Culture and You Will Have a Results Culture.
- If employees don't trust their managers or peers, it is virtually impossible to build a productive culture of accountability.
- Management is not a democracy or a popularity contest.
- It is critical that specific performance standards are established for every position and every team member.
- When setting performance standards, always **Dream Big**! What you plant in your mind is what will grow.

- Advantage Principle: Hold Weekly Accountability Meetings with Direct Reports (Team and Individual) and Expect Your Direct Reports to Hold Weekly Accountability Meetings with Their Direct Reports.
- Advantage Principle: Give Yourself Permission to Use Your Time Efficiently.
- It is a leader's job to hold everyone accountable to how they are spending their time.
- To be effective and produce the desired results, you need sufficient energy, the right skill set, the right tool set, and the right mindset.
- Advantage Principle: Positive Attitudes Are Contagious. So Are Negative Attitudes.

Part III

THE COMPANY ADVANTAGE: MARKET, COMPETITIVE, AND BRAND ADVANTAGE

ADVANTAGE PRINCIPLE: BE KNOWN—WHERE, WITH WHOM, AND FOR WHAT YOU WANT TO BE KNOWN.

Price versus Differentiation

When I ask the owners and managers of companies what they think their advantage is in the marketplace in which they compete, if I get any answer at all (often I get a blank stare), I almost always get the same basic answers. Most people say things like, "We've got better prices," "We've got better service," or even "We've got better quality." That's great, and I hope all these statements are true, but these statements are so vague that, to the customer, they are meaningless. Everyone can and does say those things without actually having the advantage.

I was once the executive director of an alliance of independent businesses that banded together to compete more effectively against the "big guys," and one of the many services of the group was to combine purchasing power and function as a buying group. Accordingly, I met with a large number of suppliers every year that wanted to become approved suppliers. Whenever they started talking about their better products, better service, and new production facility in whatever county that was hot, without defining what made their company better or different and how they could benefit our members, the meeting was virtually over. We already had approved suppliers that had quality products, quality service, and quality production facilities. No one took the time to conduct a discovery meeting first to determine what our pain points or needs were, and too many conveyed a meaningless advantage message.

In hundreds and hundreds of interviews with businesspeople, I can remember only two times when I've gotten answers to the "What is your advantage?" question that were truly differentiating in a meaningful way. These two people delivered their advantage message with high energy and no hesitation, and differentiation was defined in an impactful way—to the right "who" in the right market. And, as it turned out, those answers were given to me by two high-performing salespeople—one was a company owner that only spent 10 percent to 20 percent of their time selling yet was still a top producer. These high performers knew instinctively that a well-defined and packaged Competitive Advantage with specifics would be a powerful tool for success. But they also knew such a statement would be meaningless without defining their advantage in terms of what mattered to their target customer and market.

This part explores the three elements that are critical to building a Company Advantage (determining where opportunity and advantage intersect for your company):

1. **Market Advantage**—clearly defining your company's product and market focus (what are you selling to whom, where, and *why*).
2. **Competitive Advantage**—creating a Value Advantage and Competitive Advantage that is meaningful to your identified market and customer (why your product or service and why your company vs. the competition).
3. **Brand Advantage**—packaging and communicating your Company Advantage in a message that effectively attracts and retains target customers (being known for what you know).

Chapter Eleven

Company Advantage

Invest in Your Company Advantage

ADVANTAGE PRINCIPLE: BUSINESS HAPPENS WHERE MARKET OPPORTUNITY AND COMPANY ADVANTAGE INTERSECT.

Opportunity and Advantage

The bigger the market opportunity and correlating Company Advantage, the easier it is to achieve success in business. Conversely, either a small market opportunity and/or a weak or unpackaged advantage message makes it tougher, if not impossible, to achieve success. Throughout history, there are all kinds of successful examples of this. One of the most extreme in recent times is of course Apple's development of the smartphone, which the company first released in June 2007. In his address, Steve Jobs said, "This is a day that I have been looking forward to for two and a half years," and that "today, Apple is going to reinvent the phone." Steve Jobs introduced the iPhone as a combination of three devices: a "widescreen iPod with touch controls," a "revolutionary mobile phone," and a "breakthrough Internet communicator."[1] Apple took a standard product, the mobile phone, and through drive and innovation figured out how to make a touchscreen mobile phone with an iPod, camera, and web-browsing capabilities that was easy to use. At a time when businesspeople were increasingly required by their companies to be more mobile and more accessible to be successful, the iPhone instantly became a necessity. In 2012, five years after the iPhone's debut, more than two hundred million had been sold. To date, billions have been sold.[2]

Overnight, Apple dominated the smartphone market, and despite solid competition, they still do. Where most technology-driven products reduce their price over time, Apple is able to command a higher price even with quality competition. Apple not only identified market opportunity, but they created new opportunity and delivered a product that had a clear advantage. I was doing a training event in Chicago at the time of one of their early new product rollouts, and they had traffic cones down Michigan Avenue to control the crowd wanting to purchase their product. All of us wish we had that problem. Other mobile phone companies had a huge market opportunity, but their advantage was diminished by Apple, which put some out of business.

Now, most companies will never get to experience the intersection of opportunity and advantage of the magnitude Apple experienced. But no matter what your business is, you should always be looking for the intersection of these two items—opportunity and advantage—in the marketplace where you choose to compete.

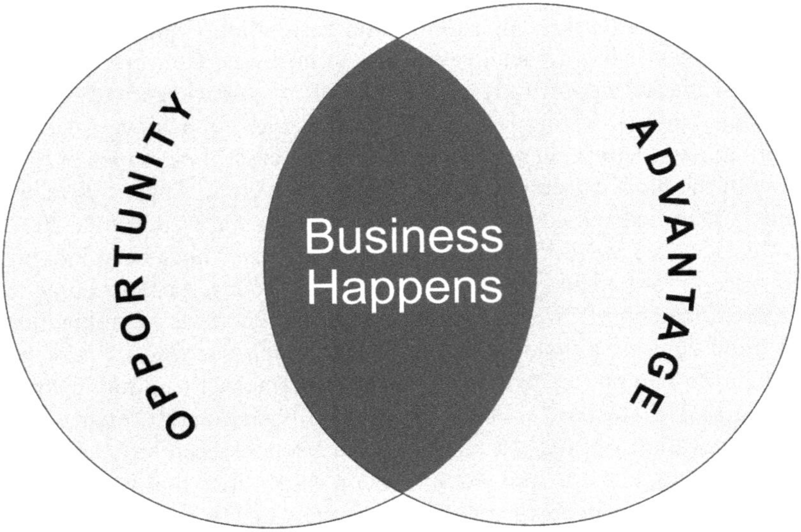

Figure 11.1. Opportunity and Advantage

On the other side of this, one big mistake I see companies make when their market opportunity shrinks is that they reduce the investment and innovation in their Company Advantage. This is a formula for obsolescence. Although I believe companies should always invest heavily in their Company Advantage, it becomes even more important when market opportunity is flat or shrinking if the plan is to stay viable in that market.

Schlitz beer is an example of the consequence of diminishing a Company Advantage, cutting corners, and destroying Product Advantage. In his article in *The Beer Connoisseur*, Martyn Cornell describes Schlitz's fall from being the top-selling beer in the United States to their collapse by the early 1980s. After a constant battle with Anheuser-Busch's Budweiser for the top spot, Budweiser pulled ahead, and Schlitz started looking for ways to meet demand while also cutting the cost of production. They changed their brewing process, and both customers and competitors noticed. Speeding up the brewing process, they used corn syrup to replace some of the malted barley, added a silica gel to prevent the product from forming a haze, used high-temperature fermentation instead of the traditional method, and substituted less expensive extracts rather than traditional ingredients. These changes resulted in reduced flavor and consistency compared to the traditional formula, and the brand quickly lost public appeal.

Schlitz's troubles compounded when they began to worry the Food and Drug Administration would require brewers to list their ingredients. Their competitors aged their beers longer, allowing protein to settle out naturally, so they did not require an artificial additive like silica gel to prevent haze. To avoid the prospect of listing silica gel on packaging, Schlitz switched to an anti-haze agent called Chillgarde since it was filtered out of the final product and would not have to be disclosed. Unfortunately, brewers did not know this agent would react with a foam stabilizer they also used, and the company ended up recalling ten million bottles of beer, costing it $1.4 million.

Eventually, the company was acquired by Stroh Brewery Company of Detroit, Michigan, and after Stroh's collapse in 1999, the Schlitz brand was acquired by Pabst. Schlitz is still made today, but it's a less expensive niche brand and sits nowhere near the heights it once reached.[3]

What might have been different if Schlitz had invested in their Competitive Advantage instead of cutting costs? Donald Keough, the former president of the Coca-Cola Company, summed this up well: "You can never cost cut your way to profitability."[4] So true.

Advantage Challenge: When considering your business, ask yourself: Is my opportunity big enough for me to be able to sustain desired growth? Do I have a strong enough Competitive Advantage? Am I able to effectively communicate that advantage to the customer? If yes, work to be intentional about how you state your Company Advantage. If not, you have some work to do!

Opportunity Matrix

The intersection of opportunity and advantage is called the "Opportunity Matrix." The Opportunity Matrix defines what you bring to your opportunity pool. In the marketplace, the Opportunity Matrix can be broken down into three levels:

- Price—You compete by delivering the lowest price.
- Value—You compete by delivering a fair price along with a superior value.
- Premium—You compete by delivering a premium product, service, and brand at a premium price.

For a good example of how these levels work in the real world, let's look at three strong brands in the automotive industry. Kia sells cars based on price (also has value offerings), Toyota sells cars based on value (also has price offerings), and Mercedes sells cars based on premium amenities (also has value offerings). Although companies should generate most of their revenue from the level they are designed to compete, they can jump one level in either direction and attract fringe business but will not have success if they try to jump more than one level. That's because when you try to be a little bit of everything to everybody, you will master nothing. Never try to jump to another category if you have not mastered the one you're in. Toyota has had huge success in the value market and decided to move into the luxury/premium market with the Lexus brand. Again, they had great success. I doubt it would be a wise strategic decision for Bentley, Ferrari, or Lexus to try to jump two levels and compete on the lowest price.

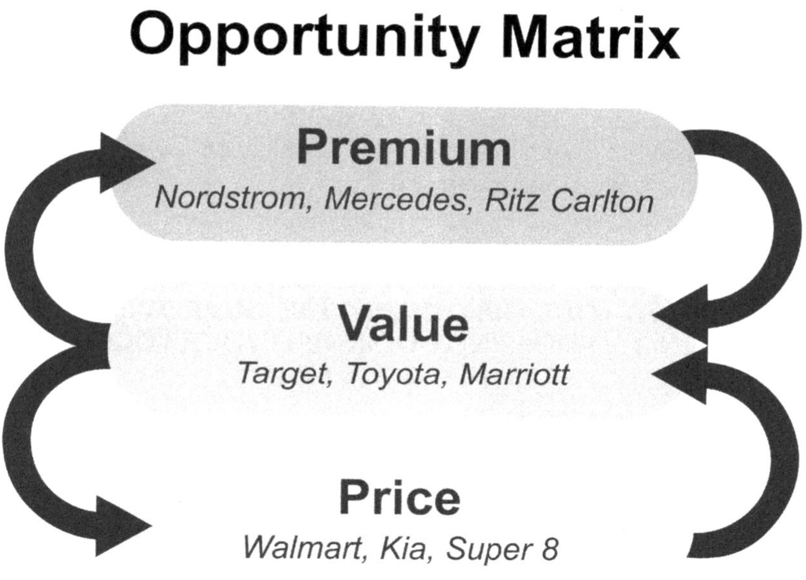

Figure 11.2. Opportunity Matrix

Another example of these three basic market levels can be found in popular department store retailers. Walmart sells products based on price, Target sells products based on value, and Saks Fifth Avenue sells products based on luxury and status. You might buy a designer bag from Target, but you probably wouldn't buy one from Walmart, even if you could find it on the shelf. By the same token, most Saks Fifth Avenue shoppers are not there to save money on low-cost necessities. Saks may sell some value brands, but they are not trying to be the low-cost provider. These retailers have been successful because they've focused their efforts on the level where they compete the best.

Be careful trying to compete with low-cost providers like Walmart unless you have a cost advantage. You will probably lose. Walmart is the largest retailer in the world, with more than a half trillion in annual sales and 11,766 worldwide locations.[5] Their key advantage is their supply chain, and their market opportunity is the world. Walmart has embraced technology and innovation to track and seamlessly restock inventory. Sam Walton's goal was "help people save money so they could live better," and their continuous investment in their supply chain allows them to achieve that goal.[6] This advantage guarantees that Walmart customers always get what they want every time they step foot in a Walmart—and at a competitive price. This aligns with Sam Walton's statement, "There is only one boss. The customer. And he can fire everybody in the company from the chairman on down, simply by spending his money somewhere else."[7]

ADVANTAGE PRINCIPLE: IT IS ADVANTAGEOUS TO EXPAND YOUR OPPORTUNITY POOL PROVIDED DOING SO DOES NOT DIMINISH YOUR FOCUS, ADVANTAGE, OR BRAND.

Although a large opportunity pool has its advantages, expanding it recklessly does not. Trying to be all things to all people makes it difficult to be focused, and losing focus is a good way to diminish an advantage. Let's look at the fast-food market. In 1986, Jerry and Janie Murrell and their sons opened a burger joint in Arlington, Virginia, and called it Five Guys Burgers. The name fit their business plan of having only a basic menu, primarily burgers and fries (no chicken). Simple, yes, but the Murrells decided they would focus on and have the best fast-food burgers and fries available anywhere.

The chain expanded very slowly. By 2001, the family had only opened four additional locations in fifteen years. Those new stores were all successful, and in 2003, the Murrells decided to start franchising. That's when real growth happened. Within a year and a half, they had three hundred locations and an incredibly loyal following. And yet the business philosophy of sticking to the basics remained. The owners haven't changed their menu much at all; for example, they refuse to expand their opportunity pool by adding a chicken sandwich. Burgers are what they're best at, burgers are what they're known for, and burgers are what their customers want.

By sticking to their initial plan, by focusing their efforts on what they do best and not trying to be everything to everybody, the company has experienced exponential growth. Today, there are more than 1,700 locations worldwide.[8]

On the other hand, Chick-fil-A has primarily chicken products on their menu (no hamburgers) and yet the company generates more revenue per restaurant than any other fast-food chain—despite being closed on Sundays.[9]

These examples show how critical market and product focus is for success, and how that focus, that Company Advantage, needs to be defined and communicated to the target customer. Chick-fil-A has cows on the billboard telling you to "Eat Mor Chikin." Five Guys has a simple, pointed message: Five Guys Burgers and Fries. With both companies, their product and market focus is clear. When defining your market focus, it is also important to know the markets you are not after.

Market and Product Advantage

Philip Kotler, an author and professor, said, "Authentic marketing is not just the art of selling what you make, but also knowing what to make."[10] Your Company Advantage should speak directly to the needs of your defined market. In defining your market and Product Advantage, you need to ask yourself these questions: What am I selling, to whom, where, and why? Having an advantage means not only knowing what to make but also knowing where to sell it, whom to sell it to, and why. The "why" in this exercise is critical. A specific product might be a good idea, but that doesn't mean it is a good idea for *your* business. Chicken sandwiches are a good idea; the Murrells decided they were *not* a good idea for a business called Five Guys Burgers. If growth is the decider, it looks like the Murrells were right about that and in a spectacular way.

This advantage of focus is applicable to all companies, including tech. When Steve Jobs was still head of Apple, he had a chief designer named Jony Ive. The two men were good friends that socialized and traveled together with their families. Jobs admired Ive's ability to generate ideas, and the working partnership between the two men led to Apple's instantly recognizable aesthetics: clean, simple, and easy to use. And yet Jobs also believed coming up with too many ideas and acting on them could have turned into the designer's greatest fault and even harmed the company. Jobs knew that too many ideas would have the dangerous potential of diluting the company's focus.

Business Insider reported that Jobs once told Ive, "Jony, you have to understand there are measures of focus, and one of them is how often you say 'no.'" Jobs believed there was focusing power in refusing an idea, even when the idea was a good one. He would often walk around Apple's offices and ask random employees, "How many times did you say 'no' today?" Having a good idea was common. Having a good idea for an Apple product was rare, and Jobs and his employees kept a razor-sharp focus.[11] I am truly amazed at how much revenue (and profit) Apple generates from so few products.

Warren Buffet, chairman and CEO of Berkshire Hathaway, agreed with this principle, stating, "The difference between successful people and really successful people is that really successful people say no to almost everything." *Accelerated Intelligence* writer Michael Simmons reports that "when Bill Gates first met Warren Buffett, their host, Gates' mother, asked everyone around the table to share the single most important factor to their success. Gates and Buffett both gave the same one-word answer: 'Focus.'"[12]

As your company grows, one of the toughest things to do will be to stay true to who you are and what made you successful. The temptation to jump on all sorts of good ideas, without considering whether they will be good for your company, will be immense. Every successful company experiences this challenge, and you will too. The Murrells and Steve Jobs were able to find ways to stay true to their vision; Five Guys Burgers and Apple have enjoyed spectacular success because, or at least partly because, of their acceptance of the immense power of NO. Jobs was not shy about giving this advice to other leaders. When Nike CEO Mark Parker asked Jobs for advice, Jobs told him, "Nike makes some of the best products in the world. Products that you lust after. But you also make a lot of crap. Just get rid of the crappy stuff and focus on the good stuff."[13] Simple and Strategically Brave advice.

Market analysis is a thorough and documented investigation of a market that is used to inform a business's planning, strategy, and decision-making activities. A market analysis considers elements such as market size and share, key market metrics (e.g., growth, profit), market barriers, market change, competition, company advantages, and so on. As business context is always changing—faster than ever with technological advances—these are things that companies should monitor and discuss regularly. Your success is not dependent on some outside force but on the choices you make and actions you take. Those choices are impacted, in part, by market analysis.

Market Analysis—Market Size and Share

I started working with two very similar companies at about the same time, and while one of the companies was in a small market with 90 percent market share, the other was in a large market with less than 10 percent market share. The company with 90 percent market share was in a great situation as they had little competition and a clear market advantage. Yet their growth was limited unless they expanded their market opportunity pool. Although the other company with less than 10 percent market share had a substantial amount of competition, they also had much greater growth potential because they had a well-defined market advantage and unrestricted opportunity. In my mind, the more competition I have the better because if I have a well-defined and packaged advantage I have the opportunity to take market share from the competition. Keep in mind that this is not a static thing. For example, at the beginning of your company's growth, when you have 10 percent market share or less, it may not make sense to expand your opportunity pool. Later, when you have 50 percent market share, you might have to ask yourself, Do I have enough opportunity to grow how I want to grow? With growth will come new and different challenges. At a certain point, if you have too much market share, you will become a target for your competition. You may have to do more business defense than business offense. When you have a large percent of market share, like 50 percent or more, you may want to make a strategic decision to expand your opportunity pool.

Market Analysis—Key Metrics of Growth and Profit (Yours versus the Market)

Profitable growth is a Vital Goal for most companies, and looking at how your metrics compare in the market you compete in can be an excellent gauge of success. If you follow proven planning and execution principles, you should be able to outgrow your competitive market many times the industry average as well as enhance profitability. If a company can sustain growth at two to three times their industry average, they are doing a number of things right and will have the resources to continually enhance their Company Advantage. Conversely, if your growth and profit are below industry averages, you're at a disadvantage and you have some work to do.

One very successful company I'm familiar with had a combined incentive goal of 35 percent growth and profit—substantially above industry averages. A branch could have 40 percent growth and a 5 percent profit loss or 10 percent growth and 25 percent profit to meet this Brass Ring goal. Not only did everyone in their company know this goal, but everyone in the industry knew their goal. Guess what? This company grew revenue and profit forty-eight out of fifty years, taking them from a few million in annual revenue to a few billion in annual revenue, and their profit grew exponentially as well. They are now the eight-hundred-pound gorilla in their industry and have ventured into additional opportunity spaces.

Amazing what clear goals can accomplish!

On a side note, often when companies first start to achieve an increased growth expansion, they panic when they experience increasing expenses for things like building expansion, equipment, merchandise, sales and marketing, and so forth. I tell these clients to rejoice! Why? Because I've yet to see a company increase growth—when done in a planned, strategic, focused, and controlled way—and not see cash flow increase as well. There may be a one-year or two-year lag, but it will come.

Market Analysis—Market Trends (Is Your Company a Leader or a Follower?)

Ignore market analysis and trends at your peril. Some very good companies have fallen victim to context changes in their industries and, as a result, are no longer in business. Some were in booming industries like mobile phones, electronics, video, drugstores, discount retailers, and so on. Make the right choices by understanding market trends or, better yet, by being the innovator and the trendsetter, or you may end up "Great to Gone" like Zenith, Blockbuster, Circuit City, Ames Department Stores (early competitor to Walmart), A&P grocery stores, or many family businesses like the local family drugstore. The family drugstore thinks they went out of business because Walgreens put up a store on the busiest intersection in town—a perfect example of effective strategy. In reality, they went out of business because they had not changed anything about their business over the past fifty years and ignored what others, like Walgreens, were doing. What if they had moved their store to the busiest intersection in town, added a drive-through, and expanded their product offering? They blame their demise on the competition, but in my experience, business success or failure is typically based on choices and actions.

Apple was obviously a trendsetter with products like the iPhone. Netflix is a trendsetter with streaming video and content. Amazon is a trendsetter with one-click purchasing as well as free shipping. But you don't have to be a publicly traded, multi-billion-dollar company to be a trendsetter. A couple companies that come to mind in Wisconsin are Culver's, a fast-food restaurant with higher-quality food than most fast-food competitors—delicious—and Kwik Trip, an amazing convenience store where you can pick up steaks and potatoes or fried chicken for dinner. Someone told me recently they have a friend whose favorite restaurant is Kwik Trip. They have both differentiated themselves in competitive market spaces and are wildly successful.

Items to consider when analyzing trends include pricing and charges, product offerings (variety and selection), innovation, service, agreement terms, and so on. Often you can look at trends and differentiate by not following the trend. For example, with most airlines you pay for your bags, but with Southwest your bags fly free.

Market Analysis—Markets to Consider

Geographic Markets—Where to Play?

Where to play is a critical question. A. G. Lafley, American businessman who led Procter & Gamble, and Roger L. Martin in their terrific book *Playing to Win* talk incessantly about the importance of "where to play and how to win" as it relates to strategic planning. Lafley used these concepts to double P&G's sales, quadruple its profits, and increase its market value by more than $100 billion.[14] Although expanding geographically can be an effective strategy to gain a larger opportunity pool, sometimes playing everywhere is not.

A company in one of my Executive Peer Groups was one of the top performers in the group and decided to make an acquisition to expand their geographic market, but it was such a "big bite," for which they were unprepared, that it derailed their results for years. You should never fear failure, but you should always be aware of the size of the bite you are taking as well as how success or failure will affect your core business. This company has since refocused and has come back strong.

A great example of keeping geographic market focus is the New Glarus Brewing Company. Founded in 1993 in New Glarus, Wisconsin, it is an independently owned craft brewery that is the fifteenth-largest craft brewer and twenty-fifth-largest overall brewing company in the United States.[15] Yet they only sell their beer in Wisconsin, a focused strategy that has been astonishingly successful. Plus, they have very good beer—Spotted Cow is a favorite! There is something about limiting where people can get your product that makes them want it more.

Product Markets—What Product(s) and/or Service(s) Do You Win With?

I've mentioned Apple many times in this book, and product focus is another example of less being more. They stay amazingly focused on trying to be the best with a few products. Yes, even they have seen a need to expand their opportunity pool through their service and content offerings but never at the detriment of their core business or brand. This allows them to invest heavily in their advantage. The more diverse a company becomes, the bigger challenge they have maintaining a clear advantage because their resources become too spread out. I think of Apple, and I think of the iPhone—a product that I can't live without and one of the most profitable items ever invented. When I think of Chick-fil-A, I get hungry for a chicken sandwich.

Prospects Market—To Whom Do You Sell?

Existing Market—Segment of people who are already being served by your company or your direct competitors. They use the type of product or service you offer either through you or a competitor. Although an important market segment, this is the market where most companies focus exclusively, which means they are missing out on creating more opportunity in the expanded market.

Expanded Market—Segment of people/companies who are not using your products or the products of your direct competitor but have the potential to be customers. In this segment, you create new demand through innovation and how you package your product or service advantage and take it to market. Often this opportunity pool can be larger than the existing segment. This is a nontraditional or an undiscovered market, a segment of people unpenetrated by you and your direct competitors who may require a new way of going to market. For example, Kleenex wasn't always selling disposable tissues. It started out as makeup remover and a cleansing tissue. However, they discovered from customer feedback that a lot of customers preferred to use their tissues as substitute handkerchiefs. Kleenex were the first facial tissue introduced to the market and the first brand of facial tissue to have a pop-up box.[16] Amazon is a company that is always changing business context and expanding markets. Amazon first changed the way we purchased books; then, with Kindle, they changed the way books are read. Eventually, they changed the way we purchase everything. When I was a kid, an "old-timer" said, "If Sears don't have it, you don't need it." I guess the saying now should be "If you need it, Amazon has it."

Customer Market—Additional Market Opportunity within Your Existing Customers?

This is the segment of people and companies who are already your customers but may purchase additional products or services. In many industries this is a huge yet often ignored market. As an example, I have insurance through many different brokers, for personal and business, yet have never received a call from one of them asking if there was additional business they could work to obtain. Think of the opportunity they are missing. It's huge!

I had a company speak at one of my Executive Peer Groups that was very good at upselling their existing customer market—way above industry standards. Yet, when I asked the owner if he ever felt they would run out of upselling opportunity since they had been focusing on this growth opportunity for years, his answer was fast and absolute: "Bob, we could double the size of our company without adding one new customer if we capitalize on upselling to our existing customers." He convinced me that he could and would. Imagine if 50 percent of your growth came from existing customers. It may not be feasible for all industries but for some it is. I've seen it firsthand.

Advantage Challenge: Identify your core products and determine your penetration of those core products with existing customers. What would growth look like if you increase that penetration by 10 percent, 20 percent, 30 percent, or more?

Market Analysis—Competitive Analysis (Who's Your Competition?)

Sun Tzu stated in *The Art of War*, "If you know the enemy and know yourself, you need not fear the result of a hundred battles." [17] Where do you position yourself in the marketplace versus your competition? It is important to recognize your competitors, but how you do that, and how your company talks about your competition, is important. Competition is not a bad thing. It makes companies improve or perish. Or as Thomas Winninger said in his book *Price Wars*, "Fish stay healthier when there is a perceived predator in the pond."[18] When looking at competition you can obsess over it, ignore it, make it obsolete, learn from it, or strategize against it.

Obsess Over It: Too many companies obsess about their competition, saying they fear or hate them or spending all their time criticizing competitors. That's useless; it is a waste of time and energy. Often companies spend time obsessing over the market leader while the market leader spends their time obsessing over how to be better—or at least they should be. The book *Blue Ocean Strategy* said it well: "The only way to beat the competition is to stop trying to beat the competition. Companies too often try to be different in the same way."[19]

Ignore It: Napoleon Bonaparte said, "Never interrupt your enemy when he is making a mistake."[20] Here's a great example of this. I was once touring a company where the owner had invited me to visit. This was a very successful company that was drastically outgrowing the competition in their market. The owner's son was giving me the tour. I asked him who their company's biggest competitor was and waited for the response. We stopped walking. The son looked at me, frowned, and thought for a long time about my question. "I'm sure we've got some," he said after a minute, and I had to laugh to myself. What a great answer! Everyone at this company was so focused on what they were doing, they didn't have time to consider or worry about who their top competitor even was. That is the kind of focus that will lead to success. Now, I'm not suggesting you should completely ignore competition; you should understand their strengths, strategies, and differentiators and have a strategy for beating them in the marketplace. But, if you do those things well, it may actually seem like you don't have any competition.

Make It Obsolete: Be so good at addressing your marketplace and the needs of your customer that your competition becomes irrelevant. Walmart did this to Ames Department Stores. Barnes & Noble and Borders almost did this to small independent bookstores, but then, Amazon did it to those big book retailers and did it so well Borders succumbed to the pressure and went out of business. Some independent bookstores focused and defined their advantage, and many survived and even thrived. In the tech sector, there are more electronics sold today than ever before, and yet Palm, Compaq, and Zenith were made obsolete by Apple, Samsung, Microsoft, and so on.

Learn From It: Greek scholar Aristophanes said, "The wise learn many things from their enemies."[21] Sometimes your competitors are so strong in the marketplace, it would be impossible not to notice them. When you do have strong competitors, one strategy is to simply make up your mind that you are going to enjoy the challenge. Do this and you are surely going to test yourself and your company, and both will get better and stronger in the process. Have a blocking strategy for what your competitors are best at, so the conversation is about your Competitive Advantages. Remember to learn from, not focus on or copy. Walt Disney concurred: "I have been up against tough competition all my life; I wouldn't know how to get along without it."[22]

Strategize against It: Your competitors are going to do what they are going to do. Whatever that is, it is out of your control. What is in your control are the strategies you develop, how you organize your day, and how you define your Company Advantage and work to earn that advantage in the minds of your customers every day. Put forth energy and focus on what you can control instead of what you cannot. Do things to outperform your competition, and you'll be surprised by how quickly you are just not interested in what they are doing any longer. The key is to use competition as a motivator to be better. Make it a habit to focus on your strategies and make your company the best. Let them worry about you.

Market Analysis—Company Analysis

A more important analysis is to look inward at yourself. Does your company have the talent, drive, resources, and advantage to excel in the markets in which you compete, or should you consider new opportunities? The areas listed below are items to review on a regular basis.

Company Analysis—Financial Needs/Strength: Does your company have the financial strength to achieve its Growth/Vital Goals? If you are struggling financially and you don't have a clear plan and strategy for improvement, you are probably going to have challenges achieving success. From my experience, the best way to get financially sound is to execute a plan, invest in your market advantage, outgrow the competition, and become Strategically Brave.

Company Analysis—Company Needs: The key question here shouldn't be "How fast *can* we grow?" but rather "How fast *should* we grow?" What are the payroll, overhead, merchandise, and administrative needs to expand into whatever new idea you are contemplating? And most importantly, do you have the resources and expertise to fill these needs?

Company Analysis—Family Needs: What are the family needs and lifestyles and how many mouths need to be fed from the business? Many family businesses don't make it past the third generation because of the expanding number of owners.[23] This is one reason growth is so critical for a family business. If, as part of the company purpose, the family has philanthropic interests, those will need to be factored in as well.

Company Analysis—Growth Needs: What are the resources that will be compulsory to grow and expand, and what are the associated costs? Growth should always be a priority as all companies have limited resources. Determine and control your growth, and your company will control its destiny.

Company Analysis—Facilities: Will your facilities support your growth, or do you need to expand? Are there operational capabilities that you can outsource? Many name-brand companies no longer own the manufacturing facilities that make their products. This allows them to focus on the other areas of their business that will drive profitable growth.

Company Analysis—Talent: Your most precious resource is talent. As we discussed in chapter 7, "Talent Advantage," I've found neglecting talent to be the biggest stall point that gets in the way of sustained growth. Make sure to grow your talent pool at the same pace as, but in advance of, your growth. If you don't, because employees are overwhelmed and exhausted, you may see growth become a negative. You never want to see this happen.

Company Analysis—Knowledge: Are you focused on training your employees for the future and the company you plan to become? Your investment in training should be substantial and sustainable. Do you and your employees have the know-how and skills required? If not, commit the resources to correct this situation.

Company Analysis—Innovation: Do you have a culture that supports innovation? Amazon, Microsoft, Salesforce, Facebook, and Netflix never rest on their laurels. They understand competition is always after market share and realize they need to always be innovating and investing in their advantage. J. K. Rowling said, "Imagination is not only the uniquely human capacity to envision that which is not, and therefore the fount of all invention and innovation, in its arguably most transformative and revelatory capacity, it is the power that enables us to empathize with humans whose experiences we have never shared."[24] The story goes, J. K. Rowling was turned down by twelve publishers before finding success with the Harry Potter books.[25] Imagine if she had given up after eleven. Harry Potter books have become the biggest-selling series ever, with more than five hundred million copies sold worldwide.

Focus on your core business in your core market first and do a detailed analysis. If you determine that you need to expand your opportunity pool, do so strategically and make sure you can deliver an advantage to that pool. Ask yourself, What advantage do I deliver to this market? anytime you are tempted to consider an expansion. Without a strong answer, stick to what you are already doing well.

A desire only to be bigger with no strategic focus—instead of a desire to be better—can lead to pursuing growth in areas in which you have no passion and that are inconsistent with your core values, offer you no Competitive Advantage, do not fit your economic engine, often force you to neglect your core business, and may compromise your values. Simple advice: don't do this!

Competitive and Value Advantage

Here is an insight I've discovered after years of running companies, consulting with both successful and struggling companies, and helping the struggling ones turn things around: the greater your Value Advantage and Competitive Advantage in the marketplace in which you compete, the more growth becomes sustainable and profit explodes. Consider Apple, Google, Microsoft, and Facebook; a huge advantage equals some of the most profitable companies in the history of business. Accordingly, companies should always invest as much as possible into maintaining and growing their advantage. It has an astounding return on investment, and the alternative is business death. Additionally, you should do whatever you can to make the competitive environment a "beauty contest" based on *your* strengths. Try to set the industry standards in your market based on what *you* do best. Then your Company Advantage will be the dominant force in the market.

Value Advantage: Value advantage is why a customer uses your product or service offering. What value do you provide to your customer? If you focus on offering value first, profits will follow. Or, as Albert Einstein said, "Try not to become a man of success, but rather try to become a man of value."[26] Think for a minute: What is the value of your smartphone (communication, information, connection)? What is the value of your Netflix service (convenience, entertainment, content variety)? Now, ask yourself, What value advantages do my products and services offer my customers?

I don't care if it's a business relationship, a friendship, or a marriage, if either party does not see value, the relationship is in trouble. I mentioned before that I was once the executive director of a buying group that made substantial purchases. When I would call one of our approved suppliers and leave a message, I would get an immediate callback. Now, fast-forward to when I was no longer part of the buying group and left some of those same companies a message. Some would call back the same as before, but there were some where I would only hear crickets. I share this story with a smile because I know it was not personal. As I am no longer involved with them becoming or remaining approved suppliers for the organization which influences purchases, some of those companies no longer see value in the relationship. The moral to the story is your company should constantly be reminding your customers and the market of the value your product or service offers. Perhaps we should remind those we have personal relationships with of the value we offer as well.

Competitive Advantage: Now that the customer recognizes they want or need your offering, your Competitive Advantage is why they would choose you over your competition. Why the iPhone over all the other phones on the market? Why Chick-fil-A over all other fast-food restaurants? Why use Google over all the other search engines? Why use Netflix over other streaming services? These companies are perfect examples of investing in their advantage. In 2020, Netflix had a budget of $16 billion for new content, approximately double its closest competitor's.[27] My take on that is they did not need to spend $16 billion on content. They could have purchased or created it much cheaper. They spent $16 billion on their advantage. Their advantage is the quantity, quality, and exclusivity of their content. Their goal is to make it so no one's content can compete with theirs. Why do you think Google provides Google Maps, Google Drive, and so on? They do it so no other search engine can match their Competitive Advantage. Have you tasted a Chick-fil-A sandwich? They are addictive. I have never seen a busier or better-run drive-through. I don't know the people at Chick-fil-A, but I can assure you they invest in the quality of their Product and Service Advantage and will never scrimp on ingredients trying to cut costs.

According to Harvard University research, the competitive position between firms accounts for 32 percent of the variation in profit.[28] I say that may be too low by a mile. In my experience, with clients in like industries, growth and profit range dramatically based on a number of variables including Competitive Advantage. Think about companies in the exact same industries offering similar products with the same information. Yet some make 20 percent to 30 percent profit while others make barely enough to get by. Some consistently grow faster than industry averages while others' revenue remains flat. The interesting part is that the differences in those outcomes are in their control. The companies that plan, strategize, execute, and invest in their advantage control their destiny. The companies that don't understand and invest in their advantage, but instead blame forces outside their control, lose.

As referenced earlier, the Growth Advantage Executive Peer Groups I moderate are a perfect example of this. We survey a variety of items in these groups including financial success, and the ranges in every survey we do are dramatic. They range from outstanding to mediocre to scary bad. You can guess which companies have developed an advantage that puts their performance ahead of their competition and which companies think their results are out of their control. There is a true downward spiral when you don't invest in your advantage.

If you know both your Value Advantage and your Competitive Advantage, and continuously innovate and invest to make them stronger, there will always be opportunity wins for you in the marketplace. One problem, however, is that many companies talk as if they have a market advantage, but the market is not experiencing it. Bain & Company conducted a survey asking executives from 362 companies if they believed they delivered a "superior experience" to their customers, and 80 percent replied they did. When customers were asked about the level of performance in their experiences with the companies they bought from, merely 8 percent of those companies received a rating of "superior."[29] It is my hunch that those companies are not delivering the superior experience that they think they are. The 20 percent that admit they don't offer a superior experience may be in real trouble!

You need to have more than an advantage in the boardroom; you also have to deliver it in the market. Every executive is going to say, "Well, sure, we've got an advantage." Whether that is actually true or not is decided, day in and day out, by your customers' experience.

Companies differentiate in a variety of ways: Walmart differentiates on price. Apple differentiates on product (design, simplicity, usability). Here are some other examples of companies that do an excellent job of differentiating themselves in the marketplace and have been rewarded handsomely for it. Netflix differentiates on convenience and content—you used to get your disks in the mail, and now you can simply stream instantly. Southwest Airlines differentiates on price based on simplicity—they use only one kind of plane. Enterprise Car Rental differentiates on how they hire, train, and promote talent—it's all about the people who work there. American Express has unrivaled customer service in their market space. Zappos differentiates on culture that attracts talent. Walgreens focuses on geographical convenience. Look around at the companies you patronize and I'm sure you can think of other examples, too. Use these insights to define how your company differentiates itself in the mind of your customer.

Advantage Challenge: Ask yourself, and your team, what is your company's differentiated advantage? Unless it immediately came to mind, you don't have it! Unless everyone in your company gave the same answer, you don't have it! When you really have an advantage, and you package it, everyone should know it.

Novelist Rita Mae Brown wrote a line often attributed to Albert Einstein that says, "Insanity is doing the same thing over and over again but expecting different results."[30] I have my own version of this famous quote. It goes like this: "Definition of insanity: Doing the same thing *as your competition* and expecting different results." Differentiation is at the heart of a successful business strategy. The sharper your differentiation, the greater your company's advantage.

In a study reported by the *Harvard Business Review*, it was found that "of companies that sustained a high level of performance over many years, more than 80 percent had a well-defined and easily understood differentiation at the center of their strategy."[31] A company's strategic differentiation and execution matter *four times* as much as the business it is in. This is one reason why variance in growth and profit is so diverse.

Advantage Analysis Graph—Which Quadrant Do You Want to Compete In?

Lower Left Quadrant—In this quadrant, the customer or market needs are the same and there is no differentiation in the offering. Purchasing decisions are going to be made based on price. Low-cost providers typically operate on tight margins and are dependent on large sales volumes. Advantage invested on in this quadrant is low price and how to deliver that price at a profit. Walmart is one of the best ever at

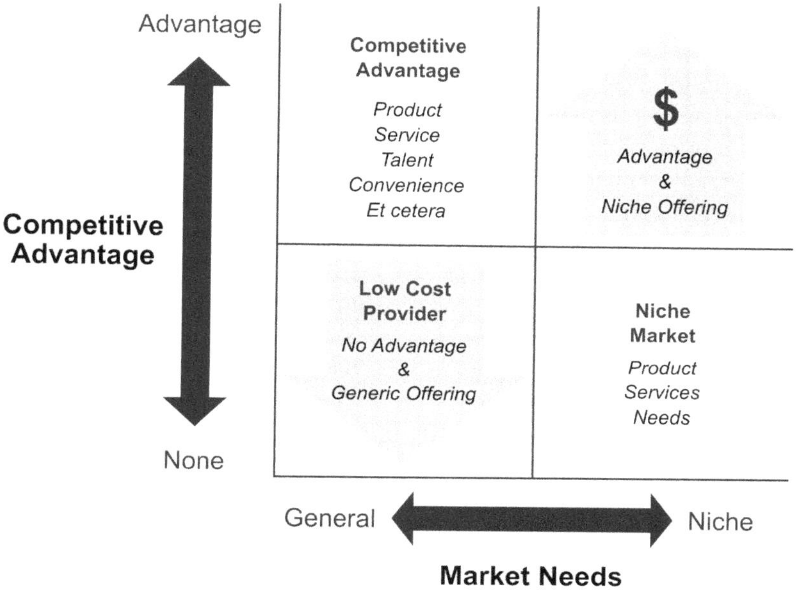

Figure 11.3. Advantage Analysis Graph

this: "Prices are falling." They started as a discount retailer in rural markets and built a supply chain scale that allowed them to take their advantage to urban markets and around the world.

Lower Right Quadrant—This is a quadrant where market needs or offerings are niche—expanded market. The market niche is defined as the service or product features aimed at satisfying specific market needs, as well as the price range, production quality, and the demographics that it is intended to impact. This is an expanded market that is often created in scale by the offering company: Apple with the smart-phone, Xerox as the first desktop copier, Amazon the first online bookstore, eBay the first meaningful online auction website, and White Castle with the first fast-food outlet and the first fast-food restaurant to sell one billion hamburgers. As there is typically high investment cost in creating this market, it is important to command a price that delivers a strong profit margin. When companies are successful in a niche or expanded market, competition will soon follow. Being first does not guarantee success unless companies can generate profit and extend their advantage.

Upper Left Quadrant—In this quadrant, market needs are the same or similar, but companies strive for meaningful elements of differentiation. This is where identifying, investing in, and packaging your advantage is critical. Companies that don't end up trying to compete on price without a cost advantage, which is a formula for disaster. Signs your company does not have a well-defined and packaged brand advantage: poor market recognition, low sales, selling bad business, low closing rate, high lost business, dwindling repeat sales, sales representative turnover, selling at low prices, disappointing profits, and meetings spent talking about competition instead of your advantage strategy. If any of these signs, or a combination of these signs, can be found regularly in your company, you have some work to do to define your Company Advantage.

Upper Right Quadrant—In this quadrant, market offering or needs are niche, and there is a differentiated advantage. Even when a company creates a new market and for a period of time has the ultimate advantage, competition always follows. This quadrant should demand the highest prices and profit margins as costs to develop business in this quadrant are typically high, especially until scale is met. Although electric vehicles have been around for a long time, Tesla was the first company to offer an all-electric car with a powertrain and lithium-ion battery that could travel more than two hundred miles per charge. Now that they have changed the minds of many consumers regarding their perception of electric vehicles and achieved market scale, many companies are aggressively entering the space and are trying to catch up and create their own advantage. Tesla is a very innovative company but, like all companies, will still have to deal with strong competition and perpetually invest in their advantage.

Having an Advantage Strategy is critical and has four key elements:

First, a Significant Value and Competitive Advantage—One that sets companies apart from the competition in a meaningful way. It does not matter what business you're in, you need a clear advantage. David Johnson is the World Famous Bushman in San Francisco along Fisherman's Wharf, a busker who hides motionless behind some eucalyptus branches and waits for unsuspecting people to wander by and scare them. As they walk by, he shakes the bush and makes "oogah-boogah" noises, startling the unsuspecting tourists. Crowds gather to watch him work, even those he has previously scared.[32] Johnson differentiated himself from other street performers and people tipped him after he scared them—a very unusual but effective business plan.

Departure from industry standards and norms is an important element of business strategy. Gary Kasparov, the best chess player of his era, said, "One does not succeed by sticking to convention. When your opponent can easily anticipate every move you make, your strategy deteriorates and becomes commoditized."[33] Don't let your offering become commoditized.

Second, a Packaged Brand Advantage Message—Something that is persuasive and speaks directly to the needs of the customer in a convincing and meaningful way. Mahatma Gandhi said, "My life is my message."[34] Your packaged brand message is the lifeblood of your business.

Third, an Advantage Focus—A central focus that gets the attention of your employees, customers, and prospects. As Bruce Lee said, "The successful warrior is the average man with laser-like focus."[35] Run your business like a focused warrior.

And Fourth, an Advantage Commitment—A commitment to investing in and keeping your advantage strong and visible. Sir Richard Branson said, "Branding demands commitment; commitment to continual re-invention; striking chords with people to stir their emotions; and commitment to imagination. It is easy to be cynical about such things, much harder to be successful."[36]

ADVANTAGE PRINCIPLE: THE COMPANY THAT IS BETTER AT BRANDING AND COMMUNICATING ITS ADVANTAGE OFTEN TRUMPS THE COMPANY WITH THE ACTUAL ADVANTAGE.

Brand Advantage—Packaging and Communicating Your Advantage

Jeff Bezos from Amazon says, "Your brand is what other people say about you when you are not in the room."[37] What do you want people to say about your company when you're not in the room? A Brand Advantage is insufficient unless you package it and communicate it in an effective way to the market. To communicate your Brand Advantage, you have to be able tell the story that relates it to the market. You also need to keep repeating it, over and over again, in new and interesting ways. You cannot get fatigued with your brand message! You need to keep your focus on it so that your employees and your customers do, too. Brand Advantage messages can even be a self-fulfilling prophecy. Repeat it enough and, if it isn't entirely true at the beginning, it will become true through focus, investment, and hard work.

Tsufit, in the book *Step into the Spotlight!*, said, "An 'expert' is not someone who knows what he knows. An 'expert' is someone known for knowing what he knows."[38] A brand is an association, idea, or concept that you own, inside the mind of the prospect, customer, and employee. It is imperative that you influence and control those associations in an intentional way. If I am referred to or known by a company, I'm known for what I know. It is a much easier process to make the sale than when I am trying to sell to a company in an industry where I am not known. Be known for knowing what you know in the markets where you want to be known.

Advantage Challenge: What do you know (do better than your competition) that you want to be known for?

Every time a customer interacts with your company, every time they "touch" your company in some way, they should have a positive experience that supports and amplifies your advantage. Each of these "touches" needs to lead to a positive message, which in turn leads to building brand credibility.

What are the benefits of branding? Branding is everything! It clarifies your message, enhances your credibility, differentiates you from your competition, communicates your Competitive Advantage and your Value Advantage, and attracts high-quality employees and high-quality customers. And that's what you want most, isn't it?

So who should you be branding to first? Yourself, of course! This is crucial. If you don't believe your Brand Advantage message, no one else will either. Branding starts within the company, not outside of it. Once you are fully behind your brand, make sure your executive and management teams are committed, then the rest of your employees, and from there, you take your brand to customers and prospects. If you don't brand to yourself first, as well as your employees, you'll never be able to brand to your customers.

How do you brand? There are many good ways. Here are three I've found to be effective:

Have a **Tagline**—A frequently repeated phrase or statement that communicates your "Advantage." This should be honest and reflect your core message. Famous examples of great taglines are all around us if you look. "The Few. The Proud. The Marines." "Bounty—The Quicker Picker Upper." "GEICO—15 minutes could save you 15 percent." "Snap, Crackle, Pop—Rice Krispies." Taglines are simple and memorable.

Have a prepared **Elevator Speech/Thirty-Second Commercial**—Be able to communicate what your company does in less time than it takes for an elevator to reach the ground floor, or about thirty seconds. This is a value proposition stated in an inviting way that can be a conversation starter or stand on its own.

Have defined **Advantage Points**—One to five advantage differentiators that distinguish you in the market from your competitors and that every employee in your company knows and can communicate verbatim.

Here's an example using Airbnb. **Tagline:** Wherever you go we have a place for you. **Elevator Speech:** We have created a platform that connects travelers with locals, letting them rent our rooms or even entire places. Travelers save money, and locals can monetize their empty rooms—we just take a 10 percent commission. **Advantage Points:** a global travel community; hosts who truly care; we're here for you—day or night; every trip is covered by Airbnb.

A few final thoughts about drafting your brand message: it needs to be simple and clear, it needs to differentiate you from your competition, and it has to communicate your Competitive Advantage and your Value Advantage. It should be unique, true, believable, consistent with your Core Values, and integrated in every customer contact.

Advantage Challenge: Complete a Strategy ROAD Map. Ask yourself: What are the Roadblocks in the way of achieving my Vital Goals? What are my greatest market opportunities? What are my Competitive Advantages? What are my competitive disadvantages? Where do opportunity and advantage intersect for my company?

Reference the ROAD Map Advantage Challenge Application (Figure A.11) at the back of the book.

Chapter Summary

- Advantage Principle: Business Happens Where Market Opportunity and Company Advantage Intersect.
- Advantage Principle: It Is Advantageous to Expand Your Opportunity Pool Provided Doing So Does Not Diminish Your Focus, Advantage, or Brand.
- Your Company Advantage should speak directly to the needs of your customers. Make sure it takes into account these three interrelated areas: Market and Product Advantage, Competitive and Value Advantage, and Brand Advantage.
- In defining your Market and Product Advantage, you need to ask yourself these questions: What am I selling, to whom, where, and why?
- Value Advantage: Value advantage is why a customer uses your product or service offering.
- Competitive Advantage: Now that the customer recognizes they want or need your offering, your competitive advantage is why they would choose you over your competition.
- "Definition of insanity: Doing the same thing *as your competition* and expecting different results."
- When it comes to your Competitive and Value Advantage, do whatever you can to make that competition a "beauty contest" based on *your* strengths. Try to set the industry standards for your market based on what *you* do best.
- Advantage Principle: The Company That Is Better at Branding and Communicating Its Advantage Often Trumps the Company with the Actual Advantage.
- Who should you be branding to first? Yourself, of course! This is crucial. If you don't believe your Brand Advantage message, no one else will either.
- A brand message needs to be simple and clear, differentiate you from your competition, and communicate your Advantage and should be integrated in every customer contact.

Wrap-Up

Growth Advantage Effect

WOW! We covered a lot in this book, and if you haven't already, it is time to get working on your Growth Advantage. Combine the elements of the Planning Advantage, the Execution Advantage, and the Company Advantage to establish a System Advantage for all the elements that contribute to your company's Vital Goals and give your team members their best chance at success. Everything we do in business should be about maximizing our market advantage, thereby creating the Ultimate Competitive Edge. In her book *Go for the Goal*, Mia Hamm, gold medalist and one of the greatest soccer players in US history, recalled an encouraging note left by coach Anson Dorrace, who nailed it when he said, "The vision of a champion is bent over, drenched in sweat, at the point of exhaustion, when nobody else is looking."[1] Building your Growth Advantage may take a little sweat, you may need to work hard when no one is looking, but I promise the outcomes will be worth it.

Now a little math to demonstrate the Growth Advantage Effect:

Let's look at two companies with $10 million annual revenue, 10 percent profit, and an industry equity value or market capitalization of two times annual revenue—meaning if they sold their business, they would get approximately $20 million. Now let's assume Company A compounded 5 percent growth and Company B compounded 10 percent growth over a ten-year period (see Figure D.1). At the end of ten years, Company A's combined profit and equity value increase would be $15,784,680—an average annual profit and equity value increase of $1,578,468. Company B's combined cumulative profit and equity value increase would be $39,406,016—$3,940,602 average annually. This is what I call the Growth Advantage Effect. Without factoring any percentage increase in profit, the annual Growth Advantage Effect would increase from $1.5 million annually to $4 million annually. Whether your revenue is $1 million or $1 billion annually, the effects are the same. Every percent increase in growth and corresponding profit has a huge compounding effect.

Growth Advantage Effect		**Compounded Over 10 Years**	
		5% Growth	**10% Growth**
Revenue Starting Revenue = $10,000,000	Annual Revenue	$16,288,946	$25,937,425
	Total Revenue Increase	$6,288,946	$15,937,425
	Average Annual Revenue Increase	$628,895	$1,593,742
	Cumulative Revenue Increase	$32,067,872	$75,311,671
	Average Annual Cumulative Revenue Increase	$3,206,787	$7,531,167
Profit (10%) Starting Annual Profit = $1,000,000	Annual Profit	$1,628,895	$2,593,742
	Total Profit Increase	$628,895	$1,593,742
	Cumulative Profit Increase	$3,206,787	$7,531,167
	Average Annual Cumulative Profit Increase	$320,679	$753,117
Equity Value (2 X Revenue) Starting Equity Value = $20,000,000	Equity Value	$32,577,893	$51,874,849
	Equity Value Increase	$12,577,893	$31,874,849
	Average Annual Equity Value Increase	$1,257,789	$3,187,485
Growth Advantage Effect Starting Profit & Equity Value = $21,000,000	Cumulative Profit & Equity Value	$35,784,680	$59,406,016
	Cumulative Profit & Equity Value Increase	$15,784,680	$39,406,016
	Average Annual Cumulative Profit & Equity Value Increase	$1,578,468	$3,940,602

Figure D.1. Growth Advantage Effect

Now that we know developing a Growth Advantage is well worth it, today is the time to get started. But remember: sustained business growth doesn't just happen. Growth must be planned for and executed, cultivated from a strategic standpoint and applied tactically at the front line, and led by the right people focused on the right objectives.

Appendix

Advantage Challenge Applications

ADVANTAGE CHALLENGE: PURPOSE

COMPANY PURPOSE (WHY)
What is your company's purpose? Why does it exist?
**Rank up to three selections with one being the highest priority.*

_____ Financial (make money)
_____ Equity (build wealth)
_____ Philanthropy (private initiatives/public good)
_____ Family (opportunity, wealth, incomes)
_____ Succession (next generation/legacy)
_____ Jobs (employees)
_____ Customer (satisfying needs)
_____ Other: ____________________
_____ Other: ____________________
_____ Other: ____________________

HISTORY (PAST PURPOSE)
What elements from your company's past should help shape its future?

1. ____________________
2. ____________________
3. ____________________

MISSION (CURRENT PURPOSE)
What are the reasons for your organization's existence today?

1. ____________________
2. ____________________
3. ____________________

VISION (FUTURE PURPOSE)
What are the future aspirations of your organization?

1. ____________________
2. ____________________
3. ____________________

VALUES (GUIDING PURPOSE)
What are the ideals and principles that guide the thoughts and actions of your organization and define its character?

1. ____________________
2. ____________________
3. ____________________

Take key words from the left that positively define the company that you want to be:

Use the key words above to create a Purpose Statement as to why your company exists:

Figure A.1. Advantage Challenge: Purpose

ADVANTAGE CHALLENGE: CULTURE

Identify and rank your company's Culture Builders & Culture Killers. Which Builders need the most work/improvement? Which Killers are the biggest obstacles to your success?

1. Which Culture Builder(s) needs the most work/improvement?
   **Rank your top three selections with one being the highest priority.*

_______Specific Goals
_______Action/Progress
_______Accountability
_______Training & Reinforcement
_______Strategic Thinking
_______Other: ____________________
_______Other: ____________________
_______Behavior Tracking & Management
_______Focused Measurement
_______Productive Meetings
_______Engagement
_______Motivation
_______Other: ____________________
_______Other: ____________________

What will you do to improve in the areas prioritized?

1. ____________________
2. ____________________
3. ____________________

2. Which Culture Killer(s) is the biggest obstacle?
   **Rank your top three selections with one being the highest priority.*

_______Complaining
_______Too Busy
_______Lack of Progress/Action
_______Bad Mind-set
_______Team Distrust
_______Other: ____________________
_______Other: ____________________
_______Satisfaction
_______Below Baseline Numbers
_______Accountability Deficit
_______Lack of Motivation
_______No Team Rules
_______Other: ____________________
_______Other: ____________________

What will you do to address these obstacles?

1. ____________________
2. ____________________
3. ____________________

Figure A.2. Advantage Challenge: Culture

ADVANTAGE CHALLENGE: TIME MANAGEMENT

List at least three (3) activities that occupy your time in each quadrant.
What percent of your time is spent in each quadrant?

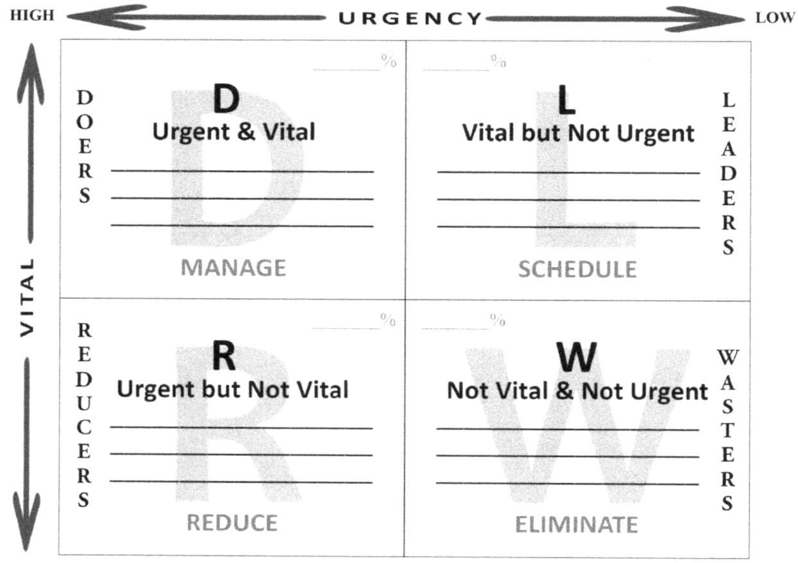

In quadrant D, I will better manage ______________________.

In quadrant L, I will schedule ______________________.

In quadrant R, I will reduce ______________________.

In quadrant W, I will eliminate ______________________.

Figure A.3. Advantage Challenge: Time Management

ADVANTAGE CHALLENGE: VITAL GOALS

Brainstorm your company's potential Vital Goals (top goals based on the results necessary to the existence, continuance or well-being of your company). Prioritize the top one, two and/or three goals worthy of your best effort.

Brass Ring = Superior standard of performance
Baseline = Minimum acceptable standard of performance
Below Baseline = Unacceptable standard of performance

Brainstorm your company's potential Vital Goals (list all ideas):

______________________	______________________
______________________	______________________
______________________	______________________
______________________	______________________
______________________	______________________
______________________	______________________
______________________	______________________
______________________	______________________
______________________	______________________
______________________	______________________

Prioritize your company's Vital Goals (three maximum):

Vital Goal #1: ______________________

Baseline: ______________________

Brass Ring: ______________________

Vital Goal #2: ______________________

Baseline: ______________________

Brass Ring: ______________________

Vital Goal #3: ______________________

Baseline: ______________________

Brass Ring: ______________________

Figure A.4. Advantage Challenge: Vital Goals

ADVANTAGE CHALLENGE: BE SPECIFIC

Are your Vital Goals specific? Ask the following questions:

Vital Goal: ______________________________

Baseline Goal: ______________ Brass Ring Goal: ______________

Is it achievable (circle one)? yes no

Is it measurable (circle one)? yes no

If so, how?

____

____

What's the upside if achieved?

____

____

What's the downside if not achieved?

____

____

Is the energy you need to expend worth it (circle one)? yes no

Are you committed (circle one)? yes no

Deadline (by when)?

____

____

Figure A.5. Advantage Challenge: Be Specific

ADVANTAGE CHALLENGE: PREDICTIVE BEHAVIORS

Select one element of growth by department and by position. Note the Baseline and Brass Ring result goals. Establish initiating Predictive Behavior goals and all follow-up behavior goals.

ELEMENT OF GROWTH:

____

Department: ______________________________

Position: ______________________________

Position Result Goal:

Baseline (weekly): ______________

Brass Ring (weekly): ______________

PREDICTIVE BEHAVIORS:

	Predictive Behavior	Baseline Goal (weekly)	Brass Ring Goal (weekly)
Step 6.	______________	________	________
Step 5.	______________	________	________
Step 4.	______________	________	________
Step 3.	______________	________	________
Step 2.	______________	________	________
Step 1.	______________	________	________

**Step #1 is the initiating behavior.*

Figure A.6. Advantage Challenge: Predictive Behaviors

ADVANTAGE CHALLENGE: TALENT ACQUISITION

Identify qualities/attributes of an ideal candidate.

How/where will you recruit ideal candidates?

What test(s)/profile(s) will you use to screen candidates?

When will you use them?

What additional steps will you take to qualify candidates?

What interview questions will you ask/what answers are you looking for?

What should be included in your Condition of Employment Agreement?

How will you measure results?

Figure A.7. Advantage Challenge: Talent Acquisition

ADVANTAGE CHALLENGE: TRAINING

Pick a position that reports to you and answer the following questions in regards to training and reinforcement.

POSITION:

____

List training priorities:

____________________ ____________________

____________________ ____________________

____________________ ____________________

How will you train each priority?

____________________ ____________________

____________________ ____________________

____________________ ____________________

How will you reinforce?

____________________ ____________________

____________________ ____________________

____________________ ____________________

How will you determine learning and application has occured (measure results)?

____________________ ____________________

____________________ ____________________

____________________ ____________________

Figure A.8. Advantage Challenge: Training

ADVANTAGE CHALLENGE: MOTIVATION

Pick one employee position and an outcome that you would like to influence with motivational activities. List two or three motivational ideas for each magic motivation question that may influence outcomes.

Position: ____________________ Outcome: ____________________

WHAT – What do you want me to accomplish?

____

____

____

CAN – Can I do it?

____

____

____

WORTH – Is it worth doing?

____

____

____

WHY – Why are you asking me to do it?

____

____

____

Management Motivational Activities:

____

____

____

Figure A.9. Advantage Challenge: Motivation

ADVANTAGE CHALLENGE: ACCOUNTABILITY CULTURE

List 3-5 words or phrases that define your company's accountability culture now. Include both positive and negative examples.

POSITIVE	NEGATIVE
1.____________________	1.____________________
2.____________________	2.____________________
3.____________________	3.____________________
4.____________________	4.____________________
5.____________________	5.____________________

List 3-5 words or phrases that describe the accountability culture you want to achieve.

1.____

2.____

3.____

4.____

5.____

Figure A.10. Advantage Challenge: Accountability Culture

ADVANTAGE CHALLENGE: ROAD MAP

Complete a Strategy Roadmap. Where do opportunity and advantage intersect for your company?

OPPORTUNITIES

What are your greatest market opportunities?

1. ______
2. ______
3. ______
4. ______
5. ______
6. ______
7. ______
8. ______

ROADBLOCKS

What are the roadblocks that are in the way of achieving your Vital Goals?

1. ______
2. ______
3. ______
4. ______
5. ______
6. ______
7. ______
8. ______

GROWTH ADVANTAGE STRATEGY

Where do opportunity & advantage intersect for your company?

1. ______
2. ______
3. ______
4. ______
5. ______
6. ______
7. ______
8. ______

ADVANTAGES

What are your company's market/competitive advantages?

1. ______
2. ______
3. ______
4. ______
5. ______
6. ______
7. ______
8. ______

DISADVANTAGES

What are your market/competitive disadvantages?

1. ______
2. ______
3. ______
4. ______
5. ______
6. ______
7. ______
8. ______

Figure A.11. Advantage Challenge: ROAD Map

Notes

PROLOGUE

1. Robert Kaplan and David Norton, "The Office of Strategy Management," *Harvard Business Review*, October 2005.

2. Alfred Lansing, *Endurance: Shackleton's Incredible Voyage* (New York: Basic Books, 2015).

3. Amy Climer, "5 Elements of Shackleton's Leadership," *The Deliberate Creative Blog*, December 15, 2016, https://climerconsulting.com/five-elements-shackletons-leadership/.

4. Lansing, *Endurance*; Climer, "5 Elements of Shackleton's Leadership."

5. Lansing, *Endurance*; Climer, "5 Elements of Shackleton's Leadership."

PART I: THE PLANNING ADVANTAGE

1. Alan Lakein, *How to Get Control of Your Time and Your Life* (New York: Signet, 1989).

2. David Anderson, "Vital Rules of Vision, Strategy & Tactics," LearnToLead, 2012, https://www.learntolead.com/articles/810-vital-rules-of-vision-strategy-tactics.

3. Dwayne Spradlin, "Are You Solving the Right Problem?" *Harvard Business Review*, September 2012.

1. CREATE A GROWTH CULTURE

1. "Meet Our Monkeys," Zappos, https://www.zappos.com/c/about-zappos-monkeys/.

2. "What We Live By," Zappos, https://www.zappos.com/about/what-we-live-by.

3. Chester Elton and Adrian Gostick, *The Orange Revolution: How One Great Team Can Transform an Entire Organization* (New York: Free Press, 2010).

4. Michelle F. Davis, "Dimon Sees Lasting Damage if Workers Don't Return to Offices," Bloomberg, September 15, 2020, https://www.bloomberg.com/news/articles/2020-09-15/dimon-sees-long-term-damage-if-people-don-t-get-back-to-work

5. Barry Alvarez and Mike Lucas, *Don't Flinch: Barry Alvarez, the Autobiography: The Story of Wisconsin's All-Time Winningest Coach* (Stevens Point, WI: KCI Sports Publishing, 2006).

6. John Wooden and Steve Jamison, *Wooden on Leadership: How to Create a Winning Organization* (New York: McGraw Hill Education, 2005).

7. "65 Bill Murray Quotes on Success in Life," Overallmotivation.com, https://www.overallmotivation.com/quotes/bill-murray-quotes/.

2. COMMIT TO YOUR VITAL GOALS

1. Nicole Sazegar, "19 Timeless Eleanor Roosevelt Quotes That Are Still Inspiring," *Entity*, September 14, 2017, https://www.entitymag.com/eleanor-roosevelt-quotes/.

2. Drake Baer, "Dwight Eisenhower Nailed a Major Insight about Productivity," *Business Insider*, April 10, 2014, https://www.businessinsider.com/dwight-eisenhower-nailed-a-major-insight-about-productivity-2014-4.

3. Paul Casciato, "Facebook and Other Social Media Cost UK Billions," *Reuters*, August 5, 2010, https://www.reuters.com/article/idINIndia-50661520100805.

4. Peter Drucker, *Management*, revised edition (New York: HarperCollins, 2008).

3. BE SPECIFIC

1. "Jane Wagner Quotes," BrainyQuote, https://www.brainyquote.com/quotes/jane_wagner_105976.

2. "Quotes," W. Edwards Deming Institute, https://deming.org/quotes/10084/.

3. Fred Reichheld, "The One Number You Need to Grow," *Harvard Business Review*, December 2003.

4. Fred Reichheld, *The Ultimate Question: Driving Good Profits and True Growth* (Boston, MA: Harvard Business School Publishing, 2006).

5. Fred Reichheld and Rob Markey, *The Ultimate Question 2.0: How Net Promoter Companies Thrive in a Customer-Driven World*, revised and expanded edition (Boston, MA: Harvard Business School Publishing, 2011).

6. Jack Welch, *Jack: Straight from the Gut* (New York: Warner Books Inc., 2001).

7. John F. Kennedy, "Special Message to the Congress on Urgent National Needs," Speech, Washington DC, May 25, 1961, NASA, https://www.nasa.gov/vision/space/features/jfk_speech_text.html.

8. Kennedy, "Special Message to the Congress."

9. Elizabeth Howell, "Apollo 11's Vintage Tech: The Most Amazing Moon Landing Innovations," *Space*, July 24, 2014, https://www.space.com/26630-apollo-11-vintage-tech-innovations.html.

4. MAKE IT PERSONAL

1. "The Man," Mies van der Rohe Society, https://www.miessociety.org/the-man.
2. "Quote by Mark Twain," Goodreads, https://www.goodreads.com/quotes/219455-the-secret-of-getting-ahead-is-getting-started-the-secret.
3. Chip Heath and Dan Heath, *Switch: How to Change Things When Change Is Hard* (New York: Crown Publishing Group, 2010).

5. USE PREDICTIVE BEHAVIORS TO TELL THE FUTURE

1. Anatole France, *La Vie Littéraire*, second edition (Paris: Calmann Lévy, 1888).
2. Brandon Gaille, "Chick-fil-A Business Model and Growth Strategy," Brandon-Gaille.com, March 2, 2015, https://brandongaille.com/chick-fil-a-business-model-and-growth-strategy/.
3. "Our Culture and Values," Chick-fil-A, https://www.chick-fil-a.com/careers/culture.
4. Jennifer L. Goss, "Henry Ford and the Auto Assembly Line," ThoughtCo, updated January 23, 2020, https://www.thoughtco.com/henry-ford-and-the-assembly-line-1779201.
5. Monte Burke, "The Most Powerful Coach in Sports," *Forbes*, August 14, 2008, https://www.forbes.com/forbes/2008/0901/092.html?sh=45c4ef413b21.
6. *Nick Saban: Gamechanger*, directed by Trey Reynolds (Memphis, TN: Flashlight Media Group, 2010).
7. "Guinea Worm Eradication Program," The Carter Center, https://www.cartercenter.org/health/guinea_worm/index.html.
8. "NWCR Facts," The National Weight Control Registry, http://www.nwcr.ws/research/.
9. "Homepage," Lose It!, https://loseit.com/.
10. Aristotle, *Nicomachean Ethics*, revised edition, edited by H. Rackham, Loeb Classical Library (Cambridge, MA: Harvard University Press, 1934).
11. "Charles C. Noble Quotes," Quotes.net, https://www.quotes.net/quote/57520.
12. John Wooden and Steve Jamison, *Wooden on Leadership: How to Create a Winning Organization* (New York: McGraw Hill Education, 2005).
13. Teresa M. Amabile and Steven J. Kramer, "What Really Motivates Employees," *Harvard Business Review*, January–February 2010.
14. Roald Amundsen, *The South Pole* (McLean, VA: IndyPublish.com, 2009).
15. Pallab Ghosh, "Researchers Praise Scott's South Pole Scientific Legacy," BBC News, January 17, 2012, https://www.bbc.com/news/science-environment-16530953.
16. Jim Collins and Morten T. Hansen, *Great by Choice* (New York: Harper Business, 2011).
17. Collins and Hansen, *Great by Choice*.
18. "Scott's Last Expedition," Scott Polar Research Institute, Department of Geography, University of Cambridge, https://www.spri.cam.ac.uk/museum/diaries/scottslastexpedition/category/chapter-xx-the-last-march/.
19. Samuel Smiles, *Life and Labour* (London: John Murray, 1887).

6. DO THE MATH

1. Joseph Grenny, David Maxfield, Ron McMillan, Kerry Patterson, and Al Switzler, *Influencer: The Power to Change Anything* (New York: McGraw Hill, 2007).
2. Alfred Lansing, *Endurance: Shackleton's Incredible Voyage* (New York: Basic Books, 2015); Jim Collins and Morten T. Hansen, *Great by Choice* (New York: Harper Business, 2011).
3. Fred Reichheld, *The Ultimate Question: Driving Good Profits and True Growth* (Boston, MA: Harvard Business School Publishing, 2006); Fred Reichheld and Rob Markey, *The Ultimate Question 2.0: How Net Promoter Companies Thrive in a Customer-Driven World*, revised and expanded edition (Boston, MA: Harvard Business School Publishing, 2011).
4. Aldous Huxley, *Proper Studies* (London: Chatto & Windus, 1927).
5. "The Importance of Customer Service at Enterprise Rent A Car," Business Case Studies, September 17, 2019, https://businesscasestudies.co.uk/the-importance-of-customer-service-at-enterprise-rent-a-car/.
6. "The Importance of Customer Service at Enterprise Rent A Car."
7. "Confucius Quotes," BrainyQuote, https://www.brainyquote.com/quotes/confucius_140548.
8. Sun Tzu, *The Art of War*, reprint (Minneapolis, MN: Filiquarian, 2007).

PART II: THE EXECUTION ADVANTAGE

1. Jeffrey E. Garten, *The Mind of the CEO: The World's Business Leaders Talk about Leadership, Responsibility, the Future of the Corporation, and What Keeps Them Up at Night* (New York: Basic Books, 2001).

7. TALENT ADVANTAGE

1. Jim Collins, *Good to Great: Why Some Companies Make the Leap . . . and Others Don't* (New York: HarperCollins, 2001).
2. "How Millennials Want to Work and Live," Gallup, 2016, https://www.gallup.com/workplace/238073/millennials-work-live.aspx.
3. Janet Boydell, Barry Deutsch, and Brad Remillard, *You're Not the Person I Hired! A CEO's Survival Guide to Hiring Top Talent* (Bloomington, IN: AuthorHouse, 2006).
4. Duff Watkins, "Employing People? Flip a Coin!" Headhunter Confessions, May 26, 2013, https://headhunterconfesses.wordpress.com/2013/05/26/employing-people-flip-a-coin/.
5. Greg Alexander and Bradford D. Smart, *Topgrading for Sales: World-Class Methods to Interview, Hire, and Coach Top Sales Representatives* (New York: Penguin Group, 2008).
6. Alexander and Smart, *Topgrading for Sales*.
7. Jack Welch, *Jack: Straight from the Gut* (New York: Warner Books Inc., 2001).
8. Marcel Schwantes, "Warren Buffett Looks for Intelligence and Initiative When Hiring People. But Without This Third Trait, 'the First Two Will Kill You,'" Inc., December

3, 2018, https://www.inc.com/marcel-schwantes/warren-buffett-says-you-should-hire-people-with-3-traits-but-only-1-separates-successful-people-from-everyone-else.html.

9. Kenneth Labich and Ani Hadjian, "Is Herb Kelleher America's Best CEO?" *Fortune*, May 2, 1994, https://archive.fortune.com/magazines/fortune/fortune_archive/1994/05/02/79246/index.htm.

10. *Glengarry Glen Ross*, directed by James Foley (Burbank, CA: New Line Cinema, 1992).

11. Tom Peters, *The Pursuit of WOW! Every Person's Guide to Topsy-Turvy Times* (New York: Vintage Books, 1994).

12. Matt Mullenweg, "Hire by Auditions, Not Resumes," *Harvard Business Review*, January 7, 2014, https://hbr.org/2014/01/hire-by-auditions-not-resumes.

13. Marcus Buckingham and Curt Coffman, *First, Break All the Rules: What the World's Greatest Managers Do Differently* (Washington, DC: Gallup Press, 1999).

8. TRAINING ADVANTAGE

1. Olivier Poirier-Leroy, "8 Michael Phelps Quotes to Get You Fired Up," SwimSwam, July 21, 2016, https://swimswam.com/8-MICHAEL-phelps-quotes-get-fired/.

2. Catherine Clifford, "Olympic Hero Michael Phelps Says the Secret to His Success Is One Most People Overlook," CNBC, February 14, 2017, https://www.cnbc.com/2017/02/14/olympic-hero-michael-phelps-says-this-is-the-secret-to-his-success.html.

3. Mark Twain, *Collected Tales, Sketches, Speeches and Essays: 1891–1910* (New York: Library of America, 1992).

4. Malcom Gladwell, *Outliers: The Story of Success* (Boston, MA: Little, Brown and Company, 2011).

5. T. J. Murphy, "CrossFit, Olympic Wrestling and Dan Gable," VeloPress, https://www.velopress.com/crossfit-olympic-wrestling-and-dan-gable/.

6. "Bio," DanGable.com, https://dangable.com/bio/#!/full-biography.

7. Rob Hodgetts, "Tiger Woods: When He Turned Down a Beer from John Daly," CNN, April 28, 2016, https://edition.cnn.com/2016/04/28/golf/john-daly-tiger-woods-beer-story/index.html.

8. "Employees," Ziglar, https://www.ziglar.com/quotes/employees/.

9. Henrik Edberg, "Michael Phelps' Top 5 Fundamentals for Pulling Off the Impossible," *The Positivity Blog*, updated April 14, 2021, https://www.positivityblog.com/michael-phelps-top-5-fundamentals-for-pulling-off-the-impossible/.

10. Benjamin Fine, "Einstein Stresses Critical Thinking; Opposing Early Specialties, He Says College Must Aim at 'Harmonious' Personality," *New York Times*, October 5, 1952.

11. Anthony Robbins, *Awaken the Giant Within: How to Take Immediate Control of Your Mental, Emotional, Physical and Financial Destiny!* (New York: Simon & Schuster, 1991).

12. Thomas Oppong, "Daily Routines of Nikola Tesla, Mozart, Hemingway, Woody Allen, Maya Angelou, van Gogh, Stephen King, and Nabokov," CNBC, February 7, 2017, https://www.cnbc.com/2017/02/07/daily-routines-of-tesla-mozart-hemingway-and-more.html.

13. *8 Mile*, directed by Curtis Hanson (Universal City, CA: Universal Pictures, 2002).

14. John Wooden and Steve Jamison, *Wooden on Leadership: How to Create a Winning Organization* (New York: McGraw Hill Education, 2005).

15. Ken Blanchard, "Feedback Is the Breakfast of Champions," KenBlanchardbooks.com, https://www.kenblanchardbooks.com/feedback-is-the-breakfast-of-champions/.

16. Angel Melendez, "Jimmy Carr Invites Miami Comedy Fans to Heckle Him Onstage," *Miami New Times*, March 27, 2017, https://www.miaminewtimes.com/arts/jimmy-carr-headed-to-miamis-fillmore-with-best-of-ultimate-gold-greatest-hits-tour-9228661.

17. Gordon Tredgold, "50 Inspirational Pieces of Wisdom from Muhammad Ali," Inc., June 7, 2016, https://www.inc.com/gordon-tredgold/muhammad-ali-50-inspiring-thoughts-from-the-greatest-of-all-time.html.

18. Wolfgang Amadeus Mozart, *Mozart: The Man and the Artist, as Revealed in His Own Words*, compiled and annotated by Friedrich Kerst, translated by Henry Edward Krehbiel (Middlesex, England: The Echo Library, 2007).

19. Harvey Mackay, "If You Don't Have a Plan B, You Don't Have a Plan," *The Business Journals*, March 16, 2014, https://www.bizjournals.com/bizjournals/how-to/growth-strategies/2014/03/harvey-mackay-you-need-a-plan-b.html.

9. MOTIVATION ADVANTAGE

1. "Motivation: The Art of Getting People to Do What You Want," *STL Blog*, https://www.stl-training.co.uk/b/motivation/.

2. "Behind the Curtain: The Late Johnny Carson's Loved Ones Reveal the Shy Loner Only They Knew," Closer, April 18, 2015, https://www.closerweekly.com/posts/the-late-johnny-carson-s-loved-ones-reveal-the-shy-loner-only-they-knew-56426/.

3. Joseph Grenny, David Maxfield, Ron McMillan, Kerry Patterson, and Al Switzler, *Influencer: The Power to Change Anything* (New York: McGraw Hill, 2007).

4. Morty Ain, "Aly Raisman: 'Everything I Put into My Body Is for Gymnastics,'" ESPN, July 2, 2015, https://www.espn.com/olympics/story/_/page/bodyalyraisman/olympic-gymnast-aly-raisman-balancing-life-gymnastics-espn-magazine-body-issue.

5. Winston Churchill, "Give Us the Tools," Broadcast, London, February 9, 1941, Transcript, https://winstonchurchill.org/resources/speeches/1941-1945-war-leader/give-us-the-tools/.

6. "Napoleon Bonaparte," History.com, November 9, 2009, https://www.history.com/topics/france/napoleon.

7. Chester Elton and Adrian Gostick, *The Carrot Principle: How the Best Managers Use Recognition to Engage Their Employees, Retain Talent, and Drive Performance* (New York: Free Press, 2007).

8. Fred Reichheld and W. Earl Sasser, "Zero Defections: Quality Comes to Services," *Harvard Business Review*, September/October 1990.

9. "Quote by Steven Wright," SComedy, https://scomedy.com/quotes/10606.

10. Richard H. Thaler and Cass R. Sunstein, *Nudge: Improving Decisions about Health, Wealth, and Happiness* (London: Penguin Books, 2008).

11. Stephen C. Lundin, Harry Paul, and John Christensen, *Fish! A Proven Way to Boost Morale and Improve Results* (New York: Hachette Book Group, 2000).

12. "Lou Holtz Quotes," BrainyQuote, https://www.brainyquote.com/quotes/lou_holtz_383260.

10. ACCOUNTABILITY ADVANTAGE

1. Sandy Gallagher, "Accountability," Proctor Gallagher Institute, March 13, 2017, https://www.proctorgallagherinstitute.com/17557/accountability.

2. *The Last Dance*, directed by Jason Hehir (Los Gatos, CA: Netflix and ESPN Films, 2020).

3. "Dalai Lama XIV Quotes," Quotefancy, https://quotefancy.com/dalai-lama-quotes.

4. Michael Gerber, *The E-Myth: Why Most Businesses Don't Work and What to Do about It* (Pensacola, FL: Ballinger Publishing, 1988).

5. Carrie Wilkerson, *The Barefoot Executive: The Ultimate Guide for Being Your Own Boss and Achieving Financial Freedom* (New York: HarperCollins, 2011).

6. Patrick Lencioni, *The Five Dysfunctions of a Team: A Leadership Fable* (San Francisco: Jossey-Bass, 2002).

7. John Rossman, *The Amazon Way: 14 Leadership Principles behind the World's Most Disruptive Company* (Seattle, WA: Clyde Hill Publishing, 2014).

8. Peter Drucker, *Managing the Non-Profit Organization: Practices and Principles* (New York: HarperCollins, 1990).

9. Mark Twain, *Mark Twain's Notebook (1894)*, edited by Albert Bigelow Paine (New York: Harper & Brothers Publishers, 1935).

10. Joe Hoyt, "Jimmy Johnson on Report of Cowboys WR Dez Bryant Missing Meetings: 'We Wouldn't Accept That,'" *Dallas Morning News*, October 3, 2016, https://www.dallasnews.com/sports/cowboys/2016/10/03/jimmy-johnson-on-report-of-cowboys-wr-dez-bryant-missing-meetings-we-wouldn-t-accept-that/.

11. Jim Kneiszel, "Drive Thy Business, or It Will Drive Thee," *PRO Monthly*, https://www.promonthly.com/editorial/2010/07/drive-thy-business-or-it-will-drive-thee.

12. "John F. Kennedy Quotations," John F. Kennedy Presidential Library and Museum, https://www.jfklibrary.org/learn/about-jfk/life-of-john-f-kennedy/john-f-kennedy-quotations#C.

13. JD, "The Best Lessons I Learned from John Wooden," Sources of Insight, https://sourcesofinsight.com/lessons-learned-from-john-wooden/.

14. Viktor E. Frankl, *Man's Search for Meaning: An Introduction to Logotherapy* (Boston, MA: Beacon Press, 1959).

15. John C. Maxwell, *Failing Forward: Turning Mistakes into Stepping Stones for Success* (New York: HarperCollins Leadership, 2007).

16. "Quote by Robert F. Kennedy," Goodreads, https://www.goodreads.com/quotes/5651-only-those-who-dare-to-fail-greatly-can-ever-achieve.

17. "Lincoln's 'Failures,'" Abraham Lincoln Online, http://www.abrahamlincolnonline.org/lincoln/education/failures.htm.

18. Deborah Headstrom-Page, *From Telegraph to Light Bulb with Thomas Edison* (Nashville, TN: B&H Publishing, 2007).

19. Jim Collins and Morten T. Hansen, *Great by Choice* (New York: Harper Business, 2011).

20. Earl Nightingale, *The Strangest Secret* (Wheeling, IL: Nightingale-McHugh Company, 1957).

21. Bill Taylor, "What Breaking the 4-Minute Mile Taught Us about the Limits of Conventional Thinking," *Harvard Business Review*, March 9, 2018.

22. A. G. Lafley and Roger L. Martin, *Playing to Win: How Strategy Really Works* (Boston, MA: Harvard Business School Publishing, 2013).

23. Kerry Lynch, "Blue Angels 'Boss' Stresses Need for Debrief in Ops," AINonline, November 1, 2017, https://www.ainonline.com/aviation-news/business-aviation/2017-11-01/blue-angels-boss-stresses-need-debrief-ops.

24. Blaine Lee, *The Power Principle: Influence with Honor* (New York: Free Press, 1998).

25. "Quotes about Preparation," LeadershipNow, https://www.leadershipnow.com/preparationquotes.html.

26. Mary Bagley, "George Washington Carver: Biography, Inventions & Quotes," LiveScience, December 6, 2013, https://www.livescience.com/41780-george-washington-carver.html.

11. COMPANY ADVANTAGE

1. Steve Jobs, "iPhone Keynote 2007," Genius, 2007, transcription, https://genius.com/Steve-jobs-iphone-keynote-2007-annotated.

2. Lionel Sujay Vailshery, "Apple iPhone Sales Worldwide 2007–2018," Statista, January 22, 2021, https://www.statista.com/statistics/276306/global-apple-iphone-sales-since-fiscal-year-2007/.

3. Martyn Cornell, "The Fall of Schlitz: How Milwaukee's Famous Beer Became Infamous," The Beer Connoisseur, January 10, 2010, https://beerconnoisseur.com/articles/how-milwaukees-famous-beer-became-infamous.

4. Donald R. Keough, *The Ten Commandments for Business Failure* (New York: Portfolio, 2008).

5. Julia Hanna, "Walmart's Workforce of the Future," Harvard Business School, July 7, 2019, https://hbswk.hbs.edu/item/walmart-s-workforce-of-the-future.

6. Chad Rubin, "Walmart Supply Chain 2021: Why It Continues to Dominate," Skubana, January 4, 2020, https://www.skubana.com/blog/walmart-leading-way.

7. Robert Reiss, "How Top CEOs Transform Companies Around the Customer, Like the New Kentucky Derby Videoboard," Forbes, April 21, 2014, https://www.forbes.com/sites/robertreiss/2014/04/21/how-top-ceos-transform-companies-around-the-customer-like-the-new-kentucky-derby-videoboard/?sh=6238ac0b32ac.

8. "The Five Guys Story," Five Guys, http://www.fiveguys.com/Fans/The-Five-Guys-Story.

9. Matthew McCreary, "Chick-fil-A Makes More per Restaurant Than McDonald's, Starbucks and Subway Combined . . . and It's Closed on Sundays," Entrepreneur, https://www.entrepreneur.com/article/320615.

10. Philip Kotler and Kevin Lane Keller, *Marketing Management*, fourteenth edition (Upper Saddle River, NJ: Prentice Hall, 2012).

11. Monica Torres, "Steve Jobs Believed So Much in the Power of Refusal That He Asked Apple Head of Design Jony Ive How Many Times He Said 'No' Each Day," Business Insider, October 11, 2017, https://www.businessinsider.com/steve-jobs-asked-jony-ive-how-many-times-he-said-no-2017-10.

12. Michael Simmons, "Warren Buffett: 'Really Successful People Say No to Almost Everything,'" Accelerated Intelligence, January 7, 2019, https://medium.com/accelerated-intelligence/warren-buffett-really-successful-people-say-no-to-almost-everything-ab78832ffebc.

13. Carmine Gallo, "Steve Jobs: Get Rid of the Crappy Stuff," *Forbes*, May 16, 2011, https://www.forbes.com/sites/carminegallo/2011/05/16/steve-jobs-get-rid-of-the-crappy-stuff/?sh=4a5ffec07145.

14. A. G. Lafley and Roger L. Martin, *Playing to Win: How Strategy Really Works* (Boston, MA: Harvard Business School Publishing, 2013).

15. Kathy Flanigan, "Holy Cow: New Glarus Makes the List of Top-Selling Breweries Again, Even Though It Only Sells in Wisconsin," *Milwaukee Journal Sentinel*, April 2, 2020, https://www.jsonline.com/story/entertainment/beer/2020/04/02/new-glarus-brewing-ranks-15th-among-u-s-craft-breweries-sales/5111781002/.

16. Visakan Veerasamy, "Kleenex Marketing Strategy: Making Content Marketing Fun," ReferralCandy, June 19, 2020, https://www.referralcandy.com/blog/kleenex-marketing-strategy/.

17. Sun Tzu, *The Art of War*, reprint (Minneapolis, MN: Filiquarian, 2007).

18. Thomas Winninger, *Price Wars: How to Win the Battle for Your Customer!* (Roseville, CA: Prima Publishing, 1995).

19. Chan Kim and Renée Mauborgne, *Blue Ocean Strategy: How to Create Uncontested Market Space and Make Competition Irrelevant* (Boston, MA: Harvard Business Review Press, 2005).

20. "Napoleon Bonaparte Quotes," BrainyQuote, https://www.brainyquote.com/quotes/napoleon_bonaparte_103585.

21. "Aristophanes Quotes," BrainyQuote, https://www.brainyquote.com/quotes/aristophanes_141557.

22. "Walt Disney Quotes," BrainyQuote, https://www.brainyquote.com/quotes/walt_disney_131648.

23. Peter Davis, "The Challenge of the Third Generation," *Family Business*, March 1990, https://www.familybusinessmagazine.com/challenge-third-generation.

24. J. K. Rowling, "Text of J.K. Rowling's Speech," *Harvard Gazette*, June 5, 2008, https://news.harvard.edu/gazette/story/2008/06/text-of-j-k-rowling-speech/.

25. Alison Millington, "J.K. Rowling's Pitch for 'Harry Potter' Was Rejected 12 Times—Read the Now-Famous Letter Here," Insider, July 30, 2018, https://www.insider.com/revealed-jk-rowlings-original-pitch-for-harry-potter-2017-10.

26. William Miller, "Death of a Genius: His Fourth Dimension, Time, Overtakes Einstein," *LIFE*, May 2, 1955, https://books.google.com/books/about/LIFE.html?id=dlYEAAAAMBAJ.

27. Sergei Klebnikov, "Streaming Wars Continue: Here's How Much Netflix, Amazon, Disney+ and Their Rivals Are Spending on New Content," *Forbes*, May 22, 2020, https://www.forbes.com/sites/sergeiklebnikov/2020/05/22/streaming-wars-continue-heres-how-much-netflix-amazon-disney-and-their-rivals-are-spending-on-new-content/?sh=7f5ce64e623b.

28. Anita M. McGahan and Michael E. Porter, "What Do We Know about Variance in Accounting Profitability?" *Management Science* 48, no. 7 (2002), http://www.jstor.org/stable/822694.

29. James Allen, Frederick Reichheld, Barney Hamilton, and Rob Markey, "Closing the Delivery Gap," Bain & Company, 2005, https://www.bain.com/contentassets/41326e0918834cd1a0102fdd0810535d/bb_closing_delivery_gap.pdf.

30. Christina Sterbenz, "12 Famous Quotes That Always Get Misattributed," *Business Insider*, October 7, 2013, https://www.businessinsider.com/misattributed-quotes-2013-10.

31. James Allen and Chris Zook, "The Great Repeatable Business Model," *Harvard Business Review*, November 2011, https://hbr.org/2011/11/the-great-repeatable-business-model.

32. Phillip Matier and Andrew Ross, "Bushman of Fisherman's Wharf Gets the Last Ugga-Bugga/D.A. Drops Stack of Complaints Over His Sidewalk Antics," *San Francisco Chronicle*, April 7, 2004, https://www.sfgate.com/bayarea/matier-ross/article/Bushman-of-Fisherman-s-Wharf-gets-the-last-3313974.php.

33. Jacob Morgan, *The Future of Work: Attract New Talent, Build Better Leaders, and Create a Competitive Organization* (Hoboken, NJ: Wiley, 2014).
34. "My Life Is My Message Gallery," Gandhi Ashram at Sabarmati, https://gandhi-ashramsabarmati.org/en/the-museum-falang/my-life-is-my-message-gallery.html.
35. "'The Successful Warrior Is the Average Man with Laser-like Focus'—Bruce Lee," *CIO Views Magazine*, October 11, 2019, https://medium.com/@cioviewssocial/the-successful-warrior-is-the-average-man-with-laser-like-focus-bruce-lee-e50f8e18ea80.
36. "How Sir Richard Branson Played a Part in Our Rebranding to Red Bee Media," Red Bee Media, November 14, 2017, https://www.redbeemedia.com/blog/red-bee-rebrand/.
37. Kate Torgovnick May, "10 Brand Stories from Tim Leberecht's TED Talk," *TEDBlog*, October 9, 2012, https://blog.ted.com/10-brand-stories-from-tim-leberechts-tedtalk/.
38. Tsufit, *Step into the Spotlight! 'Cause ALL Business Is Show Business!* (Pennsauken, NJ: BookBaby, 2008).

WRAP-UP

1. Mia Hamm, *Go for the Goal: A Champion's Guide to Winning in Soccer and Life* (New York: HarperCollins, 1999).

Bibliography

8 Mile. Directed by Curtis Hanson. Universal City, CA: Universal Pictures, 2002.

"65 Bill Murray Quotes on Success in Life." Overallmotivation.com. https://www.overallmotivation.com/quotes/bill-murray-quotes/.

"About Us." Zappos. https://www.zappos.com/about.

Ain, Morty. "Aly Raisman: 'Everything I Put into My Body Is for Gymnastics.'" ESPN. July 2, 2015. https://www.espn.com/olympics/story/_/page/bodyalyraisman/olympic-gymnast-aly-raisman-balancing-life-gymnastics-espn-magazine-body-issue.

Alexander, Greg, and Bradford D. Smart. *Topgrading for Sales: World-Class Methods to Interview, Hire, and Coach Top Sales Representatives*. New York: Penguin Group, 2008.

Allen, James, Frederick Reichheld, Barney Hamilton, and Rob Markey. "Closing the Delivery Gap." Bain & Company. 2005. https://www.bain.com/contentassets/41326e0918834cd1a0102fdd0810535d/bb_closing_delivery_gap.pdf.

Allen, James, and Chris Zook. "The Great Repeatable Business Model." *Harvard Business Review*, November 2011. https://hbr.org/2011/11/the-great-repeatable-business-model.

Alvarez, Barry, and Mike Lucas. *Don't Flinch: Barry Alvarez, the Autobiography: The Story of Wisconsin's All-Time Winningest Coach*. Stevens Point, WI: KCI Sports Publishing, 2006.

Amabile, Teresa M., and Steven J. Kramer. "What Really Motivates Employees." *Harvard Business Review*, January–February 2010.

Amundsen, Roald. *The South Pole*. McLean, VA: IndyPublish.com, 2009.

Anderson, David. "Vital Rules of Vision, Strategy & Tactics." LearnToLead. 2012. https://www.learntolead.com/articles/810-vital-rules-of-vision-strategy-tactics.

"Aristophanes Quotes." BrainyQuote. https://www.brainyquote.com/quotes/aristophanes_141557.

Aristotle. *Nicomachean Ethics*. Revised edition. Edited by H. Rackham. Loeb Classical Library. Cambridge, MA: Harvard University Press, 1934.

Baer, Drake. "Dwight Eisenhower Nailed a Major Insight about Productivity." Business Insider. April 10, 2014. https://www.businessinsider.com/dwight-eisenhower-nailed-a-major-insight-about-productivity-2014-4.

Bagley, Mary. "George Washington Carver: Biography, Inventions & Quotes." LiveScience. December 6, 2013. https://www.livescience.com/41780-george-washington-carver.html.

"Behind the Curtain: The Late Johnny Carson's Loved Ones Reveal the Shy Loner Only They Knew." Closer. April 18, 2015. https://www.closerweekly.com/posts/the-late-johnny-carson-s-loved-ones-reveal-the-shy-loner-only-they-knew-56426/.

"Bio." DanGable.com. https://dangable.com/bio/#!/full-biography.

Blanchard, Ken. "Feedback Is the Breakfast of Champions." KenBlanchardbooks.com. https://www.kenblanchardbooks.com/feedback-is-the-breakfast-of-champions/.

Boydell, Janet, Barry Deutsch, and Brad Remillard. *You're Not the Person I Hired! A CEO's Survival Guide to Hiring Top Talent*. Bloomington, IN: AuthorHouse, 2006.

Buckingham, Marcus, and Curt Coffman. *First, Break All the Rules: What the World's Greatest Managers Do Differently*. Washington, DC: Gallup Press, 1999.

Burke, Monte. "The Most Powerful Coach in Sports." Forbes. August 14, 2008. https://www.forbes.com/forbes/2008/0901/092.html?sh=45c4ef413b21.

Casciato, Paul. "Facebook and Other Social Media Cost UK Billions." Reuters. August 5, 2010. https://www.reuters.com/article/idINIndia-50661520100805.

"Charles C. Noble Quotes." Quotes.net. https://www.quotes.net/quote/57520.

Christensen, John, Stephen Lundin, and Harry Paul. *Fish! A Proven Way to Boost Morale and Improve Results*. New York: Hachette Book Group, 2000.

Churchill, Winston. "Give Us the Tools." Broadcast. London, February 9, 1941. Transcript. https://winstonchurchill.org/resources/speeches/1941-1945-war-leader/give-us-the-tools/.

Clifford, Catherine. "Olympic Hero Michael Phelps Says the Secret to His Success Is One Most People Overlook." CNBC. February 14, 2017. https://www.cnbc.com/2017/02/14/olympic-hero-michael-phelps-says-this-is-the-secret-to-his-success.html.

Climer, Amy. "5 Elements of Shackleton's Leadership." *The Deliberate Creative Blog*. December 15, 2016. https://climerconsulting.com/five-elements-shackletons-leadership/.

Collins, Jim. *Good to Great: Why Some Companies Make the Leap . . . and Others Don't*. New York: HarperCollins, 2001.

Collins, Jim, and Morten T. Hansen. *Great by Choice*. New York: Harper Business, 2011.

"Confucius Quotes." BrainyQuote. https://www.brainyquote.com/quotes/confucius_140548.

Cornell, Martyn. "The Fall of Schlitz: How Milwaukee's Famous Beer Became Infamous." The Beer Connoisseur. January 10, 2010. https://beerconnoisseur.com/articles/how-milwaukees-famous-beer-became-infamous.

Covey, Stephen R. *The 7 Habits of Highly Effective People: Powerful Lessons in Personal Change*. New York: Free Press, 1989.

Covey, Stephen, A. Roger Merrill, and Rebecca R. Merrill. *First Things First*. New York: Free Press, 2003.

"Dalai Lama XIV Quotes." Quotefancy. https://quotefancy.com/dalai-lama-quotes.

Davis, Michelle F. "Dimon Sees Lasting Damage if Workers Don't Return to Offices." Bloomberg. September 15, 2020. https://www.bloomberg.com/news/articles/2020-09-15/dimon-sees-long-term-damage-if-people-don-t-get-back-to-work.

Davis, Peter. "The Challenge of the Third Generation." *Family Business*. March 1990. https://www.familybusinessmagazine.com/challenge-third-generation.

Drucker, Peter. *The Effective Executive*. New York: Harper & Row, 1967.

———. *Management*. Revised edition. New York: HarperCollins, 2008.

———. *Managing the Non-Profit Organization: Practices and Principles*. New York: HarperCollins, 1990.

Edberg, Henrik. "Michael Phelps' Top 5 Fundamentals for Pulling Off the Impossible." *The Positivity Blog*, updated April 14, 2021. https://www.positivityblog.com/michael-phelps-top-5-fundamentals-for-pulling-off-the-impossible/.

Elton, Chester, and Adrian Gostick. *The Carrot Principle: How the Best Managers Use Recognition to Engage Their Employees, Retain Talent, and Drive Performance*. New York: Free Press, 2007.

———. *The Orange Revolution: How One Great Team Can Transform an Entire Organization*. New York: Free Press, 2010.

"Employees." Ziglar. https://www.ziglar.com/quotes/employees/.

Fine, Benjamin. "Einstein Stresses Critical Thinking; Opposing Early Specialties, He Says College Must Aim at 'Harmonious' Personality." *New York Times*. October 5, 1952.

Flanigan, Kathy. "Holy Cow: New Glarus Makes the List of Top-Selling Breweries Again, Even Though It Only Sells in Wisconsin." *Milwaukee Journal Sentinel*. April 2, 2020. https://www.jsonline.com/story/entertainment/beer/2020/04/02/new-glarus-brewing-ranks-15th-among-u-s-craft-breweries-sales/5111781002/.

France, Anatole. *La Vie Littéraire*. Second edition. Paris: Calmann Lévy, 1888.

Frankl, Viktor E. *Man's Search for Meaning: An Introduction to Logotherapy*. Boston, MA: Beacon Press, 1959.

Gaille, Brandon. "Chick-fil-A Business Model and Growth Strategy." BrandonGaille.com. March 2, 2015. https://brandongaille.com/chick-fil-a-business-model-and-growth-strategy/.

Gallagher, Sandy. "Accountability." Proctor Gallagher Institute. March 13, 2017. https://www.proctorgallagherinstitute.com/17557/accountability.

Gallo, Carmine. "Steve Jobs: Get Rid of the Crappy Stuff." Forbes. May 16, 2011. https://www.forbes.com/sites/carminegallo/2011/05/16/steve-jobs-get-rid-of-the-crappy-stuff/?sh=4a5ffec07145.

Garten, Jeffrey E. *The Mind of the CEO: The World's Business Leaders Talk about Leadership, Responsibility, the Future of the Corporation, and What Keeps Them Up at Night*. New York: Basic Books, 2001.

Gerber, Michael. *The E Myth: Why Most Businesses Don't Work and What to Do about It*. Pensacola, FL: Ballinger Publishing, 1988.

Ghosh, Pallab. "Researchers Praise Scott's South Pole Scientific Legacy." BBC News. January 17, 2012. https://www.bbc.com/news/science-environment-16530953.

Gladwell, Malcolm. *Outliers: The Story of Success*. Boston, MA: Little, Brown and Company, 2011.

Glengarry Glen Ross. Directed by James Foley. Burbank, CA: New Line Cinema, 1992.

Goss, Jennifer L. "Henry Ford and the Auto Assembly Line." ThoughtCo. Updated January 23, 2020. https://www.thoughtco.com/henry-ford-and-the-assembly-line-1779201.

Grenny, Joseph, David Maxfield, Ron McMillan, Kerry Patterson, and Al Switzler. *Influencer: The Power to Change Anything*. New York: McGraw Hill, 2007.

"Guinea Worm Eradication Program." The Carter Center. https://www.cartercenter.org/health/guinea_worm/index.html.

Hamm, Mia. *Go for the Goal: A Champion's Guide to Winning in Soccer and Life*. New York: HarperCollins, 1999.

Hanna, Julia. "Walmart's Workforce of the Future." Harvard Business School. July 7, 2019. https://hbswk.hbs.edu/item/walmart-s-workforce-of-the-future.

Headstrom-Page, Deborah. *From Telegraph to Light Bulb with Thomas Edison*. Nashville, TN: B&H Publishing, 2007.

Heath, Chip, and Dan Heath. *Switch: How to Change Things When Change Is Hard*. New York: Crown Publishing Group, 2010.

Hodgetts, Rob. "Tiger Woods: When He Turned Down a Beer from John Daly." CNN. April 28, 2016. https://edition.cnn.com/2016/04/28/golf/john-daly-tiger-woods-beer-story/index.html.

"Homepage." Lose It! https://loseit.com/.

Horwath, Rich. *Deep Dive: The Proven Method for Building Strategy, Focusing Your Resources, and Taking Smart Action*. Austin, TX: Greenleaf Book Group Press, 2009.

Howell, Elizabeth. "Apollo 11's Vintage Tech: The Most Amazing Moon Landing Innovations." Space.com. July 24, 2014. https://www.space.com/26630-apollo-11-vintage-tech-innovations.html.

"How Millennials Want to Work and Live." Gallup. 2016. https://www.gallup.com/workplace/238073/millennials-work-live.aspx.

"How Sir Richard Branson Played a Part in Our Rebranding to Red Bee Media." Red Bee Media. November 14, 2017. https://www.redbeemedia.com/blog/red-bee-rebrand/.

Hoyt, Joe. "Jimmy Johnson on Report of Cowboys WR Dez Bryant Missing Meetings: 'We Wouldn't Accept That.'" *Dallas Morning News*. October 3, 2016. https://www.dallasnews.com/sports/cowboys/2016/10/03/jimmy-johnson-on-report-of-cowboys-wr-dez-bryant-missing-meetings-we-wouldn-t-accept-that/.

Hsieh, Tony. *Delivering Happiness: A Path to Profits, Passion, and Purpose*. New York: Business Plus, Hachette Book Group. 2010.

Huxley, Aldous. *Proper Studies*. London: Chatto & Windus, 1927.

"Jane Wagner Quotes." BrainyQuote. https://www.brainyquote.com/quotes/jane_wagner_105976.

JD. "The Best Lessons I Learned from John Wooden." Sources of Insight. https://sourcesofinsight.com/lessons-learned-from-john-wooden/.

Jobs, Steve. "iPhone Keynote 2007." Genius. 2007. Transcription. https://genius.com/Steve-jobs-iphone-keynote-2007-annotated.

"John F. Kennedy Quotations." John F. Kennedy Presidential Library and Museum. https://www.jfklibrary.org/learn/about-jfk/life-of-john-f-kennedy/john-f-kennedy-quotations#C.

Kaplan, Robert, and David Norton. "The Office of Strategy Management." *Harvard Business Review*, October 2005.

Kennedy, John F. "Special Message to the Congress on Urgent National Needs." Speech, Washington DC, May 25, 1961. NASA. https://www.nasa.gov/vision/space/features/jfk_speech_text.html.

Keough, Donald R. *The Ten Commandments for Business Failure*. New York: Portfolio, 2008.

Kim, Chan, and Renée Mauborgne. *Blue Ocean Strategy: How to Create Uncontested Market Space and Make Competition Irrelevant*. Boston, MA: Harvard Business Review Press, 2005.

Klebnikov, Sergei. "Streaming Wars Continue: Here's How Much Netflix, Amazon, Disney+ and Their Rivals Are Spending on New Content." Forbes. May 22, 2020. https://www.forbes.com/sites/sergeiklebnikov/2020/05/22/streaming-wars-continue-heres-how-much-netflix-amazon-disney-and-their-rivals-are-spending-on-new-content/?sh=7f5ce64e623b.

Kneiszel, Jim. "Drive Thy Business, or It Will Drive Thee." *PRO Monthly*. https://www.promonthly.com/editorial/2010/07/drive-thy-business-or-it-will-drive-thee.

Kotler, Philip, and Kevin Lane Keller. *Marketing Management*. Fourteenth edition. Upper Saddle River, NJ: Prentice Hall, 2012.

Labich, Kenneth, and Ani Hadjian. "Is Herb Kelleher America's Best CEO?" Fortune. May 2, 1994. https://archive.fortune.com/magazines/fortune/fortune_archive/1994/05/02/79246/index.htm.

Lafley, A. G., and Roger L. Martin. *Playing to Win: How Strategy Really Works*. Boston, MA: Harvard Business School Publishing, 2013.

Lakein, Alan. *How to Get Control of Your Time and Your Life*. New York: Signet, 1989.

Lansing, Alfred. *Endurance: Shackleton's Incredible Voyage*. New York: Basic Books, 2015.

Last Dance, The. Directed by Jason Hehir. Los Gatos, CA: Netflix and ESPN Films, 2020.

Lee, Blaine. *The Power Principle: Influence with Honor*. New York: Free Press, 1998.

Lencioni, Patrick. *The Five Dysfunctions of a Team: A Leadership Fable*. San Francisco: Jossey-Bass, 2002.

"Lincoln's 'Failures.'" Abraham Lincoln Online. http://www.abrahamlincolnonline.org/lincoln/education/failures.htm.

"Lou Holtz Quotes." BrainyQuote. https://www.brainyquote.com/quotes/lou_holtz_383260.

Lynch, Kerry. "Blue Angels 'Boss' Stresses Need for Debrief in Ops." AINonline. November 1, 2017. https://www.ainonline.com/aviation-news/business-aviation/2017-11-01/blue-angels-boss-stresses-need-debrief-ops.

Mackay, Harvey. "If You Don't Have a Plan B, You Don't Have a Plan." *The Business Journals*. March 16, 2014. https://www.bizjournals.com/bizjournals/how-to/growth-strategies/2014/03/harvey-mackay-you-need-a-plan-b.html.

Matier, Phillip, and Andrew Ross. "Bushman of Fisherman's Wharf Gets the Last Ugga-Bugga/D.A. Drops Stack of Complaints over His Sidewalk Antics." *San Francisco Chronicle*, April 7, 2004. https://www.sfgate.com/bayarea/matier-ross/article/Bushman-of-Fisherman-s-Wharf-gets-the-last-3313974.php.

Maxwell, John C. *Failing Forward: Turning Mistakes into Stepping Stones for Success*. New York: HarperCollins Leadership, 2007.

May, Kate Torgovnick. "10 Brand Stories from Tim Leberecht's TED Talk." *TEDBlog*, October 9, 2012. https://blog.ted.com/10-brand-stories-from-tim-leberechts-tedtalk/.

McCreary, Matthew. "Chick-fil-A Makes More per Restaurant Than McDonald's, Starbucks and Subway Combined . . . and It's Closed on Sundays." Entrepreneur. https://www.entrepreneur.com/article/320615.

McGahan, Anita M., and Michael E. Porter. "What Do We Know about Variance in Accounting Profitability?" *Management Science* 48, no. 7 (2002): 834–51. http://www.jstor.org/stable/822694.

"Meet our Monkeys." Zappos. https://www.zappos.com/c/about-zappos-monkeys/.

Melendez, Angel. "Jimmy Carr Invites Miami Comedy Fans to Heckle Him Onstage." *Miami New Times*. March 27, 2017. https://www.miaminewtimes.com/arts/jimmy-carr-headed-to-miamis-fillmore-with-best-of-ultimate-gold-greatest-hits-tour-9228661.

Miller, William. "Death of a Genius: His Fourth Dimension, Time, Overtakes Einstein." *LIFE*. May 2, 1955. https://books.google.com/books/about/LIFE.html?id=dlYEAAAAMBAJ.

Millington, Alison. "J.K. Rowling's Pitch for 'Harry Potter' Was Rejected 12 Times—Read the Now-Famous Letter Here." Insider. July 30, 2018. https://www.insider.com/revealed-jk-rowlings-original-pitch-for-harry-potter-2017-10.

Morgan, Jacob. *The Future of Work: Attract New Talent, Build Better Leaders, and Create a Competitive Organization*. Hoboken, NJ: Wiley, 2014.

"Motivation: The Art of Getting People to Do What You Want." *STL Blog*. https://www.stl-training.co.uk/b/motivation/.

Mozart, Wolfgang Amadeus. *Mozart: The Man and the Artist, as Revealed in His Own Words*. Compiled and annotated by Friedrich Kerst. Translated by Henry Edward Krehbiel. Middlesex, England: The Echo Library, 2007.

Mullenweg, Matt. "Hire by Auditions, Not Resumes." *Harvard Business Review*, January 7, 2014. https://hbr.org/2014/01/hire-by-auditions-not-resumes.
Murphy, T. J. "CrossFit, Olympic Wrestling and Dan Gable." VeloPress. https://www.velopress.com/crossfit-olympic-wrestling-and-dan-gable/.
"My Life Is My Message Gallery." Gandhi Ashram at Sabarmati. https://gandhiashramsabarmati.org/en/the-museum-falang/my-life-is-my-message-gallery.html.
"Napoleon Bonaparte." History.com. November 9, 2009. https://www.history.com/topics/france/napoleon.
"Napoleon Bonaparte Quotes." BrainyQuote. https://www.brainyquote.com/quotes/napoleon_bonaparte_103585.
Nick Saban: Gamechanger. Directed by Trey Reynolds. Memphis, TN: Flashlight Media Group, 2010.
Nightingale, Earl. *The Strangest Secret*. Wheeling, IL: Nightingale-McHugh Company, 1957.
"NWCR Facts." The National Weight Control Registry. http://www.nwcr.ws/research/.
Oppong, Thomas. "Daily Routines of Nikola Tesla, Mozart, Hemingway, Woody Allen, Maya Angelou, van Gogh, Stephen King, and Nabokov." CNBC. February 7, 2017. https://www.cnbc.com/2017/02/07/daily-routines-of-tesla-mozart-hemingway-and-more.html.
"Our Culture and Values." Chick-fil-A. https://www.chick-fil-a.com/careers/culture.
Peters, Tom. *The Pursuit of WOW! Every Person's Guide to Topsy-Turvy Times*. New York: Vintage Books, 1994.
Platform Sports League. "Find Your 100." http://platformsportsleague.com/find-your-100/?utm_source=rss&utm_medium=rss&utm_campaign=find-your-100.
Poirier-Leroy, Olivier. "8 Michael Phelps Quotes to Get You Fired Up." SwimSwam. July 21, 2016. https://swimswam.com/8-MICHAEL-phelps-quotes-get-fired/.
"Quote by Mark Twain." Goodreads. https://www.goodreads.com/quotes/219455-the-secret-of-getting-ahead-is-getting-started-the-secret.
"Quote by Robert F. Kennedy." Goodreads. https://www.goodreads.com/quotes/5651-only-those-who-dare-to-fail-greatly-can-ever-achieve.
"Quote by Steven Wright." SComedy. https://scomedy.com/quotes/10606.
"Quotes." W. Edwards Deming Institute. https://deming.org/quotes/10084/.
"Quotes about Preparation." LeadershipNow. https://www.leadershipnow.com/preparationquotes.html.
Reichheld, Fred. "The One Number You Need to Grow." *Harvard Business Review*, December 2003.
———. "Prescription for Cutting Costs: Loyal Relationships." Bain & Company. October 25, 2001. https://media.bain.com/Images/BB_Prescription_cutting_costs.pdf.
———. *The Ultimate Question: Driving Good Profits and True Growth*. Boston, MA: Harvard Business School Publishing, 2006.
Reichheld, Fred, and Rob Markey. *The Ultimate Question 2.0: How Net Promoter Companies Thrive in a Customer-Driven World*. Revised and expanded edition. Boston, MA: Harvard Business School Publishing, 2011.
Reichheld, Fred, and W. Earl Sasser. "Zero Defections: Quality Comes to Services." *Harvard Business Review*, September/October 1990.
Reiss, Robert. "How Top CEOs Transform Companies around the Customer, like the New Kentucky Derby Videoboard." Forbes. April 21, 2014. https://www.forbes.com/sites/robertreiss/2014/04/21/how-top-ceos-transform-companies-around-the-customer-like-the-new-kentucky-derby-videoboard/?sh=6238ac0b32ac.
Robbins, Anthony. *Awaken the Giant Within: How to Take Immediate Control of Your Mental, Emotional, Physical and Financial Destiny!* New York: Simon & Schuster, 1991.

Rossman, John. *The Amazon Way: 14 Leadership Principles behind the World's Most Disruptive Company*. Seattle, WA: Clyde Hill Publishing, 2014.
Rowling, J. K. "Text of J.K. Rowling's Speech." *Harvard Gazette*. June 5, 2008. https://news.harvard.edu/gazette/story/2008/06/text-of-j-k-rowling-speech/.
Rubin, Chad. "Walmart Supply Chain 2021: Why It Continues to Dominate." Skubana. January 4, 2020. https://www.skubana.com/blog/walmart-leading-way.
Sazegar, Nicole. "19 Timeless Eleanor Roosevelt Quotes That Are Still Inspiring." *Entity*. September 14, 2017. https://www.entitymag.com/eleanor-roosevelt-quotes/.
Schwantes, Marcel. "Warren Buffett Looks for Intelligence and Initiative When Hiring People. But Without This Third Trait, 'the First Two Will Kill You.'" Inc. December 3, 2018. https://www.inc.com/marcel-schwantes/warren-buffett-says-you-should-hire-people-with-3-traits-but-only-1-separates-successful-people-from-everyone-else.html.
"Scott's Last Expedition." Scott Polar Research Institute, Department of Geography, University of Cambridge. https://www.spri.cam.ac.uk/museum/diaries/scottslastexpedition/category/chapter-xx-the-last-march/.
Simmons, Michael. "Warren Buffett: 'Really Successful People Say No to Almost Everything.'" Accelerated Intelligence. January 7, 2019. https://medium.com/accelerated-intelligence/warren-buffett-really-successful-people-say-no-to-almost-everything-ab78832ffebc.
Smiles, Samuel. *Life and Labour*. London: John Murray, 1887.
Spradlin, Dwayne. "Are You Solving the Right Problem?" *Harvard Business Review*, September 2012.
Sterbenz, Christina. "12 Famous Quotes That Always Get Misattributed." Business Insider. October 7, 2013. https://www.businessinsider.com/misattributed-quotes-2013-10.
Taylor, Bill. "What Breaking the 4-Minute Mile Taught Us about the Limits of Conventional Thinking." *Harvard Business Review*. March 9, 2018.
Thaler, Richard, and Cass Sunstein. *Nudge: Improving Decisions about Health, Wealth, and Happiness*. London: Penguin Books, 2008.
"The Five Guys Story." Five Guys. http://www.fiveguys.com/Fans/The-Five-Guys-Story.
"The Importance of Customer Service at Enterprise Rent A Car." Business Case Studies. September 17, 2019. https://businesscasestudies.co.uk/the-importance-of-customer-service-at-enterprise-rent-a-car/.
"The Man." Mies van der Rohe Society. https://www.miessociety.org/the-man.
"'The Successful Warrior Is the Average Man with Laser-like Focus'—Bruce Lee." *CIO Views Magazine*. October 11, 2019. https://medium.com/@cioviews-social/the-successful-warrior-is-the-average-man-with-laser-like-focus-bruce-lee-e50f8e18ea80.
Torres, Monica. "Steve Jobs Believed So Much in the Power of Refusal That He Asked Apple Head of Design Jony Ive How Many Times He Said 'No' Each Day." Business Insider. October 11, 2017. https://www.businessinsider.com/steve-jobs-asked-jony-ive-how-many-times-he-said-no-2017-10.
Tredgold, Gordon. "50 Inspirational Pieces of Wisdom from Muhammad Ali." Inc. June 7, 2016. https://www.inc.com/gordon-tredgold/muhammad-ali-50-inspiring-thoughts-from-the-greatest-of-all-time.html.
Tsufit. *Step into the Spotlight! 'Cause ALL Business Is Show Business!* Pennsauken, NJ: BookBaby, 2008.
Twain, Mark. *Collected Tales, Sketches, Speeches and Essays: 1891–1910*. New York: Library of America, 1992.
———. *Mark Twain's Notebook (1894)*. Edited by Albert Bigelow Paine. New York: Harper & Brothers Publishers, 1935.

Tzu, Sun. *The Art of War*. Reprint. Minneapolis, MN: Filiquarian, 2007.

Vailshery, Lionel Sujay. "Apple iPhone Sales Worldwide 2007–2018." Statista. January 22, 2021. https://www.statista.com/statistics/276306/global-apple-iphone-sales-since-fiscal-year-2007/.

Veerasamy, Visakan. "Kleenex Marketing Strategy: Making Content Marketing Fun." ReferralCandy. June 19, 2020. https://www.referralcandy.com/blog/kleenex-marketing-strategy/.

"Walt Disney Quotes." BrainyQuote. https://www.brainyquote.com/quotes/walt_disney_131648.

Watkins, Duff. "Employing People? Flip a Coin!" Headhunter Confessions. May 26, 2013. https://headhunterconfesses.wordpress.com/2013/05/26/employing-people-flip-a-coin/.

Welch, Jack. *Jack: Straight from the Gut*. New York: Warner Books Inc., 2001.

"What We Live By." Zappos. https://www.zappos.com/about/what-we-live-by.

Wilkerson, Carrie. *The Barefoot Executive: The Ultimate Guide for Being Your Own Boss and Achieving Financial Freedom*. New York: HarperCollins, 2011.

Winninger, Thomas. *Price Wars: How to Win the Battle for Your Customer!* Roseville, CA: Prima Publishing, 1995.

Wooden, John, and Steve Jamison. *Wooden on Leadership: How to Create a Winning Organization*. New York: McGraw Hill Education, 2005.

Index

About the Author

Bob Lisser, as founder and president of Growth Advantage and author of *The Growth Advantage*, embodies a rare set of credentials and capabilities that enable him to successfully help company leaders design and build their blueprint for sustained and profitable growth. Bob is obsessed with learning and driven to pass his hard-won wisdom on to others. He is passionate about helping companies that are struggling to sustain strategic growth. He is also devoted to helping leaders who want to improve their craft as well as managers and executives that get put into a position of leadership without having the skills and training necessary to be successful in their job.

Through leading organizations and companies, consulting with businesses, conducting training seminars, public speaking, and facilitating Executive Peer Groups, Bob has become a recognized expert in planning and execution, an authority in corporate strategy, an impactful speaker, a master trainer, and a powerful accountability coach. Bob's enthusiastic style helps clients grow top and bottom lines as well as become leaders within their industries.

CPSIA information can be obtained
at www.ICGtesting.com
Printed in the USA
BVHW040759120422
633936BV00010B/2

9 781538 161722